Destiny of Change

HOLT, RINEHART AND WINSTON BUSINESS AND SOCIETY SERIES
R. Joseph Monsen, *Adviser*

RAYMOND BAUMHART, S.J.   Ethics in Business

KENNETH R. SCHNEIDER   Destiny of Change: *How Relevant Is Man in the Age of Development?*

Destiny of Change

How Relevant Is Man
in the Age of Development?

KENNETH R. SCHNEIDER

Holt, Rinehart and Winston, Inc.
New York Chicago San Francisco Atlanta Dallas
Montreal Toronto London

Copyright © 1968 by Kenneth R. Schneider
All rights reserved
Library of Congress Catalog Card Number: 68-22734

2708501

Printed in the United States of America

1 2 3 4 5 6 7 8 9

To Mandy

Foreword

Industrialization, urbanization, and bureaucratization are the three main forces for change in the modern age—and technology underlies them all. In *Destiny of Change*, Kenneth Schneider analyzes these forces and their effect on the individual. The sum of his propositions points to a powerful historic shift in what he calls the "magnetic fields" shaping society. He suggests restructuring these forces and creating a more humane social setting for the individual. Always his central question is: What is happening to the individual as our society becomes increasingly industrialized and urbanized? This question has seldom been considered more thoughtfully or with greater insight than in this book.

The author argues that the very system of industrialization we have developed has produced an increasing social subordination of the individual to the prerogatives of the organization. As a consequence, our social purposes are governed by the mechanisms of the system rather than by the needs of man.

We can hardly understand contemporary society and business without considering the effect of the forces of industrial change. In a society such as ours, where change is often equated with progress, too little thought is given to improving the quality of society, that is, to increasing the variety of meaningful economic, social, and cultural options, thereby expanding the essence of human freedom.

Those interested in understanding the basic issues of our society, the forces of change, and the possible shapes of our future will find this book of keen interest. Those who already may have felt that the individual is the forgotten man in our modern industrial, urbanized, and bureaucratized society will find that the author's arguments give strong and reasoned support to what may have been only intuition. Those who may not agree with the author will at least pause and think. That this book will cause people to think about some of the most crucial problems of our society is in itself as high an encomium as I can pay. Kenneth Schneider's achievement, however, is to have written a highly intelligent book that is at the same time both stimulating and readable —a rare occurrence. Over all, this is one of the most thought-provoking books that I have read about our modern business-created society and the individual's place within this society. It should be required reading for all those who attempt to study and understand contemporary society.

R. Joseph Monsen

Seattle, Washington
May 1968

Preface

Our subject is human social development in an age of economic preeminence, organizational power, and technological and scientific expansiveness. The center of concern is the individual. The context is the community. The span is physical, economic, psychic, and cultural.

The main theme counters the popular and persistent optimism that equates technological and institutional development with human well-being—especially as the new inhuman enormity of development preempts the emotional and interpersonal foundations of individual behavior, which once derived from the social completeness and continuity of interdependence on the small human scale. Nevertheless, the general argument is optimistic.

This book is a criticism of bureaucratic institutions. However, the specific criticisms are meant to describe not their failure but rather their successes, and especially the excesses engendered by the most sudden and revolutionary nature of those successes.

But the book is not only a social criticism. It is also a protest, a hope, and something of a plan. Honest criticism calls for a personal protest, a positive seeking, a constructive proposition. Constructive propositions are sorely needed, because the world today is starved for a *social* constructiveness. That is, we must search for the positive means to overcome the rapid onset of a cultural protein deficiency that most of all deprives the individual of a rewarding interpersonal group life. This deficiency is now bluntly manifested by hippies, the urban riots (as well as the whole civil rights movement), and other protest demonstrations.

A number of suggestions and proposals are therefore offered. What we need most is a new outlook on our accomplishments and on our historic opportunities, to make them more fully beneficial to man *as a person* in his ordinary social setting.

Only passing attention is given to the nuclear threat and the population threat. These problems have been well hashed in current literature. Moreover, taken by themselves, they do not readily prompt a discussion of positive human possibilities.

We are concerned with both the advanced and the newly developing countries. However, since the most central lessons of development are to be found in the advanced countries, most of the attention is focused on that experience.

The broad concern requires a general approach, especially because human pertinency is increasingly diminished by specialization. I have not, therefore, attempted to produce substantiation in depth. My method as a generalist makes it impossible to satisfy many varied specialists, each on his own terms. The "validity" I seek is suggestive and provocative, corroboration being provided by numerous arguments and examples, aimed at a general understanding of man's condition and potential.

Except for the final and summary chapter, the argument has three main parts. Chapters 1 through 5 examine the existing state of development for its impact on the individual. Chapters 6 and 7 are the turning points and consider community and the new field of community development. Chapters 8 through 12 extend and apply the analysis of the early chapters and the concepts of the middle chapters to five fields: industry, cities, institutions, education, and planning.

Footnotes reveal my debts to persons for concepts and insights that I have tried to carry forward. Two stand out: Lewis Mumford and Robert Nisbet, for their wisdom and their humanity. Many persons kindly assisted me at some point in the writing or reviewed one or more chapters of the initial draft: Reinhard Bendix, Richard Bernhart, Karl Bode, Samuel Burneson, Delmar Dooley, James Fesler, Rochelle and Ralph Field, Lawrence Haworth, Philip Houser, Abraam Krushkhov, Marcia and Robert Leonard, Lawrence McLaughlin, Albert Mayer, David Mayer, Louis Miniclier, Melvin Novick, Richard Park, Malcolm Rivkin, Hans Singer, Joseph Sirefman, John Thomas, John Turner, Buenaventura Villanueva, Raanan Weitz, and Harvey Wheeler. Many thanks are due to Marie Otzinger, Betty Campbell, and Helen Peek for assistance in the preparation of the manuscript. Special thanks to the staff at the Lafayette College library for its excellent service and the fine spirit in which it was rendered. Special thanks also to Joseph Monsen and Robert Lentz, each for his unique assistance and thoughtfulness. None, however, gave more, encouraged more, or critically examined the development of the book more than my wife, Blanche. Her role cannot be measured; nor can it be redeemed by gratitude.

KENNETH R. SCHNEIDER

Hopewell, New Jersey
May 1968

Contents

Introduction

This is the age of development, the first challenge to stir all mankind, and no less than the awakening of man's first *universal* civilization. It is re-creating every culture with a new and common mold, penetrating all parts of every continent, restructuring the pattern of all settlements, remaking the very means to sustain life, even transforming life purposes.

The current world-wide mobilization for change culminates more than six thousand years of isolated thrusts toward civilization and some four centuries of applying scientific method to achieve that end. Only in the historic instant of the past few decades has there arisen a general recognition that international development is even possible in our time.

For one third of mankind, largely in Europe and North America, the gathering momentum of development in the past century and a half has brought about a massive urban industrialism through the perfection of technology (the organizing of specific properties of materials and machines) and bureaucracy (the organizing of specific capacities of persons and institutions). For the individual the results have been materially bountiful but also socially divisive and psychically disruptive.

For two thirds of mankind in Asia, Africa, and Latin America, development is a new imperative, a race measured by per capita income and made grim by a delicate equation of population and food. Consequently

1

the newer countries are putting a singular faith and reliance on technology and bureaucracy. Once the initial crucial problems of accelerating development are overcome by these proven development tools, the transformation of these peoples may very well be massive and abrupt. Then the throes accompanying a rapid breakup of old social patterns will be severe.

The growth of urban industrialism in the West has shifted the magnetic field of human organization. An intimate, individual-focused polarity has been overcome by an impersonal economic polarity. What once was motivated and organized in the family and local community by custom is now initiated and organized in corporate institutions and agencies by formulas, financial resources, and technical capacities; and these affect even those endeavors traditionally closest to the family hearth: welfare, entertainment, retirement, education, health. Where the individual belonged intimately and socially he now belongs only functionally. Social focus has diverged and blurred as the individual has thus become part of a larger, less *socially* differentiated mass and as social services have become isolated from one another and unrelated to the compassion of kith and kin.

The magnetic shift of human organization underlies the central argument of this book: that by permitting the magnetic field to shift almost wholly in response to technological and bureaucratic demands of change, Western society has allowed social value to drift from individual man to large organizations. As necessary as industry and industrial organization may be for human advancement, the complete remaking of society into one vast industrial cartel is an aberration in human affairs.

The technology behind industrial production is now reaching the stage where its demands on man—his physical presence in production and his bondage to its bureaucratic structure for a lifetime—can rapidly diminish. The magnetic poles that organize man can be realigned to free him from the production-consumption syndrome and to broaden all humane aspirations. The poles *can* be realigned, provided that society can break away from the proprietary grip of a runaway economy, which bears less and less resemblance to human needs and ingeniously seeks new ways to pump-prime new levels of consumption.

This view is a challenge, not a statement of pessimism or optimism. Peoples entering into the processes of change, as well as those already accelerated, are challenged to find greater human purposes in development and to command the institutions of mankind to serve those purposes more faithfully and fully. Until man reaffirms the preeminence of human association in human organization, he will lack the ethical and cultural foundations he so desperately needs in his struggle for integrity and worthiness.

Since the magnetic shift accompanying industrialization has taken place over centuries and permeates the deepest sources of human conduct, a realignment to enrich the sources of psychic, social, and cultural conduct will require many decades, if not centuries, of resolute action based on a continuing dialogue about human purposes and the changing human condition. This does not imply a return to the past, which is both impossible and undesirable, but it does mean that we act on an understanding of the past.

We can see, for example, that bureaucratic organization has skewed human activity toward a cosmopolitan pole of behavior, cut the base of vitality of the family at the other pole, and left in limbo the rich intermediate range of interpersonal association. This has narrowed the valid choices of behavior open to individuals and raises a serious question about the social plurality that Western society claims to have.

Another example is that of capacities. If civilization is, after all, the emergence of human direction in human affairs, we must recognize that increasing human capacities a hundredfold—and this is the scale of what is occurring—poses special challenges to the reasoned humane purposes of society. Heretofore one of the gravest problems of civilization has been to increase human capacities. But now in hardly more than one generation some societies will shift from human to atomic energy and acquire the cybernetic controls to free man from his former burdensome role in production. This multiplication of social power raises possibilities of profligacy as well as abundance, chaos as well as order, subjugation as well as freedom. The intellect that has focused so much effort upon enlarging man's undisciplined powers must now shift some of its concern to the excesses of a massive, crowded, and terribly powerful man-made environment.

The most dangerous excesses are those that undermine human worth. They may produce devastating environmental pollution or bleak, inhospitable cities, which are but playfields for the cheap game of profits. Consumption may turn to consumptiveness, or the individual's life may be subordinated to socially impoverishing employment. Professional imperialism may crowd out the spontaneous and spirited amateur, not only in sports and the arts, but in the recreation of producing useful goods with one's own hands.

The avoidance of such excesses depends upon the social goals that direct our growing capacities. Even a casual examination of the operating pattern of organizations, the disjointed nature of social services, and the restrictive, performance-oriented nature of education attests to the deficiency of contemporary social goals in relation to contemporary capacities.

Social goals are chiefly deficient in their service to the individual. Present "goals" define him principally in economic statistics, try to keep him adjusted only to service as a useful citizen, and take special notice of him only when he becomes a welfare or security problem. But this merely emphasizes again that social value has drifted from man to organizations—that is, to the new Big Citizens to "whom" social sovereignty ominously accrues.

When the ligaments organizing society mainly serve the prerogatives of corporate (formal) institutions, the individual inevitably falls in step. Status, locality, and association, as well as income, come to depend upon employment. In fact the essential social context and continuity of life depend almost solely upon the seeking of income. When a job is lost or changed, the whole social context is abruptly altered and continuity between the past and future is broken. Individual and family integrity are compromised not only by unemployment or relocation but by the mere threat, for these possibilities temper social conduct and all forms of membership.

A reformation of the polar magnetism in society to redirect social goals back to the individual must center upon the kinds of organization that provide social context and continuity to the behavior and the course of life of the individual. The individual must be the locus about which the determinants of organization primarily evolve.

Within the individual lies the urgent challenge of international development: to liberalize the struggle, to aim not merely to raise the gross external capacities of society, but to elevate the whole *élan* of life in every living person.

If there is a civilized meaning to the abundance now spreading throughout the West, and in promise for all mankind, it is this: We must, above all, nurture the psychic and social integrity of the individual and prevent it from being strapped to the imperious ethos of organization. We must make society organically responsive to the personality of man and not to the categories, aggregates, and processes of economic action.

Nor is democracy merely a list of rights and safeguards. We must demand more of it, more of our civilization. It should exult all of life for all men. We must direct society to honor more than its elite, to create more than a flood of artifacts, to decentralize excellence, to make knowledge more worthy than the management of power and performance, and to desanctify the will of institution, the statistics of linear change, and the mandates of the dollar.

Unquestionably, international development is the imperative of our age. But the imperative, with its inherent moral, philosophic, organizational, and scientific challenge, has no inevitable outcome. That can only be resolved by men with new wisdom and determination.

1

Man's Stake in Development

Perhaps the major fact of the decade of the 1960s is that nearly all nonindustrialized countries, independent and dependent alike, have joined the path of *development*. After the turmoil and awakening of the war decade of the 1940s, there first emerged in the 1950s a broad consensus that *all peoples could develop a high level of life through consciously taking hold of the reins of change,* and at that time a number of new countries first adopted comprehensive five-year development plans.

Earlier development in the West, however, came about experimentally, piecemeal, and (by today's standards) almost unconsciously. Today the advanced industrial countries are evolving toward over-all direction and planning to promote and guide change, especially economic change. Thus, even outside the communist countries and the newly developing countries, the concept of development has shifted from an *observation* or *prediction* about the course of change toward a *program* for controlling change.

Under varying conditions and systems, then, a broad convergence of approaches underlies the effort to increase material abundance. This convergence also underlies the basically similar problem that the less developed and more developed peoples face in the age of development. The general problems vary mostly in degree. Where they are different in kind, then it is only a matter of time—a few decades—until the basic similarity shows up.

5

Development, then, will be treated here as one general process for all countries, and the differences in the stages or character of change as normal variations in the same over-all struggle. However, since the frontiers, the precedents, the leading initiatives in any broad effort are crucial to the outcome in all countries, we shall focus upon the countries with advanced economies. And because my knowledge and observations have arisen chiefly in the United States, the discussion leans upon the particular circumstances of American development.

The problems of this book are vital to the countries now initiating development, precisely because they point to questions that the newer countries can often do more to resolve than the older, more "mature" countries. The newer countries have a fresh start in many, many ways.

This first chapter will sketch a few historic perspectives on the development of the West, consider some elements of the potential in the newly developing countries, and highlight some of the humane potential of development as a whole.

INSTITUTIONAL INHUMANITY

In 1831 Alexis de Tocqueville visited America for a few months and later wrote *Democracy in America,* by far the most penetrating interpretation of American life to this day. His keen observations revealed patterns that others had missed. Tocqueville looked to the future of the American democratic experiment with hope but also with deep skepticism. Even today his work nourishes a faith but also jolts easy assumptions about the course of democracy.

Now that urbanism and industrialism have been pieced onto the American democratic experiment, we may wonder what observations a modern-day Tocqueville might make. Possibly he would be struck with a deep anomaly, perhaps an outright paradox, in the life of the American people. First, no doubt, he would observe the magnificent growth of organizations providing for human needs: the incomparable range of schools, the impressive hospitals, the programs for care of the aged and for welfare assistance. He would find equally notable the wide range of constructive work financed by the great foundations, or that carried on by voluntary associations. All this might be described as institutional humanity.

Yet the perceptive French visitor might equally be struck by a related set of phenomena that might be called institutional inhumanity—pervasive forces, methods, and attitudes that attack the wholeness and the uniqueness of the individual, conditions that disrupt congregation and the flow of human association.

The paradox of inhumanity is demonstrated in many ways. Life and property are protected by thousands of police (which did not even exist in 1831), yet few delinquents or potential criminals can find constructive endeavor or the wide-ranging sympathetic assistance they require. The poor are given relief income and housing assistance, but their self-improvement and integrity are then severely strictured. The elderly and the emotionally disturbed are cared for magnificently by nineteenth-century standards, but they are segregated from normal involvement in society. The various kinds of socially disadvantaged and debilitated may be assisted, but only until such assistance leads to a steady job. Very large investments are made in education, but education trains millions for high technical performance, few for personal or social worth. Shopping districts and centers expend large sums for attractive store fronts and dazzling displays but virtually nothing for benches, drinking fountains, or rest rooms. Subways, though efficient, are scarce, filthy, and uncomfortable, while automobile travel, costly and inefficient, is subsidized by billions of dollars.

Tocqueville would surely be quick to observe that money, organization, and integrity are directed to the progress of large organizations and the whole society, while this "progress" often has harsh effects in the small areas of society that serve the individual. Ten million dollars is far more likely to be budgeted for *one mile of freeway* than for *forty community centers* at $250,000 each. And each mile of new urban freeway disperses thousands of persons into disorder so that the automobile may move with order and efficiency. Thus there is an implicit understanding that automobiles are served while neighborhoods are not and that highways are integrated while neighborhoods are not.

Tocqueville might suggest further that institutional inhumanity in America today results from the many divisions of life the individual must suffer. Society is now organized for efficient and unified production, but man himself is divided. His daily behavior is divided into isolated segments: commuting, work, a drink after work, family and meals, TV. His relations with others tend to be particularized, functional, and pecuniary. Special interests are all that bring individuals together; one's friends tend to be grouped by these special interests. General friendships arising from mutual personal interest are usually too burdensome to maintain, except once a year by Christmas card.

And the human institutions that have high standards of public service also splinter the individual in a similar way. Hospitals or welfare agencies may seek well-being for the individual, but they conceive of that happy state as arising from a finite number of services—as if one hundred and one discrete services might assure the good life.

The unity of our age evidently lies in the production and distribution of goods and services. These goods and services flow, as it were, on a vast freeway network with great interchanges that facilitate and sort the flow. But for man the environment has become an atomistic flux, creating a sense of movement without a sense of direction or of place. Social intercourse seems to have been reduced to calculable exchange. Life emerges as daily, weekly, and yearly contacts and routines, each to attain a calculated benefit, but each essentially barren of the interpersonal mutuality inherent in most societies.

Tocqueville might have wondered whether the divisiveness and oppressiveness of mind and emotion found in modern America are not merely new variants of the tyranny man has long suffered. Although perhaps tyranny of the past tended to be capricious, the tyranny of today is now minute and regular, as Tocqueville himself noted, but also embedded in an array of powerful institutional capacities completely inconceivable in Tocqueville's time.

The sources of our present institutional humanity and institutional inhumanity are quite diverse. Let us examine one of the threads leading to the present condition.

SUBMISSION AND CONTROL

The historic chart of physical change is a curve of acceleration. For most of history the line is a gradually rising inclined plane. But during the last century, and especially in recent decades, the line whips up toward the vertical. This curve of acceleration applies to travel speeds, volumes of trade, population, material wealth, knowledge, education—to most everything in which man has become involved.

But the curve has carried with it a human burden. The first advances of man toward civilization were the domestication of animals, the selection and propagation of seeds, the formation of stable villages and communal systems, and the evolution of tools and skill to produce, among other things, the containers that Lewis Mumford suggests are the preeminent mark of the neolithic age. These practices not only produced a new wealth and security: they imposed changes within the person. Man made himself the chief product of domestication.

The essential effect upon man was much more than what he learned to do. The changes enveloped his being. Whereas paleolithic hunters had been free scavengers of natural bounty, the settled neolithic farmer had to acquire a varied and discriminating control of environment. To do so he had to submit himself to a discipline regulated by the hunger of his animals, the demands of the seasons, and a precise sequence of cultivation. Craft skills required a new patience and discipline of hand and mind. Village life required a submission to collective necessity. External control, therefore, was always matched by internal submission. Control and submission inevitably became the paired ingredients of development.

The next transformation occured with the development of cities about 6000 B.C. A more formal specialization accompanied innovations such as metallurgy, plows, potter's wheels, looms, sailboats, large-scale construction, and, finally, writing, mathematics, and astronomy. Mumford describes the change as an "implosion" of new power to one center. It was within the city that the great division of classes took place, essentially dividing people between those who produced and those who consumed. The gradually unified control by a king over the court, temple, and granary fortified the social imbalance to which cities have always tended, whatever their glories of nurturing civilization.

The promise of cities (so fervently sought today in Asia and Latin America) was a lopsided affair from the outset. It brought men together for systematic exploitation by class control, economic concentration, military power, law, and scripture. Centralized power subdued the rural folk and taxed their production. Organized war was another direct result.

The promise of new abundance and security prompting the development of ancient cities once again paired external control and internal submission. This time, however, external control was applied to man by his fellows. Both control and submission tended to be aimed inwardly. Although control of the environment advanced impressively, the power of urban institutions systematically exploited and distorted men. "Thus by a curious act of transvestiture," as Mumford describes it, "a ceremony that began by the invocation of more abundant life, turned into its very opposite: it invited a centralized military control, systematic robbery, and economic parasitism." [1] *

Thus man first submitted himself to the necessary discipline required for simple domestication. Then he fell under the control of small urban elites, forfeiting both inner and outer control and much of his output.

Much later, when Western society was coming into its own after the Reformation, a wholly new instrument of control slowly took form. In the systematic processes evolved in bureaucracy the West's restless new institutions were able to define a new role for the individual. Both the secular state and the private corporation were able to grow to unprecedented size and complexity by rationalizing individuals and their varied skills within institutions. Bureaucracy was truly a strategic accomplishment, and in fact many or most of the feats of the West are triumphs of complex organizations, even more than of technology.

* Footnote references follow last chapter (page 267).

Today the customary forms of bureaucracy seem to be inherent in social organization. Man, however, has traveled a long trail to reach his present practices. To help appreciate their significance, we may recall elements of Max Weber's classic description: "The fully developed bureaucratic mechanism compares with other [nonbureaucratic] organizations exactly as does the machine with nonmechanical modes of production." The role of an individual is rationalized by complete separation of the office from the officeholder, which segregates "public" and "private" affairs. The individual holds an office as a duty rather than a right; specific duties are performed according to clear rules and jurisdictions; the individual office is within a strict order of super- and subordination. The officeholder receives a definite remuneration for his services, rather than exploiting his position by means of rents and enslavements (which was once the motive for the "purchase" of offices). Officeholding is a full-time profession, not an honorific vocation; its performance requires expert training; and appointments are made according to qualifications and objective standards of selection.[2]

Bureaucracy is not only comparable in character to technology but is also its indispensable corollary. Modern communication and transportation, Weber points out, were the pacemakers of modern bureaucracy, presenting organizations with problems of many specializations, vast scale, complexity, and unified operation. Weber stresses also that it is specialized knowledge that gives power—and indispensability—to bureaucracy. By being precise, unambiguous, continuous, and prompt, bureaucracy could establish and command organizations of unlimited size and complexity.

Bureaucracy, therefore, combines technology with a highly articulated control over man to achieve higher output by organization. Consequently, as Peter Drucker stresses, men no longer produce: they only serve in organizations that produce. Organizations produce by precisely combining materials, machines, and men. As they have gained new capacities, their control over man has shifted from raw physical energy to the rational abilities and skills derived from long training periods.

With bureaucracy has emerged a new kind of man, the bureaucrat, a creature as central to modern society as was the cleric to medieval society, and who contrasts with that cleric as strikingly as the modern corporation with the medieval Church. His "parish" is *the* firm or *the* agency. Through more than a century of rapidly increasing professional competence, the bureaucrat has made himself a dispassionate, rational, calculating, and disciplined instrument of organizational advantage. Both employees and consumer constituents are expendable or exploitable elements in the persuit of organizational growth and power. No other purpose is possible for the bureaucrat. His income, status, and often even his place of residence and friendships depend upon it. That is, he is not socially or economically independent of his bureaucratic identity.

This professional elite has revealed to the world an unbelievable productivity and competence through organization. Man has therefore quite willingly given the bureaucrat a free hand to use the whole of society as the staging area for the creation of productive organization, to cut through the traditional social fabric of organized behavior to build new institutional superstructures, just as Cortez' men dismantled Aztec temples in Mexico and used the stones to build Christian cathedrals. As a consequence, the organization of society has become increasingly irrelevant to the social and psychic requirements of the individual, leaving him on an ever narrowing foundation of personal integrity and stability. Moreover, he is left more helplessly open to a systematic subordination to the self-determining will of bureaucratic organization.

Today men benefit vastly from their submission to the control of bureaucracy. But that control has changed the personality of the individual, affecting personal creativity, cooperativeness, loyalty, and identity, and demands a willingness to alter most other goals or modes of life.

Yet today another new genre of control is coming upon man. Because bureaucracy has succeeded far more than anyone could have dreamed in multiplying production (and also in creating perplexing problems of abundance in the United States), a new control is emerging wholly to promote consumption among men. The most potent and obvious means is modern advertising—emotion-laden yet systematic and relentless. It is a new economic means to extend continuously the old goal of increasing output, for consumptive demand is now the major limiting factor in increasing output in advanced economies. By going beyond primary and secondary human needs in its appeals it reveals a forced ritual of gluttony, a pitiful deficiency of liberalizing social goals, and a myth carried over from the economics of scarcity

A historic cycle is now beginning to close. From the neolithic age onward man has passed through many stages, submitting in each to a discipline Freud referred to as the "discontents" of civilization. Now that we have unlimited energy and computer controls—the two major means to relieve men of work—the deprivations of human integrity no longer have the biting necessity they had even fifty years ago. With the cycle closing, a continuation of the present discipline of production becomes much more arbitrary. But the emergence of a new discipline to consume not only exaggerates the discontents of civilized society but dishonors the whole civilization.

The various elements of this discussion will be taken up in later chapters. It is more pertinent at this time to draw another perspective.

DECLINE OF DIVERSITY

The specialist has come into his own in the twentieth century. He has made a specialist of most organizations. He has spawned wide ranges of new techniques, capabilities, and interests. He has brought a wide diversity to the whole society.

Still, beneath the diverse professional and technical surface of society, there is a bewildering social uniformity. Cities are more alike than a century ago; air-conditioned buildings need not reflect their geography; national markets in food, clothing, and building materials dilute the local character of diet, apparel, or homes; uniformities of building, zoning, and subdivision codes yield suburbs that are deadeningly sterile and alike. For the individual, modular uniformity of behavior is the very real result of technological diversity.

And even as specialization requires a broad social diversity, the specialist himself is enclosed in a narrow world. As Lewis Mumford describes it, he "achieved excellence and efficiency in the part . . . but he lost his grip on life as a whole." [3] Even though specialization has greatly benefited man and given him access to the cultural diversity of hundreds of other professional specialties, it has simultaneously denied to him the wide and vital social and cultural participation that makes a whole man. Society-wide diversity is very different from the kind of diversity that is real for the individual.

There is a natural connection between technological diversity on the one hand and social uniformity and individual restrictiveness on the other. The current objectives of development are set only in the narrow terms of raising the standard of living. What goes on beyond that is looked upon by government, financial, and technical bodies as superfluous, perhaps even spurious, to development. Health and education are subsumed as prerequisites of economic improvement; only incidentally are they considered as independent contributors to the good life. The arts and humanities fare not even as well. Curiously, even the National Aeronautics and Space Administration feels obliged to justify its budget requests in terms of the potential of the space program in raising the standard of living.

The parochial single-mindedness that narrows development to economic growth raises a question about the plural vigor of contemporary civilization. A comparison with Roman and early Western civilizations may offer us some perspective.

Previous civilizations, of course, were tales of growth and decline. Relatively small populations, existing in essential isolation, were sparked and made exceptional by very small elites, were supported by brutal concentrations of limited wealth, excelled in a restricted range of endeavor, and generally rested their destinies upon one major city. These factors powerfully limited the cross-fertilization, maturation, radiation, variation, and continuity of each society's chief articles of excellence.

Ancient Rome was more fortunate than earlier civilizations because it achieved a far wider base for its development. Probably for this reason it came closer than any of its precursors to the breakthrough that had to await the Western renaissance. Its population was large; it rested in part on numerous, widely dispersed cities; it broadened its leadership somewhat to include divergent peoples. A wide range of achievement characterized its endeavors, although perhaps these were weighted too heavily in favor of law, administration, and militarism. The achievements of Greece were absorbed almost systematically, except in one critical area: nascent Greek science was permitted to stagnate. Had Rome absorbed diverse leadership more fully and stimulated innovation and scientific investigation at widespread centers of its empire, the catalytic convergence of science, technology, and administration that marks the emergence of modern civilization might have appeared a thousand years earlier.

Almost from the outset Western civilization escaped the parochial limitations of earlier struggles for higher levels of life. As Barbara Ward has emphasized, the emergence of Europe, with its vast human diversity and relative geographic proximities, was associated with "myriad new spurts and experiments, based upon the activities of thousands of different centers of economic and political power." [4] Inventiveness could appear in Italy, then France, then England. Together the variegated traditions of many centers would constantly stimulate varied new concepts, systems, and adaptations.

Europe's magnificent good fortune lay not only in having numerous centers of cultural initiative but also in achieving and maintaining a certain uniqueness at each center. Universities transplanted from France to England could become institutions of quite a different kind. Parliamentary democracy could evolve for centuries in England and Switzerland, then burst with new meaning after the French Revolution. Philosophy and, later, science could flower in separate but related centers, offering contrast that aroused envy, competition, or contempt. Landmarks of innovation could radiate to many cultures and varied institutional environments. Every new idea could be considered differently in each. Through uncountable transplantings the right degree of nurture, stimulus, or daring could somewhere produce a new maturity or provoke a radically new endeavor. Or, equally important, such exchange could cause decay of a feudal stronghold and pave the way for an ultimate transformation.

It was significant, then, that conceptions of excellence in Paris varied from those in Florence or London. It was probably more significant that cultural objectives also varied. Competition under a uniform set of cultural rules would have narrowed inventiveness just as readily as the absence of contrasting centers. Europe thus arose on the strength of its diversity.

The emergence of universities illustrates another important characteristic of Western development. Here, for the first time, arose an institutional vehicle and a cultural ideal for developing knowledge on a broad foundation. Springing from the rediscovery of Plato's academy and the tradition of the medieval cloister, and evolving from the four classical faculties of theology, law, medicine, and philosophy, the university slowly enlarged its outlook to include all areas of knowledge, all means of discovery, and all professional uses of knowledge. Under one institutional roof the professions, sciences, and humanities profited enormously by the universal access and cross-fertilization of all subjects, ideas, and methods. Each university was a grand central plaza for all events of knowledge to appear, become relevant to other events of knowledge, and radiate outward. Like the plaza, it offered free access, easy movement, and ready association of the ideas of scholarship. It had no monopoly of intellect, no single pattern of development; its purpose was facilitation, not control or uniformity. Its faith lay in the inherent worth of knowledge and in the effectiveness of undirected scholarship. The university thus furnished society with an unprecedented means of grappling with knowledge to make it serve any or all of mankind—as, for example, when Prince Henry brought together leading mathematicians and astronomers to improve navigation for exploration.

Restrictive traditions and oppressive conformities were not absent from Europe's development. But these varied from place to place, and when a restriction could be overcome in one locality it had a better chance of being overcome elsewhere. By this means a greater diversity—and tolerance—could gradually evolve within each independent center.

Diversity established at least three essential conditions for the growth of Western civilization. First, there were numerous independent centers of innovation, each with its own experience and opportunities, and each having some communication with the others. Second, each center was differently motivated, sought excellence with a different purpose, and imposed novel interpretations and uses upon its borrowings from other centers. Third, primarily in the university, an institution appeared that sought a broad compass of knowledge, giving each branch of knowledge the same independence and also the same intercommunication as existed between the urban centers of innovation.

Today, for all of our diversity of specific interests, our innovations are aligned to achieve a narrow, common set of goals and to function according to increasingly narrow rules of change. Despite its encompassing the earth, contemporary development does not have deeply contrasting centers of innovation. Japan's science, technology, and business are steadily more like Europe's and North America's. India's bureaucracy did not diverge essentially from Britain's upon attaining independence. Certain uniformities are obviously essential and follow from the nature of given materials and knowledge about them. But uniformity is not required in the goals or the style of life of all people in all countries. Moreover, the life of the individual in thousands of local settings need not be homogenized. Variety, distinctiveness, and vital involvement for the human being are in danger of being preempted by the Big Citizens and their monolithic goals of development.

DENIAL OF EXCITEMENT

As the world strides through the final third of the twentieth century, the overpowering interest of development lies clearly within the realm of economics—not in philosophy, drama, or poetry, as in the development of Greece, nor in the spirit of universal man, as in Renaissance Italy, but rather in bread and electricity that are made by machines. To be sure, the old excitements of mankind, such as sculpture and poetry, are still around, and even flourish in some nooks of society. As everyone can see, however, they are not a part of the excitement of the times, not part of the general motivation, not written into the goals, not patronized by the world developers.

On further consideration, one wonders what happened to the excitements of development, the excitements of life that should inject a sharpness into fresh civilizing winds. They are not found in the Aswan High Dam, except by a few Egyptian bureaucrats and engineers; not in the Asian or Pan American highways, for these are but a series of contracts; not in the new Indian Institutes of Technology, for these are grim struggles to train technologists. The whole business of development—and development does highly resemble the utilitarianism of business—is governed by a stern fiat of cultural and interpersonal austerity under the forebodings of the "dismal science" of economics.

The fact that diverse social and cultural objectives are not part of development is probably a principal reason for the low level of excitement. Actual problems of poverty themselves cannot explain a lack of inspiration. Serious challenges put in perspective of broad civilizing goals should sharpen rather than dull men's motivation. Overcoming poverty would not seem to be a very lasting or deep motivation among men. It is not surprising, therefore, that a part of the "excitement" associated with contemporary development is negative in character, namely, that of the hippies. Very notably, the hippies have only arisen in those parts of wealthy countries where the kind of development the world now seeks is most clearly revealed.

So today all nations are divided into two groups: the rich and the poor. Economic assistance weighs heavily in the relations between them. Everywhere the rallying cry is gross national product; each percentage point of change on the scale of growth measures the degree of success—or failure—of a government and its assistance group. The goal is simple: to bring about the singular economic "take-off" that Walt Rostow symbolized so pertinently.

The concern is essential, of course, and even represents a new spirit of commonwealth among men. But it is a dominating *economic* concern, nevertheless, and like any other single overriding objective—becoming a concert pianist, following a monastic life, or going on a crusade—economic development can overpower all other human motives and reduce all events solely to its own terms. Already to a significant degree the sciences, civic life, architecture and urban design, welfare legislation, recreation plans, even colleges and universities are difficult for us to understand without reference to their economic potential or economic necessity. This is plainly evident, for example, when a park or university is called into being solely to spur the economic vitality of an area.

Unfortunately, development in our day is chiefly characterized by its impersonality—that is, by economic growth models, high finance, bureaucratic organization, and technical specialization. These features do not arouse the excitement that all men should have while creating a new civilization: the excitement that arises when personality is intimately a part of a cultural adventure; when it directly builds and shares something that is much larger than the individual; when it links the past and the future with the present role of the individual; when it bears upon and relates friends, family, community, the young and the aged, the high and the humble, all in a highly personal way.

Cultural excitement is inevitably personal, and to be stimulated and broadened it must find a personal setting. The individual human setting apparently cannot be too small without losing its stimulus, or too large without losing personality. It thus appears that a certain finite range of interpersonal behavior often had the effect of permitting if not stimulating a certain line of endeavor to flourish, such as Greek humanism, when in a broader-gauge and more outwardly aggressive society, such as our own, the spirit of mutual discovery might have suffocated. It is somewhat dubious whether the accomplishments of Athens in the fifth century B.C. could have come about within the organizational and technological exploitiveness of twentieth-century society.

We must ask, therefore, whether the wider and more humane possibilities of future development might be oppressed by excessive external variations of life as the past too often was oppressed by internal provincialism. Perhaps both conditions can deny the intimate social diversity that is at the base of a cultural excitement. Isn't this a question we dare not overlook.

Aside from the inherent value of seeking out the excitement in our development potential, it may be that the spirit in which men take up the development challenge may also be as valuable in practical terms as the professional, specialized, and bureaucratic approaches that dominate development practice today.

CAPACITIES FOR DEVELOPMENT

Despite the present concentration on the economics of growth, economic progress has been disappointing in the newly developing countries. Economists watching the barometers of growth and the temperament of rising expectations worry lest the dichotomy between the rich and poor become nationally and internationally explosive. They see that economic growth in many poor countries hardly keeps up with population growth, while many already wealthy countries bask under rapid economic advance and relatively low-population increase.

The current weight of argument is that economic foundations must be built before the luxuries of affluence may be indulged in. This argument is true only in the narrowest economic sense. What is more important is that liberal human purposes can make the period of struggle for development itself into one of man's most exciting ages and give the society some of its finest traditions. At any level of affluence the excitement of life is more a matter of vision than of means. And those who would shelve their broader visions of society for another day inevitably depress both its present and eventual possibilities.

But there is also a question about the simple effectiveness of a monolithic concentration upon the economics of growth. There is already widespread evidence over a number of decades that projects in agriculture, education, village industries, cooperative development, and even community development in which appeals are made to the economic motives of village people (according to the Western understanding of motives) are simply not effective. Even when one assumes a general desire for material gain, there are just too many conflicting values and vested interests, confused patterns of leadership and organization, superstitions, and static conceptions of life to permit material values to become effective.

The economist with a singular motive of economic growth too easily overlooks the profound inner changes of bringing hundreds of millions of people from an essentially neolithic life into a frame of mind reasonably compatible with a money economy, modern administration, urbanism, and industrialism. Given a universal taste for money, can we still expect traditional peoples to quickly shake off the security of community, the comfort of old beliefs, the web of family welfare, the peace of the rural village life, and the simple familiarity of one's locality for the uncertain rewards of a laborer's day wage, a submission to imposed performance and working hours, the bewildering pecuniary relationships among unknown persons, and the social formlessness of cities? Economists are still too deeply burdened with Adam Smith's economic optimization of human behavior. They still too often plan for investments in health and education and then assume that improved health and higher grade levels will underwrite other investments in production. Their calculations of economic change thus ignore social changes. The consequences are costly errors that delay the economic progress they seek.

The economist may have thus overestimated the economic potential in the 1960s. But he may be underestimating the potential for the 1980s and 1990s, as the long-term catalysts now observable have their inevitable effect and the psychic and social motivations of many millions of people are reshaped into powerful economic drives. The present pessimism derives from disappointments about growth in per capita output, particularly in agriculture, and a continuing high population growth. This pessimism has been "projected" to the year 2000—an assumption that the economic record of the next three decades of concerted effort will be no better than that of the first.

To be sure, the present hurdles are massive. Rapid population growth and lagging food production are now paramount *practical* considerations. We may, for example, expect that food will be especially critical in India in the coming few years. However, it is important to remember that the population problem itself is partly a result of development progress. Health has been initially more responsive than food production, and so lower death rates have created a zooming population, a food deficit, and a drag on over-all economic growth.

Although these problems must be faced with vigor and even with a certain increased urgency, the solutions may appear much earlier and more suddenly than is now generally expected. In the face of the scientific revolution now affecting agriculture in the West (creating a massive surplus) and the demonstration that so small a country as Japan can independently feed most of its 100 million, a world food crisis after one or two decades could only be interpreted as a dereliction on the part of the world's leadership. Similarly, considering the inexpensive birth-control devices now becoming available and the large-scale national family planning programs now getting under way after twenty years of debate and experimentation, a runaway population after a decade or two would amount to a simple abdication of human direction in human affairs.

Only a historic view of a whole century or more will bring into perspective the full magnitude of the productive power now being created. The acceleration of change and its geographic spread since 1945 are utterly phenomenal in history. And most of what is taking place in the new countries has hardly begun to surface in economic accomplishment, and may not before the late 1970s. But when that variegated energy gets into motion, probably by the 1980s, the economic thrust may be overwhelming.

These predictions are not based on statistics, but rather on the determinations of men, perhaps best evidenced by the current frustrations over efforts to radically increase production. These frustrations speak for new, more resolute levels of action in the second and third complete decades of development. After all, these frustrations have arisen only in the first fifteen years of a mounting effort by many countries to develop. And the results in many sectors, such as in health and government administration, are very encouraging at that.

The paramount features of development in the new countries in the 1960s are the immense capacities for economic growth that are steadily and surely being set up. Time is needed for accumulation, organization, and adjustment before these capacities can actually show up in "output."

The United Nations declared the 1960s to be the Development Decade. But more likely it will be remembered as the decade of preparation for economic development, including such activities as gaining independence for most of the remaining dependent peoples, building government bureaucracies, improving health and expanding education, improving transportation, expanding community development, promoting the creation of cooperatives and other enterprises, expanding the capacity of financial institutions. The 1960s is the decade of the preinvestments, the river-basin and mineral surveys, the founding of technical schools, the making of plans, the political adjustments, the first groping experiences. The 1960s will be known for these beginnings, which will provide the basis for dealing more effectively with population growth, food output, and industrial production in the 1970s.

Universities, more than most institutions, affect the transfer of capacities for development. Before 1950 Africa south of the Sahara and outside South Africa had not one university and only a few minor colleges. Between 1950 and 1965 no less than three dozen universities were established, most of them after 1960. What is just getting under way in Africa is more advanced in Asia and Latin America. The Philippines boast of several hundred thousand college students and India more than a million—comparable in number to the United States in the interwar years. In the Philippines quality of instruction has been low, and in India classical studies have predominated—but higher quality is now sought in the Philippines, and India is moving strongly toward science, engineering, and agriculture.

The point is that the wherewithal for world development is now available and being disseminated. The science and technology required for the task are proven and in use, and so is man's ability to organize himself institutionally and economically.

However, although the mobilization of such an array of forces may bring an end to dire poverty in the coming decades, the present tendency to narrow social motivation to that objective alone may undermine man's belief in what he is doing and, ultimately, in himself.

"It is impossible to escape the conclusion," wrote Robert Nisbet in 1953, "that man's belief in himself has become weakest in the very age when his control of environment is greatest."[5] Now, as man moves headlong into economic development, the peculiar social enzyme that has weakened belief during the West's development seems assured of further rapid growth with the world's material progress. Whatever the specific cause, man's diminished belief cannot be separated from the incessant growth of functional and impersonal forms of organization at the expense of organization that centers on association, belief, heritage, family, and community.

Man himself must always remain the measure of all things. But this measure may be discarded in favor of self-perpetuating necessities, success, or power—of which no society has been more enamored than the West. At this critical juncture of history, when the lessons of Western pioneering can be put into perspective, and when new countries are first entering into their radical transformation, man dare not underplay himself. He does if he elevates industrial growth (with its ignition system of science) to the goals of development. He does if he believes other questions of human development can await an industrial base.

Amid the promises and urgencies of the times, man stands between two specters. The one—overpopulation, lagging food production, and low rates of industrial growth—is now reasonably well defined. There is an evident determination to overcome it. The other—the threat to the role of the individual person in a world of preemptive technology and aggrandizing organization—has yet to be effectively recognized. This specter, therefore, is the more dangerous one.

The powerful torque of our gathering power, turned on in the flight from scarcity, in the coming decades may establish an industrial society so attuned to the economic imperatives of every problem that it can only approach man's predicaments through calculation of their economic effects. At that stage man will be hard put to resurrect his human legacy.

LIBERAL EXCHANGE

Today the world is engaged in a gigantic dialogue, the most conscious, systematic, continuous, awesome dialogue in history. It is taking place primarily between the two segments of world society called rich and poor. It is the dialogue of development. Food and population are included, and the undisciplined capacities arising from development are not—and so the dialogue itself shows the shortcomings of the whole development enterprise.

The traffic consists of traveling students and professors, specialized advisers and demonstration projects, books and equipment. The subject is *Western know-how*, and the flow of information and ideas is really that of a Western monologue. Rote accumulation of skill remains the unquestioned ideal, the skill being the know-how to increase gross national product.

The dialogue has the earth-shaking importance of reforming and remaking civilized man, not only where he is economically backward, but where he is advanced as well. In the wider reaches of the human potential both parties in the dialogue have an equal amount to learn. Both are teachers in the broader context.

As it is, the one-way, know-how nature of the international dialogue shows how we have closed our minds to the wide range of the human adventure—both those of us who consider we have arrived and those who feel a compulsion to follow. World society is converging along a monistic trail toward a nonexperimental hardfastness and the acceptance of a single measure of worth.

Let us examine the dialogue more closely. The West has sought to improve the flow and the effectiveness of its know-how but it has not sought to pass on the lessons of its own "mistakes." One does not find offices in the U.S. Agency for International Development or in the U.N. Development Program that evaluate the West's pioneering experience in development, seeking to improve strategy and tactics in the new countries.

Such offices might call in some of the world's most imaginative philosophers to examine, for example, the deep social costs of the main thrusts of economic advance. The record of rapid declines of employment in agriculture and mining (especially the declines requiring migration between regions) at given stages of development suggests a challenge to prevent similar stagnation in the future. Then, too, chaotic urbanization might well be prevented in the new countries. A broad philosophical review of this experience might highlight opportunities to make the city both a better means to promote development and a better goal of development (a better human habitat). Chaotic cities are merely one evidence of a general failure of the West to realize maximum social and cultural benefits from its development.

Just as these problems of Western development have generally been overlooked in the development dialogue, so have many of the West's finest traditions. Little effort was required to convince developing peoples (perhaps prematurely) of the benefits of the welfare state, but the ideals of parliamentary democracy, public service by individuals and by organized philanthropy and such institutions as universities, not to speak of the broad cutural heritage, have been neglected. These are serious shortcomings of both vision and diplomacy.

Not only has the West too narrowly focused the dialogue, but there has been scarcely any counterdiscussion to broaden it. What might be communicated to the West from Venezuela, Nigeria, or Pakistan? If such countries could grasp the various alternatives of development open to them and could select and reorganize them to improve their general results, they might then enlarge the whole human experience. They might say, in effect, to the Europeans and North Americans, "We inherited your experience. It was primarily technical, institutional, and economic, because that was where you invested your main efforts. Now we offer you a primarily social experience of potential value, the outcome of our effort to improve the beneficial uses of industrialization and to avoid some of the pitfalls evident in your earlier evolution."

A vital and two-way dialogue, with more selectivity and penetrating criticism on both sides, might also be advanced by the unique cultural vantage points each country brings to international development. Every new nation faces the problem of translating its own inheritance of tradition into a rich coalescence with industrialism and urbanism. Efforts of this kind should give variety to an otherwise homogeneous process of international development.

Thus, India might plan the location and size of industrial plants, their internal organization and authority, employment and training policies, tenure and fringe benefits to preserve certain family or religious traditions. Conversely others, such as the caste system, might be discouraged by developing an accepted new framework. In any case, technology and bureaucracy should be exploited discriminatingly to strengthen selected values and traditions.

The implication should be clear. Many of the best opportunities for adjusting technology and bureaucracy to social and cultural prerogatives are in the so-called developing countries. Costly research to achieve purely technical and scientific advances must continue for some decades to be the burden of the wealthier countries. The developing countries, however, can become active centers for the liberal interpretation of industrialization—that is, for the drawing of larger human benefits from development. This role is limited in the present industrial nations by the bias of their tradition, by invested interests, and merely by their long-established way of viewing all technical and economic establishments.

A more liberal and multilateral exchange in world society must await, first, a general awareness of the full potential of two-way reciprocity of the experiences of development, and second, the availability of highly trained innovators to manage the liberalizing experiments in the developing countries. Here also the economically advanced countries might provide some assistance—for everyone's long-term benefit.

INSPIRED DEVELOPMENT

A multilateral dialogue among many centers having independent development purposes and styles might well inspire the future course of development. The dialogue among European countries in their centuries of growth presents an imperfect yet instructive example. No one national style dominated for very long. Each country made a contribution according to its unique experience. Every country learned from—and competed with—the others. The inspirations, from the university ideal to the rights of man, were raised higher because each country brought a unique perspective to bear upon them.

The enormity of our task in world development is conception and inspiration, not achievement. Economic development is now largely assured, despite many serious hurdles ahead. What is more problematic is that we comprehend the radical nature of our revolution and conceive what it might, can, and must (or must not) do for us.

Complicating the problem is the East-West ideological conflict, which forces the West's own sociopolitical dialogue and self-criticism into a rigid and reactive pattern. The importance of democracy, for example, at least in times of great change, is not so much in its present values or manifestations as in its interpretive and directive influences. A freely interpretive approach to democracy would help radiate its predominantly political application into the social and cultural arenas. But East-West tensions have hardened conceptions and limited the range of democracy during the course of change.

At present the results of technical and bureaucratic power are bulldozing human emotions into a social abyss. The inspiration for development cannot rest on upward projections of growth statistics, which simply extend the past into the future. It must be of a different character, express a different mood. The inspiration must be a statement of life that controls and qualifies the elements of change—technology and bureaucracy most of all.

Of course, we cannot ignore the two-thirds of humanity who suffer grave physical deprivation. We must be sympathetic with their frame of mind which, strangely like our own, cannot readily seize the full opportunity to grow, as we cannot seize the full fruits of our growth. The question for them as for us is to widen the horizons of life, even while the means to life are being enlarged.

2

Emerging Corporate Citizenship

The first chapter highlighted man's stake in contemporary development, particularly the price of narrowing our objectives to technical and economic means. The present chapter discusses some features of the narrow base of development, first in industry and agriculture, then in corporate and economic terms. The concluding section describes a few practical consequences of that narrow base. The general significance is a new corporate citizenship and a new locus of social sovereignty.

INDUSTRIAL POWER

Historically, the central tradition of industrial production falls into several clear stages. Handicraft, the first, was marked by one or a few craftsmen working in a small shop, usually in a family's living quarters in a crowded part of a village or town. Each man was the chief energy source, acquired all skills needed to complete a product, and used simple hand tools. Normally, he was involved in all stages of production, from procuring raw materials to disposing of his product to the user. He had a unified interest in a product and in the whole process that brought

25

it into being. The "industrial" unity harmonized with the unity of family and community.

This was characteristic until the modern era. Society, strongly supported by the Protestant ethic, had been subtly preparing itself for its race to production since the Reformation. Then, hardly two centuries ago, a series of forces brought the factory system into play in Europe. The most important features of the factory were a central source of power (initially the water wheel), large-scale machines (beginning with textiles), and large numbers of workers. The advantages of central power and large machines offset the special efforts required to organize and discipline large numbers of men for effective production. Most workers without skills were in effect regimented nervous systems and supplementary sources of power. Each man's interest was restricted to a specific task of production. The rationale of work increasingly differentiated materials, machines—and men—to achieve the ends of production. The scope of freedom and interest of the individual was fractured, as were his relations with his coworkers.

However, the factory itself was not new with the eighteenth century. Factories existed in the Middle Ages, in the Roman Empire, and in Constantinople, Antioch, and Tyre. Even water power had been used before. But these earlier factories were essentially isolated events, whereas the factories in England, Europe, and America after 1760 fit into a general pattern of growing and changing economic activity. Even before 1700 there had been an increasing amount of foreign trade, improved financial and organizational structures, improvements in equipment, and some scientific discoveries capable of industrial application. These were strongly bolstered by Arkwright's water wheel and Watt's steam engine. Factory expansion also closely paralleled improvements in transportation. Hence a broad social organization and an economic base capable of supporting higher levels of production were of equal importance with internal factory development in bringing about industrialization as we know it.

Soon a profound rationalization began, including the standardization of parts, continuous process (culminating in the production line), and new levels of integrating manufacturing, assembly, storage, and distribution. Although Eli Whitney produced firearms with standardized parts in 1793, a mature rationalization was not demonstrated until Henry Ford mass-produced automobiles on his assembly line more than a century later. The plants simultaneously became larger, often employing tens of thousands of workers. The rigors of synchronizing men to machines increased as the whole plant depended more on the balanced performance of each part.

Today the onset of automation is demonstrating an enormous new potential in productivity. Yet automation itself is but one of four profound revolutions in industry, according to Robert Brady.[1] The chemical revolution has affected the entire materials base for industry, not only in making available a vast array of new materials but also in expanding the uses of older materials such as metal, coal, and wood.

New sources of power, with more varied applications, are another revolution. The problem of energy supply for the next seventeen centuries has been theoretically "solved" with presently available uranium and thorium, based on estimated consumption in the year 2000.[2] Since a pound of uranium is the energy equivalent of 1300 to 1500 tons of bituminous coal, transport costs are negligible, so that simple energy shortages no longer need prevent development in any region of the world.

The third revolution is in electronics and automation. The three major steps in achieving automation are: (1) automatic handling and processing of materials; (2) integration of production equipment guided by built-in automatic transfer devices; (3) the inclusion of computers that "read" and automatically "correct" the process.

All three revolutions are intimately related, of course, and all depend upon a fourth, which Brady calls the standards and specifications revolution. This involves "comprehensive and exacting systems of nomenclature, formulas, process and equipment controls, and precise standards for guiding each and every step in production. . . . The results . . . are extraordinary, and in the main are as little understood in theory as they are revolutionary in practice." [2]

These mutually supporting revolutions have come about only because of an overwhelming concentration of interest by the whole society, which Brady aptly summarizes: "The new patterns of industrialization, like the spread of Christianity under the Caesars or of democracy after the Illuminati, are everywhere the order of the day." For the new scientifically oriented industrial technology "most developed and underdeveloped countries alike seem prepared to modify, alter, or, *in extremis,* sacrifice whatever stands in the way in the forms of law and custom, politics and religion, economics and standard of living." [3]

With such a concentration of interest, the revolutions in industry and their extension to all peoples are virtually inevitable. Yet, simultaneously, the signal reversal of human submission to machines and organization now appears possible. Automated production of all common products is solidly on the horizon. The time is approaching when *man will no longer be required substantially in production,* only in preparing for production and perhaps in managing its largess. Machines and industry, so long in the ascendance over the integrity of man, have now begun to make man virtually obsolete in the gross fabrication of material necessities. Even as industrial organization makes this final insulting gesture to men, the human menial regimentation, so systematically devised in the drive for production and so rigorously pressed in the nineteenth-century factories, may now decidedly decline.

Symbolically the onset of automated production seems to complete a cycle begun when a pair of hands first pounded stone upon stone to produce an ax or an arrowhead. Although important industrial revolutions undoubtedly lie ahead, the momentous revolution for man himself is now on the threshold, virtually exempting him from deadening toil and tedium.

However, completing the cycle presents to the whole society many radical challenges, of which only a few implications are evident now. Our whole modern social mechanism and style of life, built about the organization of productive work and the social means to make *men* productive, are certain to be profoundly affected; these include the form and the character of government, cities, education, media of economic exchange, social and economic policy, social hierarchy, family relationships, and individual self-images. For example, the purely social importance of earned income that forms the basis for ambition, status, courtship, and male roles in the family will decline or disappear, likely producing a new instability in interpersonal behavior.

The interlocking web of life built around work, which was so laboriously incorporated into man's social make-up over thousands of years and which is so dominant in modern society, will certainly lose its moorings. Man will lose his most essential work to machines, he will also lose his most pervasive social organizing force, the very force that now more than ever provides man with his essential link to society.

Freedom from daily toil has no current meaningful precedent to guide man, not even any ground rules, in economic thought or social theory. Certainly the theories of both capitalism and communism are caught short (and lose much of their contentious meaning). Furthermore, sudden and vast new levels of productivity may overwhelm the slow evolutionary adjustments that society has normally depended on in the past.

The West's momentous race for production, now joined by the peoples of the East and the South, is presently reaching a point that no man soberly anticipated a century ago. Society is moving at an ever greater momentum on a trail it has not traveled before, and it moves without headlights or road map. We are even without utopian visions to reveal new human possibilities.

INDUSTRIAL AGRICULTURE

The first area to begin showing the magnitude of change imminent for industry is agriculture. And in agriculture deep public concern for accelerating technical change is contrasted sharply with ignorance and inaction in meeting the consequent human problems.

Modern agriculture is indeed a proud accomplishment, but it has left a social skeleton in the closet. In the United States the rapid growth of productivity per acre and per man since the 1930s has cut in half the number of farms, bringing not only a migration of a part of each new generation to the city, but a massive and forceful close-out of millions of farmers and a decline of many farming regions.

The question for us is our way of perceiving "progress" in productive agriculture and our way of ignoring its human results. The question strikes at our habit of overlooking the huge social eddies in the mainstream of economic progress.

The typical farm family of antiquity could feed but itself and a fraction of the needs of another person. By 1940 the American farmer could feed eleven persons; by 1965, about thirty persons. Furthermore, since 1950 the largest farm "problem" has been to restrict farm production to a reasonable range of food demands. All in all, the recent revolution in agriculture has made it possible for nine tenths of the population to be free of food production. Historically, only about a tenth were free of this necessity. And productivity continues to rise.

The direct application of science and technology to farming has lifted a tremendous physical burden from the body of man. But the rural way of life has been sacrificed as the scale, capitalization, technology, and education required for modern farming have increased. Isolation is gone. The large farm family has lost its usefulness, along with the family cows, hogs, chickens, and garden.

All of this could not have been foreseen. But our aims in agricultural progress have not been very clear or very consistent. On Hilgard Hall of the College of Agriculture at the University of California, Berkeley, is lettered the poignant phrase: TO RESCUE FOR HUMAN SOCIETY THE NATIVE VALUES OF RURAL LIFE. There is special irony here, for the work carried on inside Hilgard Hall has helped destroy the traditions of rural life. Hardly a better illustration could be found than in California's own fields.

The southern part of the San Joaquin Valley is dominated by large, intensively cultivated irrigated farms, some of more than 10,000 acres. Typically cotton, potatoes, and alfalfa may be planted in carefully planned proportions and locations on each "farm" to reflect soil conditions, market conditions, full utilization of the long growing season, and government acreage allotments. Each spring these factors are evaluated by full-time economists, agronomists, and soil specialists to determine that season's best mix. Foremen operate from radio-equipped pickup trucks. All work is organized from a corporation yard, with its own office, shops, and stored equipment, often including bulldozers and fleets of cotton pickers. Cotton gins, packing sheds, or dehydrating plants may be operated as wholly-owned independent companies.

These are but the external manifestations of the shift of farming from a way of life to an industrially organized business. The owners are businessmen more than farmers; they rarely work the land themselves. Their concern is mainly finance and management. The owner's personal life and his family's are hardly related to a rural environment—regardless of whether they live in a town or on the land. The same is true of his employees (no longer hired hands), whose wages, benefits, and working conditions parallel those of industrial corporations. The only exceptions are transient workers, and their numbers have steadily declined since World War II.

The California example illustrates the industrialization of land—what is called "agribusiness." Another example, the chicken broiler industry, illustrates the industrialization of a commodity—a case of pulling chickens out of farming and making them a nonagricultural business. Until about 1925 chickens used for meat were culled from egg-producing flocks each spring and marketed as "spring fryers." The broiler industry [4] was subsequently founded on extremely rapid specialization that achieved high-volume, high-quality production by highly integrated industrial organization, creating for the first time a national market, and later even an international market.

The war created a special profit in broilers because meat rationing did not affect chickens. Interest then centered on breeding new lines of chickens for their meat qualities, period of growth, and feed utilization. The expanded markets brought large capital into play. Breeders, "grow-out" producers, and processors were quickly differentiated, and all this was managed through complex contracts. National markets helped affect an overwhelming concentration of production in about a dozen intensive growing areas, mostly in the South and East.

But perhaps the most important change was the concentration of production into fewer and fewer hands. According to one observer, some ninety companies accounted for 75 percent of the production (as integrators) in 1962. Significantly, Ralston Purina was said to be the largest. This company was in 1967 the fifty-ninth largest industrial corporation in the United States. Hence very little reason remains to classify the broiler industry as agricultural.

Meanwhile, there was virtual chaos for farmers, especially for the thousands who tried and failed to make the far-reaching adjustments the new industry required. "Broilers," said one industry survey, "illustrate an industry of almost explosive growth during the postwar years, of severe instability, and of dynamic structural adjustment to the changing external and internal forces." [5]

Shakedowns of this kind are not uncommon or even new. Anyone traveling in New England can find remnants of old farmhouses on thousands of abandoned farms, the artifacts of the struggle of many generations. These farms came into being with colonization but were defeated when more efficient farming in the Midwest created and then dominated the national market for major foodstuffs after the Civil War. Similarly in the West one may find traces of many agricultural towns that did not make a go of it. Settled with high hopes and great energy, these, too, had to be abandoned because there was not enough water, or the right soils, or sufficient transportation. Human aspiration, health, and even lives were lost in the larger regional development.

Examples such as California agribusiness and the broiler industry illustrate two especially relevant points. The first is the demise of the rural way of life. What is important is not just that rural life is disappearing; rural life was probably doomed at the onset of modern industrial production. Nor was it all that grand. Very probably the rural way of life had no more intrinsic validity than our concept of the "noble savage," or any other long-established social tradition. But it was a way of life, and it was cherished by most of those who knew it.

The second and far more important point is the way in which major social and economic changes are conceived. It is striking to see how much public and private effort is put into the promotion of change and how little to constructive channeling of the sweeping effects of change. The disappearance of the rural way of life was actually a painful expulsion of a part of society out the back door, not only because abandonment of farms was and is not the choice of most rural people but also because there are no programs to rectify economic hardship or to assist in occupational and social readjustment.

True, the effects of sweeping events can seldom be foreseen. But that is not true of long transitions, when their general dimensions and character can be described, evaluated, and projected. Today we can make reasonably accurate forecasts about the forced depopulation of the rural areas, and the specific nature of the problem is well known. Whereas there were 6.8 million farms in America in 1935, the number dropped dramatically to 3.7 million in 1962.[6] But more than 2.7 million farms in 1959 had *gross* incomes of less than $10,000 and produced less than 30 percent of the value of agricultural production.[7] Thus more than two thirds of all American farms face early consolidation or abandonment. It has been predicted that there will be only about 300,000 or 400,00 commercial farms in the United States by the year 2000.[8]

It is now quite predictable, therefore, that by the end of the century about 3 million more farms and farm families will be left high and dry—in their way of life and in their means of livelihood. What kind of good life can they look forward to? If the past offers a clue, society's response to their plight will be less energetic than its continual pressing for their expulsion through economic and technical progress. The general acceptance of drastic subversion of a population in favor of the advancement of an industry was well illustrated by an agricultural management consultant, who predicted that there will be only 500,000 farmers in the United States by 1976. "But," he quickly added, "*they* will be immensely prosperous." [9] (Italics supplied.)

As with industry, a full cycle will soon come historically to a close in agriculture. The pattern of life appearing in neolithic times, and persisting through earlier periods of civilization, is now coming to an abrupt end. But behind the unlimited abundance so clear to the statistician is the cruel economics that is bringing defeat to the majority of farmers. And after defeat, after a bewildering migration to a city and a painful readjustment, the result is the exchange of a way of life for an occupation, an exchange of deep values for an income.

In the flush of economic success society has lost sight of the hardship of the concomitant declines. It has not "looked into the eyes of the wounded." [10]

CORPORATE LIFE

Whatever human promise is arising from sheer industrial and agricultural productivity, there is still no assurance that the promise will be fulfilled. For all results of technological progress are mediated through the modern corporation.

If modern man in the age of development can reaffirm his human purposes in society, and imprint them on all human institutions, then the faith that man has put in technological progress is likely to be rewarding. However, should corporations follow a course of institutional self-interest, expressed in unlimited striving for profits, growth, and social power, and if these interests command the primordial position in society, material progress will likely be achieved at the expense of traditional values and rights centered on the individual. If the course of agricultural progress is representative, the future terrain is not bright, perhaps even ominous.

Massive and complex industry could not have developed without the new capacities to organize men, skills, knowledge, and ideas so well demonstrated by the modern corporation. Adolph Berle has called it one of the "master tools" of society. This instrument permits virtually any arrangement of proprietors to mobilize any volume of resources and men to perform any variety of tasks. Through contractual relationships the effective strength of any one corporation may be linked to that of any other. The corporation is indeed a master tool.

The corporation shares many important purposes, approaches to organization, and functional characteristics with government agencies, unions, professions, and nonprofit organizations, even universities and philanthropies. But our interest centers mainly upon the private stock corporation.

Much of the significance of corporations stems from their sheer size. The largest 500 in *Fortune* magazine's list claimed 60 percent of the sales of the 200,000-odd industrial corporations in the United States and 70 percent of the profits in 1965. In 1967 nearly fifty firms employed more than 50,000 persons. General Motors alone employed 745,000, sold $20 billion worth of goods, and earned nearly $2 billion in profits. And the corporate concentration goes on unabated. The 500 largest industrial firms of 1961 acquired 3400 other firms between 1951 and 1961—an average of almost seven per company. In the 1960s a new general phenomena appeared— conglomerate mergers; their story is yet to be learned.[11]

The prominence of the corporation in American life is but vaguely understood. Only occasionally is there a recognition by management of the gross magnitude and depth of corporate influence. William Gosset, vice president of Ford, has said that "the modern stock corporation is a social and economic institution that touches every aspect of our lives; in many ways, it is an institutional expression of our way of life. During the past 50 years, industry in corporate form has moved from the periphery to the very center of our social and economic existence. Indeed, it is not inaccurate to say that we live in a corporate society." [12] What features of the corporation make America a corporate society? That is, what gives corporations their deep influence upon the life of the family, the institutions that render service to the family, the character of entertainment and education, the form of cities, the life goals and ambitions of the individual?

The interest of every commerical company in the well-being of the whole society is inalterably shaped by two basic conditions. The first is the necessity to make a profit; the focus this imposes upon every company is widely appreciated and requires no further comment. The second is the performance of specialized roles. However diversified a General Electric or an RCA may seem to be, each performs in an extremely narrow sector of the total economy. This inevitably influences a corporation's outlook—for instance, on what part of the economy should expand, on what kind of public transportation policy should be followed, on whether there should be foreign aid or not. Specialization and special interest are so strong with us that even government agencies, which should have a far more comprehensive outlook, continually stake out proprietary interests and strive for growth in the best *laissez-faire* tradition.

Under such conditions, corporations, unions, agencies, and professions alike tend to promote their single purposes out of all proportion to a balanced appraisal of social needs: General Motors may promote automobile transporation beyond all sense of rational use, or the Bureau of Reclamation may press for dam construction on any river simply upon a favorable cost-benefit calculation, or the American Medical Association may openly promote a proprietary view of health. Even America's best-known example of multipurpose development, the Tennessee Valley Authority, has increasingly narrowed its emphasis to electric power production, the area offering the greatest growth potential.

Since these special interests and the persistent search for profits are combined with great size and the exercise of important social power, corporate management has drawn new criticism in recent years. One argument revolves around "administered prices," holding that, since price competition has diminished for many large firms, commodity prices are set without a significant market influence, thus guaranteeing high levels of profits and permitting higher advertising budgets with the purpose of increasing market penetrations. This policy is sometimes described as taxing the consumer. Also criticized is the tendency of corporations to retain earnings for capital expansion, thereby avoiding managerial restraints associated with outside financing. This practice has been described as investment without investor consent or equity, and Walter Reuther condemns it as "inequity capital." A third criticism involves the demise of the stockholder as an effective agent controlling the corporation. This control has shifted to professional management, and typical stockholders retain in effect only the right to petition for profits on their investments.

Daniel Bell of Columbia University has suggested that what is at stake is the "legitimacy of power." He points out that United States Steel Company, after its 1957 price increase, could make a profit while operating on as little as 32 percent of its capacity. With this kind of economic flexibility the steel industry as a whole could "take" a three-month strike, according to Bell, without affecting average profit. This means that the strike is financed by the consumer.[13] It is not without some merit, then, that the term "private government" has come into use, meaning that a concentration of social power has taken place without legitimate means for the public interest to be expressed in the management.

What appears singularly important in these arguments is that today each has a factual foundation, whereas in 1800, 1850, or perhaps even

1900 there was little basis for raising or discussing them. They reflect a new society and new conditions our social philosophy has not prepared us to interpret, and they pose questions of freedom our system has not yet made inviolable. In an address entitled "On Living in Freedom with Bigness," Adolph Berle has said, "let us . . . in the name of elementary reality, have done with the nonsense that a free market, unaided, maintains freedom of individuals to live as they choose—if indeed it ever did. . . . That occurs only when the state maintains free market conditions by restricting in large measure the very freedoms of contract and property which the free market is assumed to provide. . . ." [14]

What are the sources of contemporary corporate power and how is it expressed?

One important power, which has been given relatively little attention, is the power to decide what product to manufacture or sell or what service to provide. A company may decide to make toys of war or toys of education. It may decide to make paraphernalia for indulgence or equipment for skill formation. A television network may choose programs that play upon emotions or programs that strive for importance or excellence. A construction company may decide to build houses or build viable neighborhoods. In an age of affluence, when necessities determine only a part of expenditures, this power cannot be ignored. Nor can it be explained away by consumer response, for decisions are often made prior to known responses, and are reinforced by limited selection, massive advertising, misleading overpackaging (which puts quality into the package rather than the product), and other factors.

The rise of affluence also opens wide the door to advertising, particularly to newer, more penetrating forms of advertising, because of the flexibility of purse and leverage of appeal that arise with increasing wealth. And advertising penetrates even the design and purpose of products. Automobile manufacturers have evidently decided that Americans should buy transportation as women buy clothes, by annual style flourishes and for nonfunctional effect. Advertising is of such importance that we shall examine it separately in the next chapter.

Research is a distinct corporate tool of incomparable significance in this age of change, for it is a power over the direction of social innovation. Its importance is evident in the growth of corporate research expenditures from $510 million in 1941 to $6.5 billion in 1965. The rising trend can be seen in another way. In 1964, Xerox, a fast-growing company, increased its research and development staff by 400 persons to a total of 1100 while its production force increased only by 700 and its marketing organization by 1400, for a total company employment of more than 11,000. By the sheer numbers involved, research is evidently a central element of corporate strategic power.

Corporate research and innovation raise the question of possible influence upon all social innovation. It is not just that research into automatic coffee dispensers and cosmetics will take precedence over basic physical science or humanly pertinent social science. What is more deeply involved is that product innovation associated with the growing tendency toward creating and exploiting an irrationality in the relationship of the individual and his material needs will overwhelm or snuff out other innovation in society, which might, for example, liberalize education or make the physical city socially relevant. We cannot be sure that this condition is not already influencing the direction of change.

The broad purpose of research itself and the character given to it by corporate control are equally ponderable. And what are the implications of large research staffs working on assigned subjects for "profit"? What influences will be fed back to university training, to the universities themselves, and to the tradition of free scientific inquiry—especially its ideals of objectivity? If corporate research is creating a new tradition in science, how will it define the new purpose of science? We shall return to this problem later.

Another extraordinary power of corporations is their influence over the physical form and institutional vitality of the city. Good cities or bad cities are the way they are because, more than anything else, businesses want them that way. This is the power behind the renaissance in Philadelphia and Pittsburgh. It is equally behind the stupor of New York, Houston, and Los Angeles. Whether business wants unhampered freedom to build anything anywhere or whether it wants an optimum physical, economic, social, and cultural setting for carrying on its affairs and for its employees is all too often the crucial difference between civic stupor or renaissance. The mind of American society responds first to economic potential, and unless local economic leadership takes a liberal initiative, little of value can be expected.

Corporations are powerful also because they have an unusual and growing grip on the allegiance of their employees. This is not happenstance and it is not a natural loyalty, such as that in the family. It occurs because companies have devised particular ways of shaping rewards to influence careers at every turn. In recent years management has shifted its conception of the employee from a current expense, when he was needed primarily as unskilled or easily replaced labor, to a capital investment, as he has become a highly skilled specialist of long-term benefit to the company. Some of the means to implement this shift include successive longevity increases in wage, parallel increases in vacation and sick-leave benefits, accrual of nontransferable pension funds, and special insurance and health benefits.

But another strong factor supports allegiance to companies and conformity of behavior. Not a few writers have noted the individual's deep personal dependence upon his job, job status, and regional home location—all occupational determinants that strongly structure his membership in society. Yet this membership is always a conditional one, for the organization may terminate employment and with it disrupt the individual's place in group life. Even a distant threat of dismissal establishes a pervasive pressure of conformity upon the person. Conformity, therefore, creeps into the base of personality, minutely and imperceptibly molding the "organization man" described by William H. Whyte.

Finally, immense power rests within the corporation's huge and flexible financial resources. Numerous companies are able to make large investments, sometimes in the hundreds of millions of dollars, in projects that will not begin to "pay off" for ten or more years. This was true of subsonic jet transports, despite government support, and far larger corporate investments are required for supersonic transports, excluding government cost-sharing during development. These resources can be concentrated, or they can be dispersed in many projects and regions. Unprecedented volumes of resources are thus joined with broad flexibility of action in the national and international arena.

These powers of modern corporations are strikingly new. Only since World War II has organized research become an effective tool in the corporate chest. Similarly the personnel policies that have made man a capital investment—and corporate "property"—are quite recent. Although advertising is old, its use as a power to influence rather than inform is largely new. The manufacturer's wide freedom to determine the kind and character of its products has arisen mostly with the onset of general affluence. The businessman's influence in civic affairs may not have changed, but his direct affect on the form of the city has increased as more kinds of industrial plants have become "footloose." And in corporate resources, many a company has recently multiplied its assets tenfold in hardly more than that number of years. Even General Motors, already a giant in 1925, increased its assets thirteen times by 1964.

Each power, then, is new in fact or new in scale, still far from mature, and still largely an unknown quantity in the long span of time. The corporate powers, still in nebulous constellation and still changing and growing, pose a most baffling and profound question, a question not without its somber possibilities. If effective corporate control rests very largely with self-perpetuating management, and if only a failure to make a profit is likely to disrupt that control, it might well be that this "master tool" of society operates without an effective rudder concerning the deeper interests of society.

But even now new tools are being added to the corporate chest. Examine the field of education. Note the entry of many industrial corporations into educational systems, producing not only audiovisual and automated instruction equipment but also the accompanying instructional materials. Note also the industrial companies that have contracted to manage training centers for the Job Corps: Litton Industries, Xerox, RCA, IBM, General Electric, and others.

Traditionally, urban subdivisions have been the province of small independent developers and contractors. But now, as the scale of development approaches that of new cities of 100,000 and more, some of the largest industrial companies are entering this field. General Electric is reported to be preparing to do so. The Aluminum Company of America is already so engaged.

Evidently, traditional manufacturing is not a sufficient challenge for these companies and does not offer them acceptable growth possibilities. Opportunities in urban development and education must therefore seem bright. But how subtly will future city-making then favor a physical and institutional pattern of life more firmly gripped by corporate commercialism? And how imperceptibly will the preparation of automated educational materials impress upon young minds the singular virtues of the organizations that organize so well their dynamic society?

Put in the broad perspective, the corporation is still a new part of our tradition, but already it runs deep. It serves a mighty purpose and must play a mighty role in our thinking about the future. Yet shouldn't we, if we are to take hold of our destiny, shape the institutions that shape us? Shouldn't we benefit from *all* aspects of institutions, not just their productivity? In an age of almost unlimited power we must make our values and purposes clear and inject them into the form and character of our institutions.

In an age of massive institutional power Adolph Berle reminds us of the importance of guiding social action by a sound philosophy. Berle refers to St. Augustine's reflections about the fragmented Roman Empire: St. Augustine "knew," says Berle, "as men in power in this time did not, that whatever institutions they built derived permanence, continuity and significance from the philosophy more than from the power." [15]

This observation has been made in another way. Edward Mason suggests "that this powerful corporate machine, which so successfully grinds out the goods we want, seems to be running without any discernible controls. The young lad mastering the technique of his bicycle may legitimately shout with pride, 'Look, Ma, no hands!' but is it appropriate for a corporate society?" [16]

Ultimately, critical judgments about corporations as well as other institutions will revolve around the way they structure ordinary human relationships. At present they emphasize the pecuniary and hierarchical; they give weight to specialized and functional contacts between individuals at the expense of the social; they defer to all technical advantages and economic margins. Corporations seek to refine contacts between men to the preciseness and advantage they have achieved in the machine.

Somehow, the corporate vehicle has brought people together for a journey in such a way that the people can find no use for one another except that they happen to be going in the same direction. But why are we thus together? Where are we going? Cannot a better goal be found for going and for being together?

MONOLITHIC POWER OF ECONOMY

The sum of industrialization, agricultural transformation, and corporate power constitutes an economy of incontestable strength in shaping human social organization. But the power of economy is greater than that. Its organizational strength is joined with a deep economic ethic of belief, motivation, and precedence in social behavior that weighs heavily in such distant matters as marriage and birth rates, suicide and mental illness, delinquency and public morals. The obvious power of the economy, together with many evident side effects, strongly supports the conclusion that the American people acquiesce to economic determinism in their personal, interpersonal, and organized life.

Unless we accept the notion that the means to support life should dominate all patterns and interests of life, we should ask whether our contemporary economic pattern is not "overbuilt" in its determination of the motivation and behavior of the individual. And, considering the enormous increases in productivity taking place and in prospect, we should ask whether the prevailing dominance by economics will not become less necessary and therefore even more overbuilt in the future. Shouldn't economics penetrate social belief, behavior, and organization only as far as is necessary to produce the material basis for a worthy, challenging, exciting, and varied human existence? And aren't there even then certain social goals that might take precedence over certain extra levels of abundance?

One challenge of affluence, therefore, is that we come to terms with the new materialism, and especially with the institutional foundations that underlie affluence. Everyone is a materialist, like it or not. What is important is that before we can enjoy material wealth, or be freed from it, we must put all things in a proper context, so that they will not require burdensome attention. The poorest men are materialists, too. But materialism nearly always dominates their thinking and behavior. Those who have enough wealth to assume survival and minimum comfort may subordinate these objectives to others they consider more worthy and rewarding. In other words, unless we should suddenly find inherent value in endless acquisition, we should be able to decrease the attention we give to material needs as rapidly as machines can be made to fulfill our requirements.

Unfortunately, much contemporary Western materialism has become a game of acquisition. And the game has achieved the status of an independent or inherent value, an anticipated response, and an expected challenge throughout society. It has become a deeply institutionalized tradition with a self-disciplined ideology.

But the most important effects of an overbuilt economy are upon the family, community, church, and structure of urban living. The family in most traditions was both a unit of production and a unit of consumption, and these functions gave it unity and strength. Its property could be used either to increase production or to satisfy current needs. Both production and consumption operated together and were emotionally and socially meaningful to the individual. Today, however, corporate production has severed the two functions, leaving the family a unit of consumption. At the same time the family has been shaken loose from the appendages of grandparents and uncles and from its community home base. Children remained full members but lost their useful role. Accountably, there was an increasing dependence upon the job, the dollar, and the anonymous market.

The prevalent small town of the eighteenth or nineteenth century provides another perspective. All "goings on" were completely within the scope or knowledge of each individual or family. Most individuals spent their lives locally and were acquainted with or knew about all other residents. Every school or church served the whole town, even though but a portion of the town might be active in each. Contacts between two individuals were likely to be varied in character and carried on wherever they should meet—which was a frequent occurrence—in the store, shop, church, council, or community celebration. Practical affairs seemed to be subordinated or peripheral, concluded somehow as the outcome of an important personal association between individuals. Although work was longer and harder, casual associations and personal diversions were easily interwoven with useful and productive contacts.

The waning of community of this kind, which will be examined in more detail in Chapter 6, can be associated with large-scale employment and the tendency to promote an interchangeability of persons, the segregation of functions and specialization of contacts between persons, the strict measures of performance, and mass urbanism. What was unified and familiar became divided, specialized, and impersonal.

The powerful economic stamp of the American government was felt from the outset. The Protestant ethic was well developed by the time the

Constitution placed a high premium on property rights, and this was fundamental in promoting growth. Major legislation granted lands to the railroads, to homesteaders, and to special *agricultural* and *mechanical* colleges. The Congress gave free mineral and grazing rights on its land, supported a strong banking system, and encouraged mass immigration to fill labor-hungry factories. Education sought to develop "useful citizens" with practical know-how. Thus, broadly speaking, the government became imbued with the Protestant ethic—which was really an ethic of economics.

Although many elements of the ethic arose from the church, many also returned to influence the church. In the latter half of the nineteenth century, for instance, members often used the church as a basis for personal reputation, a good source of business contacts, and even a primitive credit reference agency.

Especially on a new continent with a mobile population whose old ties and institutions had been severed by emigration, the excitement of land, minerals, production, and sales could become powerful. New frontiers, new products, new organizations, and new markets were food for the popular imagination. New traditions and new institutions could coalesce around business enterprises and more easily influence the foundation for the new social system. Economic initiative predominated, and in one way or another all group behavior had to respond.

Land was especially important. It had long been a marketable commodity (not a public trust), and its use in forming the city served exchange and profit more than livability and civic life. Acreages were chopped into easily traded parcels to bring about an incredible hash: an absence of clear centers or boundaries, imbalance in the location of living and working areas, invasion of living areas by commerce and industry, unlimited expansiveness, indiscriminate puncturing of living areas with transportation lines. The ramrodding of railroads and major thoroughfares through all areas of the city reinforces Lewis Mumford's observation that the American city was an area to be passed through in space and time.

The management of urban land solely as a private marketable commodity not only assured that the prices of land in working-class areas would press upon the tenants' last dollars, but prompted a type of congestion that guaranteed deterioration in short order, especially since the method did not provide for parks, school sites, and other public places. The congestion caused others to seek ostentatious plots to demonstrate their wealth in open amenities, thus providing for themselves the spaces and many of the facilities that more properly—and more adequately—might have been provided publicly. Consequently, even in living areas the urban layout was derived from the same principles: land was conceived only for the economic aspects of its development and for its trading qualities. Community integrity and a livable urban form were hardly conceived, let alone realized.

Without an over-all articulation of urban form, work tended either to be too painfully close or too dismally far from home. Without deep social values to guide the urban form, the mere calculation of travel time and cost of investment were the only meaningful criteria of "house hunting," save class snobbery. Excepting schools, local institutions to serve the family were without general meaning. And without unified neighborhoods, shopkeepers were free to maximize their service areas by locating along raucous boulevards or at dangerous intersections. Indeed, for cities without the basic physical and institutional forms upon which higher human values could accrue, all that was left was economic "maximization" of functional advantages.

Cities are reputed to be the physical embodiment of a culture. Any broad examination of the American city will make evident that its assemblage, mood, and power are overwhelmingly economic. This is probably the clearest evidence that the economy is an overbuilt structure.

FUNCTIONAL ORDER

The overbuilt economic structure is also revealed in the extent to which strict functionalism is stamped on social action: the individual's daily routine, the behavior of the family, the organization of public affairs.

Industrial development means, among other things, that the effective level of interdependence of life for the individual is raised from a few hundred persons, or a few thousand, to millions and hundreds of millions. As the level has risen, its character has changed as well. The essential interdependence is no longer between individuals but rather between vast and complex organizations. The individual has become simply a ward of these organizations. More importantly, where once economic activities were incorporated within larger *social* traditions, social traditions now take their form from the *economic* order. Individual behavior is divided into particular and discreet functions and carried out in separate compartments.

A few examples will illustrate how behavior is fragmented by the functional structure of the environment.

I first consciously experienced such bald functionalism at a large university in the early postwar period. For some time I felt vaguely at sea, but for no definite reason. There were no demanding problems, yet the uneasiness persisted.

My weekly activities included about fifteen hours of lectures, about fifteen hours of part-time work, affiliation with a university-related church group, and my family life at home. I was reasonably absorbed in each, but that did not seem to matter. I wanted to share my experiences and thoughts with those about me, but I could not, for I was living in four worlds that could not be related. I was the only common element among them. I might be involved in all four in one day, but each shift put me among different kinds of people who were together for different reasons. Only incidentally did others have reason to know what I did elsewhere. If I spoke of studies at work, I elicited kindly diversions of conversation. If I spoke to another student about an incident at work, the result would be comprehension but little else.

Behavior at the university was equally splintered. Every student followed a separate trail. The normal five subjects not only segregated thought into separate packages, but also separated students socially and intellectually.

This compartmentalized existence was not a threat to stability, nor was it a momentous trial. But it was a serious deprivation of mutuality and a fragmentation of social identity. Academically, the excitement every subject had to offer was reduced to an acquisition, a performance, a credit and a grade, and, most of all, a necessary function. Obviously all needs were served: education, finances, social participation, and family, but all remained just functions.

What happens to the individual in this kind of environment is matched by what happens to family and locality. The Los Angeles metropolitan area dramatically exemplifies urban development under the influences of technology, affluence, and particularly the automobile. At its more distant fringes (some fifty miles out) are the city of San Bernardino and a complex mixture of incorporated and unincorporated urban sprawl. In the city of Rialto (1960 population, 18,000) lives a family whose husband works in the city of Fontana (population, 14,000) and whose wife works in the city of Colton (18,000). The children go to school in San Bernardino (91,000) and the family attends church in the city of Redlands (26,000). They shop in several unrelated regional shopping centers as well as in the older cities of their "principal" occupations. The radius of daily operations ranges up to fifteen miles.

Some of the consequences of this pattern of life are immediately apparent. The house at Rialto tends to become fragmented into its constituent functions: a command post, a financial institution, a hotel, and a restaurant. The members of the family have few common friends. The

second family car is not a luxury, but a necessity, because public transportation cannot economically serve families in low-density suburbs who
travel so far in so many directions. The mother is forced to be family
chauffeur for the children under driving age because few friends or
activities are within walking distance.

And the splintered family life is paralleled in the civic affairs of the
various municipalities. The family votes in Rialto, although it has vital
interests in other cities; yet even to vote in that one city is confusing.
Since several special utility districts and the school district overlap the
city of Rialto, the political organizations, issues, and personalities all become obscured. It is most difficult for the family to see or act upon the
larger civic interests, for there is no community or commonality to give
the issues focus. The family is reduced to searching for its own particular
interests, which tend to become functional and special.

The utility and school districts were originally formed *ad hoc* to provide specific services to specific areas. Some of the services were taken
over by the cities when they incorporated because municipal boundaries
and those of the districts were not identical and because vested interests
had evolved. Because of jealousies and suspicions, some cities had incorporated merely to prevent being annexed to others. Nor did the relatively flat terrain help in defining municipal boundaries. Strips and
enclaves are common. Thus the governmental structure has tended toward an unhealthy, irrational pattern of special interests. Frustrations
and conflicts have cause to grow rather than diminish over the years.

The experience of the family in Rialto, the confusions in public affairs,
and my experience of functional splintering in college are not unique—nor are they diminishing. They illustrate changes in life resulting
from society's quite unconditional acceptance of industrialization, corporate initiative, and economic preeminence.

3

Production-Consumption Inquisition

The productive side of life has not developed without influencing the institutional base of society and its balance of powers. In this chapter we shall examine some elements of the changing structure and then concentrate on the institutions with the overwhelming social initiative.

COMMANDING INSTITUTIONS

From antiquity civilization has been identified with a few paramount institutions. The family, with its blood extensions of clan and tribe, was powerful until modern times. The church had a steady ascendance until a few centuries ago, but, like the family, it has lost initiative and power as the secular state has emerged. Finally, economic organization has come of age and now rides on a crest of rapid growth.

In every age the principal establishments jockey for allegiance, for control over education of the young, for ethical initiative, and for naked power. One institution usually has the upper hand, but the others generally sustain a balance. A family may achieve unchallengeable control

45

through kingship or a whole dynasty. Sometimes an oligarchy or dictator may assume complete control of the economy and strive to transfer the sentiments of religion toward itself. But the other groups, nevertheless, tend to place a check on more extreme actions. The West has tried to maintain an open society through constitutional restraints in which all institutions function relatively freely, and this is properly placed among its finest heritages.

The family is the only major institution based on the basic biological functions of life. Nevertheless, reduced to its conjugal members and offspring, it has lost many of its old prerogatives. The stray grandparents, aunts, uncles, and cousins who could once have claimed a place at the hearth must now live in isolation or in segregated "homes." Prejudice against nepotism effectively kills family power except in certain economic establishments. The family has also lost the cohesiveness of common work as well as its role in the community. Reduced as if to a tough spore, it maintains a deep resilience, but has long since lost its zestful continuity.

Although the churches have lost much of their initiative, they fight a rear-guard action to save certain traditions. But their role weighs heavily toward simple conservatism rather than a response to social debilitation and personal disorientation. There is little evidence of their offering a profound or realistic social defense against the schismatic forces of the Big Society.

The secular state is very much another matter, having benefited from the combined attention of many great social philosophers and men of action. Consider the conceptual and practical accomplishments of constitutions, balance of powers, federation, bureaucracy, bills of rights, political parties, universal suffrage, tax systems, and international law. The results are evident also in the effective claim that states make on loyalty.

Economic organization is the newcomer among the commanding institutions having an independent social power. Until business acquired size, distinctive leadership, and a clear self-consciousness, it had little leadership significance. But late arrival has not prevented the economic order from achieving great power of scientific innovation, financial manipulation, and popular taste formation.

The professions at one time also might have evolved into a separate commanding institution. However, today they are but a vague appendage of the economic establishment, by spirit and by involvement, and their separate historic ethic appears to be mostly vestigial. Surprisingly, in terms of independence and initiative the philanthropic foundations and private social service organizations (such as the Boy Scouts, YMCA, and Red Cross) reveal a sudden historic emergence. Although the foundations are generally endowed by massive personal fortunes not likely to become available again in the future, the service organizations draw the bulk of their support directly from the people, providing a base of power comparable to that of the churches.

But in the contemporary jockeying among the commanding institutions, none matches the initiative and privilege of the large corporation. As we have noted, the varieties of power still coalescing under the corporation posed questions that reach into all levels of human behavior.

As yet the powers of the corporation have not been called to the same social accounting as the powers of the state. They respond to no broad franchise of a scope equal to their powers. The government presents no serious impediment, even from the antitrust point of view, and the recent flurry of conglomerate or mixed mergers is little affected. Indeed, antitrust action does not attack the contemporary *social* problems arising from corporate behavior at all. The whole federal influence is muted because there is not the obvious flagrancy of injustice or violation normally required to bring about new forms of legislation. Furthermore, the complex and varied nature of the effects of economic power are not amenable to single acts of legislation.

One suspects that the question of corporate power will be seriously raised as the industrial system moves beyond fulfilling primary and secondary material needs and desires and goes more deeply into synthetically aroused consumer indulgence. Therefore it is important to look into the corporation's continual sharpening of its diverse, articulate, and penetrating tools—tools that seem to render a magnificent service but that all too often pass through the thin line that separates service from exploitation.

WILL OF CORPORATIONS

Let us recall again the incomparable reflections on America by Alexis de Tocqueville more than a century and a quarter ago. Tocqueville was concerned with a "species of oppression by which democratic nations are menaced. . . . The first thing that strikes the observer is an innumerable multitude of men, all equal and alike, incessantly endeavoring to procure the petty and paltry pleasures with which they glut their lives. Each of them, living apart, is as a stranger to the fate of the rest; his children and his private friends constitute to him the whole of mankind. As for the rest of his fellow citizens, he is close to them, but he does not see them, he touches them but does not feel them; he exists only in himself and for himself alone." Above such men, Tocqueville saw an absolute power, "minute, regular, provident, and mild . . . to keep them in a perpetual state of childhood. . . . For their happiness such a [power] willingly labors, but it chooses to be the sole agent and the only arbiter of that happiness; foresees and supplies their necessities, facilitates their pleasures, manages their principal concerns, directs their industry. . . ."

Tocqueville continued:

"The will of man is not shattered, but softened, bent, and guided; men are seldom forced by it to act, but they are constantly restrained from acting. Such a power does not destroy, but it prevents existence; it does not tyrannize, but it compresses, enervates, extinguishes, and stupifies a people, till each nation is reduced to nothing better than a flock of timid and industrious animals. . . ." [1]

These were brilliant prophecies, for the reality is with us today, not only in the obviously totalitarian regimes, but at home in the huge organizations that seek to win loyalty to a multitude of brands, designs, and gadgetry. Tyranny is generally thought to have its source in government; yet Tocqueville's words today seem strikingly relevant to the economic establishment. Even without the word "power," which I inserted and bracketed in place of the word "government," the excerpt above refers more aptly to economic seduction than to government paternalism. Tocqueville himself, of course, sensed the materialistic base of a provident tyranny.

But the business philosopher, Peter Drucker, has also raised the question of totalitarianism, especially in connection with the shift of productivity from the individual to the institution. What makes totalitarianism "total," he said, "is that it completely denies the person. This could never be done in a culture in which the individual by himself can be productive, that is, socially effective. Any tyranny, however brutal and arbitrary, has limitations if it cannot make the whole of man's social life subject to its commands." [2]

Business has always been conceived in the limited terms of producing goods or services to make a profit. This was a limited social ethic and it was matched with very limited means. Now these means have grown immensely in scale, financing, technology, specialization, diversity, bureaucratic articulation, and geographic coverage. Advertising has helped business to penetrate the mind of society, and planning helps it to penetrate the future. But these immensely expanded means have not been matched by an expanded conception and ethic of the role of business in society. And they are protected by an ideology of *laissez faire*—of noninterference in the functions of business.

The discrepancy between the technical means and the social ethic is augmented in the universities by advanced schools of business administration and by the connections those schools have with the sciences and professions. These schools have raised the status of the calling, intensified the self-consciousness of the ideology, and established a professional commitment to this newest commanding institution.

Among the tools business schools employ to sharpen the young entrepreneur for corporate life is the concept of decision making. Professor Norman Martin defines it as "a present commitment to a particular line of action based upon anticipation of the future course of events." This means that, "in a sense, the future must be brought into the manageable present." The question is, in other words: what line of action will be most effective? It is not the question asked, for example, in the liberal arts education at Amherst College: how does one estimate the consequences of his action? Therefore the definition is of especial interest for what it overlooks.

Evidently, decision making is an action-oriented process with the overriding and simple objective of maximizing profits. By definition and by implication the term is ethically aloof, and this is confirmed by its literature. Thus its underpinnings are ethically permissive. Particularly in the absence of a broad base of social concern, decision making presumes a linear scale of benefits, a singular concept of success, and a monolithic basis for social action. The value is simple, functional, pecuniary, and undeviating. The term, therefore, as a tool of advanced management, epitomizes both the vastly expanded means and the ethically constricted role of modern business.

Business management, according to the implicit dictates of decision making, is comparable to competitive sports, having overtones of spirit, vigor, fair play, and success according to proven merit. But the analogy breaks down because sports are played according to carefully established rules of conduct, whereas business operates in a far more complex terrain with many gaps and inadequacies in the rules. And these gaps become wider as the powers of the corporate players become more diverse and massive. Originally competition was sought as a means of protecting the public from the evils of monopoly. But competition that continually concurs in adopting new marketing practices, advertising techniques, research findings, and more comprehensive approaches to penetrate and control consumers and the very structure in which society functions has become as questionable as monopoly. Consider how the very nature of the following are influenced: the content of mass media (limiting ideas and criticism); character of education (for producing and consuming); form of cities (designed to market land and automobiles); structure of transportation (to promote the most expensive kinds: aircraft and automobiles); extent and character of social welfare and public housing (largely to maintain labor reserves and maintain purchasing power); pattern of recreation and entertainment (emphasizes only those activities requiring expensive equipment or passive watching).

Decision making is not questioned here because of breaches of conduct, but rather because of the lack of definition of what constitutes a breach at the stratospheric level at which corporations now affect society. In these times of corporate expansiveness a serious disequilibrium has thus arisen between the power of business and the social ethic it should serve. Ultimately the implications are as ethically profound as the material results have been revolutionary.

A few cases will illustrate some of the gaps in the ethic. At the entrance to Uris Hall of the Columbia University Graduate School of Business is an inscription quoted from A. N. Whitehead: "A great society is a society in which its men of business think greatly of their function." Although the School of Business is concerned with educating only the business elite, its curriculum does not seem to press upon men to think greatly of their function. Only one of more than one hundred courses in thirteen classifications in the two-year master degree program pointedly refers to a broad framework within which business serves society. The description of the course, "Conceptual Foundations of Business," states that "the student taking this course should acquire a well-developed philosophy of business and be better equipped to perceive the broad significance of specific business policies." There is no suggestion of serious self-criticism of the role of business in society, whether philosophically, socially, psychologically, or institutionally. Yet self-criticism would seem to be fundamental if businessmen thought greatly of their function.

A more revealing case is the doctoral program at the Graduate School of Industrial Administration, Carnegie University. Significantly, it encompasses not only industrial administration but also economics and psychology.

According to the school's bulletin, a major emphasis in industrial administration "is placed on the analysis of human behavior in complex organization." This objective is carried over into economics, where studies "may employ statistics or simulation techniques together with concepts from psychology in order to isolate and evaluate critical behavioral parameters in consumption or investment relationships." Similarly; "the Doctoral Program in Psychology emphasizes scientific and quantitative analysis of behavioral phenomena. . . . Students interested in decision making, group behavior or personnel testing may concentrate in Organizational and Industrial Psychology. Students interested in man-machine systems may concentrate in Engineering Psychology. Students interested in general experimental psychology may choose to concentrate on Physiological and Sensory Psychology, Learning, or Social Psychology and Personality."

The aims of research at the school are focused sharply. One team, for example, "starting with practical problems of how top-management decisions can be made better, was led to techniques of mathematical modeling and computer simulation that are revolutionizing psychological theories of human thinking and problem solving." Other studies have included "interpersonal influence on preference and judgment, effect of communication on speed and accuracy of group problem solving," and "investigations dealing with the situational determinants and the physiological bases of reaction to fear producing stimuli, with particular emphasis on the endocrine system."

Using the academic sciences with characteristic thoroughness, the school includes among its facilities a behavioral science laboratory. One research room is devoted to experiments in psychoendocrinology and another to the observation of group organization behavior, and there is equipment for the study of the perceptual processes.

The purpose of all this, of course, is to improve administration. And to do so, the faculty is evidently impressed with the control of human behavior. This is revealed not only in the program in psychology but in the basic courses in administration. For example, the first course on the list is "Behavioral Science and Administration." Here "attention is given to the systematic development of knowledge about human behavior and to its implications for organizational design and management practice." Similarly, the course on "Interpersonal Skills in Management" stresses "the use of generalizations from the behavioral sciences in the orderly, creative solutions of practical administrative problems," including "communication, influence, control and managing for innovation and change." Other courses follow a similar vein.

This astonishing arrangement at Carnegie University clearly subordinates both economics and psychology to industrial management. These two social sciences have thus been refashioned into narrow tools of business enterprise.

What is signally important here is how knowledge and the search for new knowledge are narrowed to the interests of one profession, and especially how sharply that knowledge is aimed at the use, manipulation, and control of human beings. In the absence of clear, broadly framed social goals that limit and restrain this use of science and also free it for other more liberal purposes, we must ask what is in store for the tradition of disinterestedness in the search for truth, the liberal purposes of higher learning, and even the independence of universities.

Clearly the behavioral sciences as represented in the School of Industrial Administration at Carnegie are not serving the liberating purpose Whitehead envisioned in the early 1930s. He had hoped the social sciences would help make the new large scale of business more civilized. It is especially ironic, therefore, that while business has indeed incorporated the social sciences within its concern, the result has been a narrowing of science, not a broadening of business.

Of course the social sciences should provide useful knowledge for the various social professions, including business. Quite properly the social sciences should be incorporated into the training programs of law, education, business, and even be used for relevant applied research. This is a calling of great importance. What is missing is a truly liberating foundation in the social sciences, a foundation supporting a directive liberal philosophy of business that will enhance *all* goals of society.

Knowledge of the social sciences is a power, like all knowledge, and the social sciences are precisely a power over people. Yet they are used without a liberal and independent rudder that can prevent them from being manipulated by American society's largest interest group of Big Citizens. The power of Big Business echoes hauntingly the words of Tocqueville: a power that is "minute, regular, provident, and mild."

A textbook, *Organization*, by two faculty members at the Carnegie Graduate School of Industrial Administration provides some additional revelations. The authors, dealing with the methods of organizing employees in industrial systems, describe the approaches followed by the early theoreticians in this field: "In time and motion study . . . the goal was to use the rather inefficient human organism in the productive process in the best way possible. This was to be accomplished by specifying a detailed program of behavior that would transform a general-purpose mechanism, such as a person, into a more efficient special-purpose mechanism." The authors say that "in this model, leaders are limited in their achievement of organizational goals only by the constraints imposed by the capacities, speeds, durabilities, and costs of these simple machines." [3]

The authors compare the two early stages of "organization theory": "The study of organizations was generally dominated in the first quarter of this century by the point of view of scientific management; in the second quarter by the interests and approaches usually labelled 'human relations.' In the former case, the human actors in organization were viewed primarily as 'instruments' that could be described in terms of a few physiological and simple psychological properties. In the latter case, the human actors were endowed with feelings and motives, but relatively little attention was paid to their properties as adaptive, reasoning human beings." Finally, the authors state their own position: "Our analysis of cognition fits into the broader outline of organization theory not as a substitute for, but as a supplement to, these earlier approaches." [4]

Noteworthy is the authors' attitude toward the methods and techniques of the earlier approaches, criticizing not the dehumanized utilitarian objectives of the organizations themselves, but their relative backwardness. This is made clear when they say: "we hope . . . that we have pointed to a hundred opportunities for using human behavior in organizations as an empirical testing ground for some of the central generalizations and major methodological innovations of the behavioral sciences." [5]

The terms of the authors are scientific in character, and the setting for them is higher education—amid a tradition of search for truth and of supposed good will. But here we see an application of science not to human welfare (hardly even in narrow materialistic terms) but to the conditioning of the human will, "minute, regular, provident, and mild."

The methods followed at Carnegie are not unique, of course. A far from atypical statement from the *Harvard Business Review* predicts with a peculiar detachment the personal adjustment problems of middle managers resulting from automation in the 1980s: "One can imagine the major psychological problems arising from the depersonalization within management and the greater distance between people at different levels. . . . In particular, *we may have to reappraise our traditional notions about the worth of the individual as opposed to the organization.* . . . This kind of inquiry may be painfully difficult, but will be increasingly necessary." [6] [Italics supplied.]

The authors stated the question succinctly: it is whether man or his institutions are to be the real citizens of the republic.

But the problem is most complex. Whitehead felt that "the change of scale in modern industry has made the whole of previous literature on the topic irrelevant, and indeed mischievous. . . . Unless the twentieth century can produce a whole body of reasoned literature elucidating the many aspects of this great topic, it will go hard with the civilization we love." [7]

WILL OF ADVERTISING

Advertising has recently found a vast, astonishing new role in society, assisted by many important developments of our time: the technology behind communication, the growth of mass media and mass entertainment, high productivity and popular wealth, specialization and professionalization, and large-scale commercial organization. In exploitation of these developments, $15 billion is spent annually in the United States for advertising.

The new role is revealed by the three stages in the natural history of advertising, each progressively magnifying its extent and intensity. The first was *information* ("We have a new shipment of textiles from England"). This emphasizes communication more than influence. The second stage was *competition* ("Our washing machine will give twice the service"). Competition advertising suggests rapid improvements in efficiency, cost, durability, and total service. It competes for *the* consumer's dollar. It also symbolizes a rapid growth of new products, which come to be considered essential: appliances, ready-made clothes, automobiles, and packaged foods. The third stage of advertising is *expansion* ("You have earned a special holiday"). Stress here is put upon spending an increasing income for more variable purposes. This new power of advertising associated with general affluence pushes consumption toward the level of productive capacity. All three stages are represented in contemporary advertising, often in a single advertisement.

There is also a natural history of the kinds of influence each stage of advertising tends to carry. *Information* advertising informs us about the kinds of goods and services that are available; this is absolutely essential for normal trade. *Competition* advertising strives to make the individual brand-conscious—and increasingly conscious of style changes associated with mechanical improvements. Certain characteristics of consumption are impressed upon people: keeping up with the newest models, conspicuous consumption, and the attractiveness of such features as size, power, gadgetry, plush. *Expansion* advertising includes most of this but also moves into far more rewarding territory, well characterized by the motivation research that increasingly underlies it. *The goal is to influence the life of the individual.* Emphasis shifts in a subtle manner away from the product, especially from price and durability, to the consumer himself.

The consumer, not the product, gets the chief attention. The product is presented as a counterpart to personality, a part of one's style of life. Thus, advertising may promote an indulgence in articles that are close to the body and promote vanity: fine clothes, liquors, tobacco, and other creature comforts. Or it may appeal to the *man* of world travel, the *man* of importance, the *man* of good taste. Or it may promote a town-and-country squire complex. Naturally this life-style demands a station wagon, trailers, boats, golf clubs, skis, complete workshop—and these are required for personal adequacy.

The power of expansion advertising emerges only in a setting of free expenditure by a large, affluent population. As long as the consumer's immediate choice was between a side of bacon and a sack of flour, the advertiser's maneuverability was narrow and his budget narrower. But when the choice is between a small yacht and a trip to Rome, the advertiser's purse and persuasiveness become enormous.

Advertising has been controversial ever since it became competitive. Our question here, as for all business activity, is the loose ethical code with which advertising is moving into the roots of personality and culture. Is sophisticated, penetrating professional persuasiveness to be the omnipresent hand that guides the natural selectivity of our senses, the monitor that tracks down our moods, the steamrolling of fact and opinion that compromises judgment and even the whole intellect? The question is sharpened by the long-range possibilities of motivation research, assisted by the large body of social-science knowledge and by the social scientists themselves.

Even with motivation research, some advertisers deny that they are "diving, deep down, into the dark waters of the Freudian seas." [8] Others, such as Pierre Martineau, believe that "advertising essentially is dealing with a primitive, prelogical process of the mind—with the compulsion to action initiated by suggestion. . . ." [9] Since advertising is accepting the philosophy that Martineau espouses, his views are worth examining in his own words:

"The credo of the Advertising Federation of America begins with the statement that good advertising aims to inform the consumer and to help him buy more intelligently. This is an admirable statement of principle; but if we only provided information, we would not accomplish what we set out to do—namely, to persuade people. Nowhere in the credo is expressed what every single competent advertising man is trying to achieve: The attachment of psychological associations to his product by combining emotive and esthetic appeals with the sales logic.

"The point is sometimes made by ethical objectors that motivation research is wrong because it will permit advertisers to manipulate people against their wills, to sell them things they don't want and don't need. This is a rather silly argument. Wasn't advertising trying to create wants long before motivation research was ever heard of? People didn't realize they needed air conditioners, electric washers, and power lawn mowers for their homes until advertising created the desires for these products. If motivation research will help us to be more efficient in our advertising appeals and techniques, certainly no one will insist that we should deliberately avoid the use of something in order to give the consumer more of a sporting chance. On the contrary, it would seem to me that the morality is all on our side if we can use our advertising expenditures more efficiently, if we can achieve more effectively what we have long since been trying to achieve." [10]

"For the purposes of advertising . . . we are primarily interested in singling out only those motive forces which are manageable by the creative people. Many obscure and complex factors which may be important clinically are just too subtle for the creative people to reckon with. Cigarette research reveals that masochistic tendencies (deliberately hurting oneself) are important motives in smoking, but for the advertising man this leads nowhere." [11]

"The president of the advertising agency for an automobile having a very poor sales year attributed this entirely to the fact that the car was a poor value. Therefore, his primary advertising theme was devoted to convincing the public that it was a good value. But in our research at the same time, which cut through these consumer rationalizations, it was obvious that the car buyer was really objecting to something else—not value per se, but a radically different styling." [12]

"One of the most successful beers started out as a popular-priced beer in its own market. When it decided to expand its distribution, it raised its price to become a premium beer. The price jump also permitted much larger advertising funds, which were used very skillfully to create much greater desire on the part of the consumer. The beer has infinitely better sales success with the higher price. In the consumer's mind, it has more value today because it has more desirability." [13]

"If a chewing gum features flavor in Maine advertising, then people in Maine will insist that they chew gum for flavor. At the same time, people in Texas will assert that they chew gum to relieve tension, if this is the theme of the Texas copy. This isn't bad—it's good. Advertising does put words into people's mouths." [14]

"When I tell my youngster, 'Pick up your things and come in the house,' I am neither being informative, expressive of feelings, nor sociable. I am directing someone what to do. That's the purpose of advertising—to persuade someone either to adopt a new habit or to keep on doing what he is already doing. We are trying to influence somebody else—which is why editors pontificate, politicians orate, ministers preach, why parents and teachers criticize. All of them are attempting to direct, control, or influence the behavior of other persons. This is directive communication." [15]

". . . The average American doesn't think that he is being manipulated by advertising. Instead of turning away from it, he wants advertising." [16]

Little comment is necessary about the intent of those in the fifteen-billion-dollar advertising industry who adhere to the general views and practices described by Martineau. The question is what additional techniques and insights will come into use in the coming decades, as advertising becomes even more important in the structure of the economy and as greater sums are expended to bombard each individual. This concern is heightened by the direct influence of advertising over all the major media of mass communication, especially the press and broadcasting.

A surprising feature about advertising professionals is their remarkable lack of awareness about the broader implications of their newer practices. Vance Packard has noted how a large proportion of advertisers, "particularly from the research organizations, were so frank and detailed about their findings and operations that while I admired their candor, I at times wondered if they had become insensitive to some of the anti-humanistic implications of what they were doing." [17] Perhaps it is in this unknowing, unexamined acceptance of influence and persuasion, rather than in willful hidden influence, that a mild and provident tyranny may be arising. Perhaps, also, with enough pragmatic testing of advertising no deep-down Freudian insights may be needed; successive approximations in striving for influence might do the job perfectly well.

How easily a more complete influence might be gained with enough intensive effort—and how easily successive approximations might work —is shown by an example not directly involving advertising, but revealing a persistent, pervasive, and, to a degree, monopolistic control of communication. It involved the experience of a professor of sociology as a young man in his native Germany in the 1930s. Few people, he reported, would have had greater reason to resist the ideas of the Nazi than a Jew. Yet, despite his overt will to deny within himself the attitudes of the Nazis, he found that bit by bit their less noticeable social values were becoming absorbed into his own values. Despite his deep resistance—the same resistance that many people nowadays assert of themselves concerning advertising—the pervasive sentiments that the Nazis had inculcated into German society in so short a time reached into his behavior and belief as well.

As modern advertising seeks to create desires, to form tastes, to influence men by their emotion, it begins to shape its own ideal of personality, its own definition of society. It does this, not for any visible social goal or imputable evil, but as the incidental outcome of razor-sharp competition to improve margins of profit.

It is indeed unfortunate, therefore, to see how extensively the academically trained social scientists, particularly psychologists and sociologists, have committed themselves and their knowledge to the service of advertising—especially to the deeper levels of persuasiveness. No less disconcerting is the training universities provide in advertising techniques. One wonders whether the influence of Freud and psychoanalysis has not been felt far more widely in public persuasion than in psychiatry and clinical psychology.

Martineau, excited by the prospects of the social sciences in advertising, tells us that "the primary task facing the creative man in advertising is how to get at people's feelings." How, he asked, can the advertiser "communicate convincingly with the third ear, with the levels of intuition far beyond reason? . . ." He thus aims advertising squarely at the motive roots of personality and culture.

The ethical question behind the formation of personality—the question of individual or institutional citizenship—is very significantly a matter of privacy, and Vance Packard states it clearly: "At times it is pleasanter or easier to be nonlogical. But I prefer being nonlogical by my own free will and impulse rather than to find myself manipulated into such acts. The most serious offense many of the depth manipulators commit, it seems to me, is that they try to invade the privacy of our minds. It is this right to privacy in our minds—privacy to be either rational or irrational—that I believe we must strive to protect." [18]

MAN AS MEANS

Even a brief look at our economic system and its patterns of competition, power, and reward shows that business's interest in the individual is not to fulfill his material needs. Rather, it seeks to have the individual serve two related functions, both necessary for the health of the system: he must work to produce goods and services and he must consume them.

Naturally all of this is necessary. Men desperately want the necessities of life; and who but men will produce them? But, given this necessity, do not industrialization (mass production, mass markets, mass consumption), corporate pressure for endlessly higher profits, and the ability of advertising to expand consumption imply that social purposes have shifted subtly from man to the economic system? How far has man become the means to improve the performance of the massive social apparatus? How far has this subordination reached into the sources of human conduct?

Judged by bureaucratic practice, the industrial and commercial organizations work best and control the individual best when the person is autonomous, freely moveable, specialized, and expendable. Historically, industry could use only individuals who had been emotionally separated from the small local groups with powerful traditions. Ideally, the new man that emerged with industry was merely individuated, not the strident individualist depicted in literature. The individualist could break traditions, move to the frontier, establish new enterprises. But he was rare. The type of person required in the large factories was the separated and conforming individual.

And in production itself the individual has now lost his ability to define his own conduct. Originally, according to Peter Drucker, man as a hunter and a scavenger both produced and subsisted independently. Later, he was able to produce independently with independent skills, but subsisted dependently by trading with the local division of labor. Today, most men both work and subsist dependently. The worker is divorced from the product; he merely works within a process; the organization determines the kind and character of product and the organization produces it. Production has lost its character-giving strength for the individual.

Consequently, Drucker observes, "social status, social prestige, and social power cannot attach to the individual's *work*. They can only attach to the individual's *job*. They can flow only from his membership, status, prestige, and power within the organization." [19] Drucker discusses the Great Depression of the 1930s to illustrate the significance of the shift: "It is not primarily the economic impact that 'made' unemployment the nightmare" that it was during the Depression. "We were able to keep the great majority of the chronically unemployed and their families on an economic level . . . probably well above the level any but the very rich could have lived on only a century ago. . . . The main effect of long-term unemployment is not physical, but psychological: loss of self-respect; loss of initiative; finally, in extreme cases, loss of sanity. Denied access to the organization without which, in an industrial society, nobody can be productive, the unemployed becomes an outcast whose very membership in society has been suspended." [20]

The individual's self-image appears to have come into a historic crossfire. From one side, the industrial society insists upon increasing the precision of human response; this requires many years of training and of grooming a particular motive and mood. Many traits of personality are greatly influenced by the demands of employment, yet the individual's personal identity with the organization is highly conditional; anyone can be deprived of his membership in the organization at any time by termination of employment, undercutting his basis for social membership.

From the other side, industrialization has massed huge populations into sprawling cities. What differentiation the city has acquired has followed from industrial, trade, and transportation imperatives, while the living, social, and cultural spaces are essentially those left over. The differentiation of the society as a whole has followed from the same economic imperatives, leaving noneconomic institutions that are essentially derivative—filling, in effect, the leftover social spaces. The family, the church, and the informal associations, therefore, tend to form a fragmentary pattern. No social institution or group of institutions has much opportunity to establish substantial life goals independent of the individual's vocation. Noneconomic institutions are unable to provide anything like balanced nourishment for personality. Yet, although economic organization has become a paramount social institution, setting the major guideposts for the course of life, it resists honoring man—as the traditional paramount institutions do—by celebrating birth, sanctifying marriage, or mourning death. These are "social services" it is hardly organized for or interested in providing.

But production is only one part of the economic system's interest in man. The drift, or perhaps the drive, to consumptiveness raises another specter. Long ago hard work and forbearance of spending characterized the original Protestant ethic, which Max Weber associated with the rise of capitalism. But the grueling sixty-hour work week has given way toward a thirty-hour week. Forbearance, too, has largely disappeared with the weakened restraints of religion, the temptations of wealth, the rise of advertising. After centuries of instilling in man a conforming discipline to produce, powerful efforts are mounting to equate this with a conformity to consume.

The specter raised, already real to a degree, is that of an institutionally promoted gluttony. A particularly vivid illustration is found in an amazing triptych painting, *The Garden of Delights*, done by Hieronymous Bosch, a Dutchman, sometime between 1490 and 1516.[21] The three panels depict life in heaven, on earth, and in hell, each in lurid detail. Bosch's hell stars the devil, of course. But it is the devil's own condition that seems to epitomize the hell: he is eternally feasting while eternally defecating! What greater hell could there be than a gluttony dominating the processes of life!

The parallel for affluent society may seem distant, but can we be so sure? Like a starving man who comes upon food and compulsively engorges himself, society is coming upon wealth from a condition of historic deprivation. But even then the comparison is inadequate. It does not consider that the filled belly will at a fairly predictable point reject further intake; yet there appears to be no comparable point when systematically promoted material consumption will level off. Moreover, our economy has vested interest in unlimited increases in consumption. Already a sizable part of our national wealth is directed to mobilizing systematic techniques to see that vain consumership is not tamed, abridged, or diverted. And all this seems to be but the ongoing expression of traditional commercial interests carried toward their logical conclusion in the age of abundance.

There is particular cause for concern when a problem of society moves toward the base of personality. That this is the case appears evident in the vast "literature of alienation" to which Robert Nisbet has called attention.[22] Especially the diverse sources of this literature are impressive, including theology (Buber, Maritain, Niebuhr, Tillich), psychiatry (Sullivan, Fromm, Horney), social science (Durkheim, Malinowski, Thurnwald, Mead), and, not the least, the major writers (Proust, Mann, Joyce, Kafka, Eliot). Inevitably their interpretations vary widely, but their themes and vocabulary (disorganization, decline, insecurity, break-down, instability, frustration, anxiety) carry a common reverberating ring of clashes between man and his society.

Philosophers in many ages have looked to material advances of society to free the spirit of man. But we face a paradox in which man's free spirit is in danger of being denied and subverted by the same organizational devices by which he has sought to free himself.

4

Personality Under Pressure

We have been considering how the initiative and momentum of the economy and the corporation overrun the individual. We now turn to some corollary influences that guide the normal patterns of thought, that affect the directions and results of science, that make us dependent on the professional, and that define the use of our leisure time.

RATIONAL AND EMOTIONAL ORIENTATIONS

Samuel Goldwyn, the motion picture producer, once said: "America is a happy-ending country." He implied that Americans do not appreciate dramatic plots questioning human outlook or purposes, and certainly not unrelenting tragedy.

A success-oriented country, whose most significant goals are firmly set in accumulative terms, does not relish questioning about human ends or about the ironies that inevitably arise in human endeavor. Questioning raises doubts, and doubts are subversive to a firm discipline. Indeed, rather than doubt, the discipline required for material progress demands repeated reassurance by strong and successful models of endeavor.

What is required of men in an acquisitive society is behavior with measurable results. This is a powerful cultural edict that tends to deny all variant feeling. For the errant personality, the culture demands "an inquisition within," according to Freud, and eventual submission to its demands for conformity.

Goldwyn's remarks are a poignant reminder of how each age refashions the individual according to its own peculiar "social logic." Behavior, modes of thought, interpersonal responsiveness, self-esteem, formal beliefs, and unconsciously formed views of life all have been remade to respond to urbanism, industrialism, and bureaucracy. Although social logic prevails in all societies, no other has shaped the person with the synthetic mold so immediately and demonstrably in man's own hand. A vivid demonstration is found in contemporary views about rational and emotional behavior.

Our social conditioning shows individual emotion and rationality as contrary forces contending for possession of the person—one useless and potentially sinister, the other useful and honorable. Most public expressions of emotion connote an irrationality, instability, or uncontrolled passion, and except on the most unusual occasions they are condemned as unmanly, naive, or egoistic.

Such views are revealed in our attitude that totalitarianism is an irrational aberration of society. We "insist upon making the irrational and the evil interpenetrating essences of one another," writes Robert Nisbet. "Because totalitarianism is manifestly evil we suppose that it is also fundamentally irrational. And because we have thus proved it to be irrational we comfort ourselves with the belief that it must be destroyed by its own departure from reason . . . we merely delude ourselves if we do not recognize in it elements of, almost overpowering rationality. . . . It is rational in that it seeks to eliminate from culture all of those ceremonial, ritualistic, or symbolic features inherited from the past that constitute by their existence obstructions to the achievement of a perfect mobilization of the popular will. . . . To start out with the assumption that totalitarianism is irrational, and hence doomed to self-destruction, is to start out with an extremely unintelligent view of a form of society that has used all the rational arts of modern public administration, economic management, and social psychology to maintain itself and to make its identity ever more emphatic in the minds of its people." [1]

But rationally organized behavior has parallel uses in the contemporary urban and industrial system. We need not imply a totalitarian takeover to suggest that our large institutions actively use their rational arts to press their own interests over those of the individual. But the same rational arts that deeply penetrate and give external order to an immensely complex society also imprint a structure and orderliness into the individual's mind, suppressing or blotting out feeling and values not compatible with the system.

The denial of emotion is the denial, ultimately, of personal experience. Experience is quite meaningless without the interpretations, the content, the purposes rendered to it by the emotions. This applies to scientific and intellectual endeavors no less than to artistic or purely personal experience. But even at home we tend to deny responses revealing varied emotions, since family life has been increàsingly conceived as preparation for entry into the larger rationally organized world. Society rarely encourages the development of deep personal experience, although the broader range of emotions is required for a full, varied, balanced, and humanly responsive life. By contrast, Freud asserted in his famous little work, *Civilization and Its Discontents,* that primitive man "knew nothing of any restrictions on his instincts. As a set-off against this his prospects of enjoying his happiness for any length of time were very slight. Civilized man has exchanged his chances of happiness for a measure of security." [2]

Obviously, man's mind must acquire discipline to achieve orderly thought and to maintain the social orderliness and security upon which happiness rests. Orderly thought, however, does not arise specifically from either suppressing or promoting emotional experience, any more than worthy emotional experience arises specifically from either attaining or denying rationality. In reality, of course, the two areas are not separable; nevertheless, the capacity for enjoying life, which is founded in feelings, should not be confused with the capacity for human performance, which is founded in a disciplined mind.

The irony is that current pressures for rationality in men and organization, tending in fact toward lockstep utilitarianism, accompany a growing irrationality in human affairs. Is not the existentialists' equating of reality with absurdity but a blunt recognition of this fact in society, if not an abject capitulation to it? Are not public services tending to include only those activities which cannot be made profitable to private enterprise, rather than those requiring particular forms of social responsibility? Are not sweeping social fads generated by the highly organized mass media?

The hard fact about our rationalizing individual human behavior is the incessant and pernicious companionship of a deeper irrationality in society as a whole. We make rational the microcosmic functions through training, clear methodologies, and formal organization, but leave the macrocosmic level of social events in chaos. There is a high level of internal rationality, for example, in saving-stamp companies, but an external irrationality in the way they influence the larger economic processes of marketing. There is a high level of internal rationality in advertising firms (and even a rationality in their priming the pump for economic growth) but an irrationality in their effect upon the larger functions and purposes of society. To a degree, this larger irrationality creeps into such basic commodities as steel and chemicals (not to speak of such products as automobiles or television sets) in that their use may be promoted far beyond any rational social purpose.

Thus there is generally a clear rationality of the functioning of society up to the level of individual corporations, agencies, professional societies, and such, but an irrationality in their larger social consequences. This bespeaks the powerful social sovereignty of the Big Citizens. It also shows up in the kinds and levels of planning society does, which we shall take up in Chapter 12.

An important example of irrationality is seen in the profession of traffic engineering, which has been established principally to rationalize the movement of automobiles. It has devised numerous methods to increase street capacities by 10, 50, and sometimes even 100 percent and has established specifications for freeways with five times normal street capacities. But an enormous fallacy arises under such micro-pragmatism. The automobile demands more than twenty times the surface space of an individual, and when that space is provided, the city grows to match the automobile's scale. The automobile then feeds on its own growth. Freeways, therefore, can never be sufficient. More importantly, the city is made uninhabitable for people.

If our rationality is clear in the smaller units of behavior and increasingly unclear in the broader ranges of social action, this is because we are rational in dealing with methods and means but irrational in dealing with purposes and ends. We break up broad social purposes into specific social needs, then endow these fragmented purposes with specialized organizations that provide special services. But then the organizations acquire their own purposes beyond those for which they are created. Thus, while our perspective is narrowed, these organizations take on special interests that subvert the larger social possibilities.

Yet any society that takes pride in its humanism should not deny that *"the function of reason is to promote the art of life,"* as A. N. Whitehead emphasized in his book, *The Function of Reason.*[3] In the end, what is rational *for* man is what has deep meaning for him as a human being. But today this is denied, is preempted elsewhere. Especially now that many former pressing economic goals have lost their meaning, as has the naked drive to production, "the going becomes the goal," as Mumford has stressed. Accordingly, Allen Wheelis notes that "without meaningful goals modern man has, understandably, no sense of direction; for he does not look where he is going. Like an anxious soldier on the drill field he covertly watches those around him to make sure he stays in step. . . . He is burdened by a sense of futility and longs for something or someone to give meaning to his life, to tell him who he is, to give him something to live for." [4]

Whenever we press for rationality without respecting the emotional basis for normal human motivation and behavior, we seem to subject reason itself, or the results of reason, or the goals providing the objectives for rational behavior, to peculiar inversions. Perhaps we have yet to recognize the full paradox of externalized human objectives that are not balanced by, and possibly guided by, nonrational inner feelings.

Freud offers an interesting reflection on the problem. Civilizing a newborn child, he says, is a process of taming the id, especially the sexual and aggressive tendencies, through the superego, or the internalization of prohibitions of behavior. He emphasizes the "extent to which civilization is built up on renunciation of instinctual gratifications. . . . This dominates the whole field of social relations between individuals." [5] Freud later remarks that civilization, in commanding and prohibiting the instinctual gratifications severely, "troubles too little about the happiness of the ego, and it fails to take into account sufficiently the difficulties in the way of obeying it—the strength of instinctual cravings in the id and the hardships of external environment. Consequently in our therapy we often find ourselves obliged to do battle with the superego and to moderate its demands." [6]

The emotions, including joy and sorrow, gladness and disappointment, love and hate, pride and shame, communicate the human meaning of events and motivations. These are the foundations for worthy relationships and for individual depth, although under bureaucracy they tend to be reduced to anger or pleasure, reflecting one's performance. The emotions also give the individual a vent to relieve normal frustrations and anxieties, which, if bottled up, can lead to serious internal or external conflicts. Powerful proscriptions upon human expression both deny individual feelings as well as interpersonal association. What is denied between persons also tends to be denied within one person.

One result is extremism. Efforts to magnify the outward manifestations of rational behavior and suppress inward experience call out protest or rebellion in the individual and make him susceptible to movements with an antidemocratic purpose but with rational programs: the Ku Klux Klan, the Birch Society, the Minute Men, and the American Nazi party. Such groups have deep roots in the prevailing American traditions: white Protestantism, capitalism, individual enterprise, the right of individual defense, and nationalism. But almost certainly these organizations would do appreciable harm to the very traditions they presume to represent if they were to gain substantial national power. The Black Muslims hold a stance outside the deeper American traditions precisely because these traditions have been largely denied to Negroes.

Although the raw drives of man must be tamed, their harsh repression seems questionable. In Freud's view, civilization "obtains the mastery over the dangerous love of aggression in individuals by enfeebling and disarming it and setting up an institution within their minds to keep watch over it, like a garrison in a conquered city." [7] And conquests usually make a subdued people susceptible to other dangers. Is there, perhaps, a connection between the suppression of emotions and their exploitation in advertising? Is it possible that by suppressing emotions in the "productive" side of life we are opening for exploitation precisely the same emotions, and perhaps the whole foundation of personality, in the "consumptive" side of life? May not one be the counterpart of the other, the two poles of the same magnet?

PRESSURES OF SCIENCE

The many branches of science are, of course, rigorous users of rational thought. Indeed, without highly rational propositions, methods, and interpretations there can be no science. But science is not thereby exempted from the peculiar problems posed by rational and emotional orientations in organized life.

The broad distinction between the natural sciences and the social sciences may help illustrate how the sciences suffer from similar inversions of intent and outcome, and how these reflect upon the larger social question.

The natural sciences are the primary source for virtually all basic technological improvements in contemporary society. Their findings are rapidly interpreted for possible professional uses in engineering, medicine, agriculture, and business. There is a smooth continuum of communication from basic research to applied research and development, heavily backed by the wealth of both the enterprise system and the government, and material innovations are assured of a speedy introduction. However, it would be a mistake to overlook the disconcerting fact that this process just as readily serves inane entertainment by color television and wasteful competition in outer space as it assists in saving life. And still the undifferentiated flow of innovation increases steadily.

A century ago there was a considerable popular suspicion concerning science. This has now largely disappeared, precisely when science has proved itself one of the most radical faiths that has ever come to man. We should not be misled by the conservative demeanor of science and of most scientists. Hardly has there been in modern times a public figure more humble than Albert Einstein, and hardly has there been a man whose work has been more radical and ominous for all men than the same Albert Einstein.

The contemporary faith in science is a belief in the value of untrammeled search for knowledge. The goal is a *search* for knowledge, and does not incorporate values about the *uses* or *benefits* that should result from knowledge. Essentially, the goal is procedural rather than substantive, and reflects upon the process of coming to know rather than upon the effects of knowing. The stress is to preserve the integrity of the methods and means that "push back the scientific frontiers." This, it seems, really means "to seek whatever may come" (if we are to remain unbiased and objective in observation and experimentation). The faith assumes that all knowledge is useful, directly or indirectly (also that knowledge is good for its own sake, although this ideal no longer carries much actual weight, if it ever did); it should therefore be sought on all fronts (and nowadays as rapidly as possible).

We often hear of the "productiveness of science," and this term suggests an obvious parallel to the productiveness of industry. The methods and means in both cases are broadly intended to increase institutional capacities. And unlimited increases in "productivity" in almost any field are looked upon as desirable, if not essential, for scientific and industrial progress. One suspects, however, that difficult problems are posed by this approach in science, just as by the unlimited expansiveness of industrial production and corporate enterprise.

Of course, the importance of unfettered search for truth is a valid defense for the integrity of investigation. But this defense also serves moral aloofness and in some cases a social irresponsibility. Manifestly the work of science is far from an aloof matter for society. The advancement of science is no longer just a scientific matter. Science is and must always be prized, but only in balance with other goods. Kenneth Boulding puts this in ethical terms: "The greatest ethical confusions," he says, "have arisen because people have assumed that if something is good it should be pursued indefinitely. . . ." [8]

The hard question facing science is that in ignoring the uses and benefits of knowledge—and society has to assume relevant and useful goals of science—three patterns of direct misuse of science have arisen in the twentieth century: research primarily for new destructive capacities (atomic weapons, biological warfare, rocketry), research primarily for competitive adventure of the whole society (space programs, supersonic transports), which diverts resources from more pressing matters, and research to promote economic consumption (motivation research, marginal differentiation of drugs, cosmetics, wines, tobaccos, and so on).

Were the uses and benefits of knowledge an important part of the faith of science, our present scientific-technological arms races might have been quite different. What most deeply motivated the physicists in the United States to produce an atomic bomb during World War II was the fear that their colleagues in Germany were well on their way toward producing one. But had there been a long-standing and powerful ethic among scientists that prohibited or moderated direct research for destruction, the scientific arms race might never have arisen. In any case, no Hippocratic oath of science existed.

And, in the absence of a clear ethic of the uses and benefits of knowledge, certain effects waylay the freedom of science itself. Having no substantive goals to give positive direction to their endeavors, scientists are open to the bidding of the market for their services. Government agencies and other organizations willingly supply both the budgets and the purposes. The scientists lack a bargaining power to negotiate for research funds and projects compatible with the scientific ethic. Thus a significant traditional freedom is compromised, particularly in large-scale research organized by sponsoring institutions.

"If science wishes to continue to guard its freedom," warns Don K. Price, "it might well begin to worry about the prospect of a society dominated entirely by technological purpose." [9] Hence, in the absence of a broader-based ethic, the growth of "technological purpose" can be disastrous not only for any liberal democratic tradition, but for science itself.

RESTRAINTS OF SCIENCE

Of course, the laboratory researcher cannot take the world's burdens on his back (though some might say that he already has). Under our specialized division of labor, it may be argued, problems of social balance, adjustment, and continuity should be handled in other provinces of society. But if we should turn to the social sciences as a basic source of social amelioration, as the natural sciences have become the basic source of material innovation and change, we encounter a quite different setting. We seem to shift from a scientific activity that dynamically feeds consumable knowledge into the "production-line process" of society, as it were, to a scientific activity that is constrained from dealing constructively with the inundation from the natural sciences.

Not infrequently one hears a social scientist say, "We do not have enough knowledge to act." Such a statement, it seems, reflects more of the character of the social sciences than of their scientific knowledge.

The social sciences are traditionally divided into arbitrary segments of human behavior (economics, political science, sociology, anthropology, geography, and some aspects of psychology and history). This prompts the growth of certain specific aggregations of knowledge, but does not call forth the broader concepts that explain how most human activities blend into wholes. And, unlike the natural sciences, where there is a reasonably direct relationship between, say, physics and the several branches of engineering, or between chemistry and chemical engineering, the social sciences lack clear connections with related professions, such as education, law, administration, or urban planning.

Moreover, the social sciences and social professions do not have the elaborate mechanisms to convert theoretical knowledge into practical application—there is no well-developed middle ground comparable to "R&D." Nor do the social sciences reveal mature interdisciplinary fields such as biochemistry, geophysics, or neurophysiology. Excepting perhaps psychology, social science research is almost entirely observational, rarely experimental; for data, studies overwhelmingly rely on existing social phenomena, rather than on experiments using controlled variables. Experiments naturally have severe humanitarian and political limits. The result, nevertheless, is a form of research tending to bear upon transient rather than inherent nature, and upon present conditions rather than upon the varied human potential.

Then there are powerful social inhibitions operating on social scientists, making large segments of research peripheral, innocuous, and frequently irrelevant to basic knowledge or any other perceived human purpose. Research objectives become confused because the study of man simultaneously presents questions of ends of life as well as of means. One suspects that an aura of scientism too often hides a fear of important and therefore controversial research—a fear reflecting public suspicion that through such research society might be presented with a new Marxian manifesto.

Maintaining a show of objectivity is a major problem in the social sciences. Outright acceptance of human problems with obvious political repercussions makes any researcher suspect of simple credulity, if not radicalism. But, ironically, an atomic scientist is in some respects freer to work on weapons of mass extermination than a sociologist is to even hypothesize about the major social roles of corporations.

Every science of man must also deal with anomalies and contradictions of human behavior, so that significant research findings become suspect among scientists of other theoretical or methodological persuasions. When this uncertainty is reinforced by the hesitant philosophies and unsure traditions of social science, the social scientist is naturally reluctant to become pertinent in human affairs, as the physiologist *is* pertinent in medicine. Then excessive restraints and irrelevancies become understandable, if unfortunate.

The sciences of man are still very young. Yet, as long as social scientists argue insufficient knowledge to act, and then retire to esoteric studies, there is not likely to be a break into new and fertile grounds of endeavor. As long as knowledge is incomplete, as it will always be, this argument can be advanced. For this reason we can thank those who did not understand fire that they learned to use it. We can also thank the users of fire for our learning more of the nature of fire.

Still there is an all-too-human tendency for social scientists who refuse to direct themselves to abiding social questions (in the name of objectivity) to slip into them obliquely and unconsciously. In these cases we cannot be hopeful of the results either. In 1961 the distinguished sociologist Lloyd Warner, author of the Yankee City Series of studies, gave three lectures at New York University, and these were later published as *The Corporation in the Emergent American Society*. In his first lecture, Warner ascribed objectivity to himself when he said, "Whether what is happening is good or bad, or neither, it is not my purpose as a social scientist to say, but rather it is my task to make sense of it and communicate what the evidence indicates." [10]

Warner's lectures were given to the School of Business Administration. The interests of business seem to have been the norm for "objectivity" in discussing the emergent society, for he put both the family and individual completely in its service. "The small autonomous family," he asserted, "freed of strong kinship ties, not only provides an ideal place for training the autonomous persons in their formative period, but later in their lives gives them the freedom to move in the highly fluid world of today." And he concluded: "In our kind of world, given its basic beliefs and its emergent character, we cannot continue advancing unless we are able to produce autonomous personalities." [11]

In these remarkable passages, Warner, speaking as scientist, thoroughly undermines the aloofness he set for himself, as when he speaks of the "ideal" of "autonomous personalities." His emergent ideal seems to be the "larger community . . . where direct action, communication, and face-to-face relations continue through the emergence of the great complex organizations in all parts of our lives, technological, moral, and sacred; largely because of this men frequently interact with others over the whole United States." [12]

Under a cloak of scientific manner, Warner attacks the traditional family, dismissing the significance of local roots for individuals in society. He speaks of freedom, yet his freedom is a detachment of the individual from his local roots, only for reattachment to the bonds of the corporation. This, he admits, will require "adjustment, readjustment, and adjustment again." [13] Warner's personal views are one matter; it is something else when he speaks as a scientist and presents them as objective findings. When these values support a radical extension of human alienation we need to know that they are personal or political, not scientific.

This pitfall is widespread in American social science, and it raises again the whole question of the objectives of the social sciences. "The great object of social science, as of all science," writes Kenneth Boulding, "is to find out what is *possible*. The 'laws' of science are in fact possibility functions."[14] Possibility functions point beyond what is to what can be, to a dynamic kind of knowledge. This is particularly important today, for the development of possibilities is powerfully present in the natural sciences and conspicuously lacking in the social sciences.

Consequently the natural sciences have created a flood of innovation, of which much is converted into useful (and not-so-useful) applications in society. The flood has dissolved an old way of life and only partially built up a new socially and culturally coherent way, despite the vast "possibilities." But still the possibility functions of the behavioral sciences remain mostly dormant, except by spurious intrusion.

What is most seriously lacking is a vigorous, organized "R&D" to span between the various branches of social science and the many professions that bear upon the form and function of society. A fully developed intermediate research discipline, far more independent and articulate than what is now called applied social research, may have even more importance for the social sciences than it has had for the natural sciences. Much will depend, of course, on how fully and broadly experimental such a discipline could become.

The new discipline would be directed to contemporary pressing questions of society. The research would be *professional* and *solution*-oriented rather than *academic* and *knowledge*-oriented. This implies different research questions, different methods, and different results—and a different frame of mind. Most of all, the professional solution-oriented studies would be socially purposeful, concerned wholly with the uses and benefits of knowledge.

Professional solution-oriented social science might well be a boon to academic social science, though always indirectly and incidentally to its own objectives. Since society is a creation of man and demonstrates human purpose, much important—and basic—knowledge may be derived from useful and purposeful experimentation, especially if the social experiments are carefully defined. For example, new urban development patterns might be combined with varied institutional forms in an effort to broaden the alternatives of valid behavior open to the individual (see Chapter 6 for a description of one possibility). These experiments, if followed closely by academic social scientists, should be highly relevant to theoretical pursuits. Since purely theoretical experiments dealing with society are too often impractical or narrowly restricted, the wide range of potential solution-oriented experiments opens a new range of opportunity for the academic social scientist.

Experiments might also aim at finding the best social use of technical innovations, such as new modes of transportation or radically new methods of housing construction. Maximum social utility, minimum social dislocation, and the many indirect social possibilities may be included in comprehensive local experiments. In this way, positive experimental action will help realize the fullest potential of the natural sciences, and will also help minimize the narrowly exploitive development of many present technical innovations.

If it is scientifically desirable that a chemist synthesize a new material, a biologist evolve a new plant strain, the physicist isolate a new electronic property, it should also be scientifically valid and desirable that the social scientist develop hypotheses for the evolution of human institutions, for the rearrangement of work and production, and even for improving the moral order. But he also requires organized and practical means for experiment with concrete situations, without which theory rests on very shifty ground.

If society prizes its science and if science prizes its potential for social advancement, they must together find a way to make social science pertinent in human affairs and, equally important, a way to make the experimental method directly applicable to social change.

PROFESSIONALIZING PRIVATE LIFE

In the Middle Ages the learned professions included theology, law, and medicine. There were also the craftsmen and their guilds, but for most things men worked on the principle of self-help. Today engineering, teaching, agriculture, social welfare and business have become prominent professions. Even science has been professionalized as a regular and significant service to society. Most commercial services, crafts, and occupations have now set about making their calling professional by means of lengthy training courses and by control of membership. And nearly all professions have long since subdivided themselves into numerous specializations. All along the spectrum of human activity few gaps have escaped the specialized hand of the professional.

For the person one result is evident enough. The meaning is dependence—not only in the larger cities, where self-help and informal cooperation are minimal, but everywhere, because dependence is indispensable to the kind of society that modern man is now building. Increasingly it is a setting of television entertainment, air conditioning, prepared meals. We seem to want these things. But are we not thereby diminishing the normal range of human behavior?

In human terms, professionalism means an abdication by the individual of his judgment and action to the man with trained knowledge and skill. According to Robert Heilbroner, the advanced specializations are forcing the individual into "an ever wider, more demanding engagement with his society." [15] To be able to benefit, the individual must himself become professionalized and specialized; otherwise he becomes merely ineffective—socially most of all.

The more specialized men become, the more of life's chores each man hires out to other specialists. Self-help is made difficult or impossible by partial or complete monopoly of equipment, parts, training, licenses, franchises. If specialization were carried to its ultimate, everyone would provide one specialized and uniform service and would receive all goods, services, and cultural benefits from other specialists.

Will everyone then suckle from everyone else in a perfect symbiosis? And will the selection of professional services be the only initiative the individual will retain outside the monopoly of his own profession? Will the experimental humanism of the amateur in man be abolished? The perfect symbiosis would, in fact, be a perfect monopoly of skill, organization, and authority by outside operatives over the action of the individual. This is the logic of professionalism carried to its limits.

Let us examine some other implications. It is elementary in biology that the advanced development of man was possible precisely because he was nonspecialized; Mumford says that man was "omnivorous, 'handy,' omni-competent, yet always somewhat unformed and incomplete." [16]

Perhaps we owe the ancient Greek flowering of the human spirit to the Greek respect for the imaginative wellspring of the amateur, and to the public honoring of spontaneous creativity and contribution by the common citizen. "He not merely performed military service at call, contributing his own equipment," says Mumford, "but he served in the assembly and the law courts, and if he did not become a contestant in one or another of the games, if he did not act in the theater or sing in the chorus, he would at least have a place, in his turn, in the great Panathenaic procession. Almost every male Athenian, at one time or another, had to take part in public business, as a member of the ecclesia or assembly, and in seeing that its decisions were properly carried out." Thus, men participated for what they were as persons, not because they held licensed skills, and for the rich variety of doing, not because their performance was required to maintain and promote production and consumption. To continue with Mumford: "Work and leisure, theory and practice, private life and public life were in rhythmic interplay, as art, gymnastics, music, conversation, speculation, politics, love, adventure, and even war, opened every aspect of existence and brought it within the compass of the city itself. One part of life flowed into another: no phase was segregated, monopolized, set apart." [17]

Perhaps any valid civilization must profoundly center upon the vigor of the individual person, his glory and magnification, his surge for life's wonder and beauty, his richness and depth of experience, his audacity and confidence in his own being, his intimate association and personal sharing of other men's experience. Can that happen in a tightly professionalized society? Or will our own civilization make us all wards of cultural and material providers?

But even more simply and basically we must also ask about the professionalization of our private lives. What does urban man make today that he uses? What does a man do without the consent or assistance of an expert or authority? What habits or customs are not sanctioned, promoted, or devised by professional innovators or persuaders? What group activity is carried through without a standard kit, manuscript, program, or device? What is a man's personal experience against the vicarious experience presented to him by experts of the mass media? What is a man's opportunity for nondirective common association rather than special-purpose contacts?

Perhaps all gross necessities are best provided by competent specialists working in efficient organizations; even so, we still must ask: what is happening to the open-ended possibilities of life—the very openings that new productive capacities were to enlarge? The answer: Exactly the same thing. Professionalism is steadily commandeering the traditional role of the amateur in sports, music, art, drama, and poetry by invidious comparison. Professional competition has depressed the confidence of the amateur; so he abandons his endeavor or shamefully keeps it to himself. And those amateur efforts which prosper are largely dependent upon professional composers, managers, suppliers, and instructors in defining the nature of the endeavor. What better way is there to kill personal spontaneity and initiative?

The man—the amateur—is now divided. On the one side he has become a productive professional and on the other a consumptive layman, and by this segregation of his behavior he loses his completeness. He loses the completeness of the beginnings and ends of actions, of conceptions and culminations, of change and continuity. He loses the completeness of the setting of events, the continuity of association, even of space and time. Finally, he loses the completeness of understanding; while purely intellectual understanding may increase, personal comprehension assuredly diminishes.

The layman—no longer an amateur—becomes a mere spectator to the specialized humdrum of life. He is unable to honestly enjoy or appreciate works or performances because he cannot feel a part of them. Even his judgment and criticism have been professionalized. The layman at the theater merely joins a formal but socially formless crowd, in human isolation from both other spectators and the performers, and he must try to imbibe the subtler elements of the professional technique. Or, in actual isolation, he watches a sterile box with hypnotic half attention. Thus the coldly professionalized and corporately organized culture still slowly takes over from the spontaneous local folk culture in all parts of the world, a tradition that once carried deep personal memories from generation to generation within its forms of art and entertainment. Its important continuities give way to the contrived, the recorded or reproduced, the imposed and changing styles of the professional innovator.

THREAT OF LEISURE

Suddenly in history man's burst of productive energy has yielded not only improved living but also a growing amount of free time. Like so many modern developments, free time has caught man off-guard. The present restlessness about it reveals once again how our means are habitually getting beyond the ends we have set for them.

When we classify leisure time as a problem, as society now does, we are saying not only that it has come to us as a surprise, but that we don't know what to do with it. The leisure "problem" starkly drives home how our work has gotten a peculiar hold on us, from which we cannot easily free ourselves. The term "leisure" itself today implies the time left over after work on "worthwhile" things is complete. When we perceive leisure as a problem we are saying, in effect, "Now that we are achieving the material benefits of life, what else is there?"—a remarkable revelation of our lack of social or cultural purposes.

The problem of leisure—which is really the absence of positive cultural ambitions—uniquely plays into the hands of professional recreational and cultural providers who are willing to channel all of life's impulses (like all of life's necessities) to commerical advantage. Here is another symptom of the domination of our motivations by productive and consumptive behavior. On the productive side, instead of a new vision that redefines work, activity, and interest to enrich the whole of life, we merely become anxious to use leftover time "more profitably." Instead of finding new opportunities for self-satisfying achievement in the freedoms inherent in the new automated technologies, we reveal a compulsive desire to be specifically busy or useful. Free time is conceived merely as a by-product of work. Vacations are hardly more than paced itineraries.

On the other hand, efforts to break the productive compulsiveness too often lead merely to an equally frenzied consumptiveness. Most new activities, such as skiing, skin diving, and sky diving, all require major investments and are therefore sanctioned and promoted in the economy, as are camping, boating, fishing, golfing, and various forms of racing when properly equipped. That so many activities are taken up on individual impulse or social fashion and soon dropped suggests the compulsiveness of the behavior and the pressures for consumption behind it.

On those occasions when the drive to be useful or active is broken, the outcome is often the complete lassitude of the beach or the bar. But even then the essential pattern of consumption remains unchanged: Leisure activities are expressed in the succinct terms of production and consumption.

The picture is the same when we shift from the individual to the organizational side of leisure. Where there is mass wealth and free time there is high profit in mass culture. Such culture tends toward professional entertainment, where the doing and the observing are unalterably divided. Since the professional is interested in the productivity of his art, not in the doing as is the amateur, there is a pull toward an extravaganza effect, a striving to excite the imagination of large crowds through costly productions. But costly productions can be financially ruinous, and so efforts are made to attract ever larger crowds. This is invariably accompanied by an emphasis upon crowd control and upon narrower ranges of taste, and ultimately by efforts to manipulate those tastes. This practice owes much to the tradition of P. T. Barnum, the Prince of Humbug, and to his shows and circuses in the nineteenth century, carried on by Cecil B. de Mille and other Hollywood producers.

An extraordinary new humbug and extravaganza was demonstrated at the 1964–65 New York World's Fair at a cost of about $500 million. Some pavilions could manage forty thousand visitors per day, and long lines were common at most of them. Yet many exhibitors expressed disappointment at their attendance figures. Here were demonstrated the central features of the extravaganza effect: high capacity and high-volume attendance, involving for spectators the frustration of waiting in queue and, for exhibitors, disappointment or financial loss.

Both the spectators' frustrations and the exhibitors' heaviest costs revolved about crowd control and crowd processing. One method, used by General Motors and Bell Telephone, consisted of mobile audio-equipped seats that continuously moved past animated exhibits. A given scene might be visible precisely ten or eighteen or thirty seconds, no more and no less. Significantly, IBM gave more attention to its "People Wall," or elevator grandstand, than to its exhibit. The United States pavilion used many such grandstands on a wide-track railroad to pass through a series of sound and sight scenes.

General Electric's exhibit was a merry-go-round of six theaters rotated around five stages for five-minute stops at each. Not an actor appeared on any of the five stages, where animated mannequins described what G.E. was doing to bring about "The Wonderful World of

Tomorrow." While the crowds were entertained by robots, they were captive to a G.E. staff of more than two hundred live guards, guides, and hostesses who channeled them into line, into and out of the revolving theaters. This highlighted the fact that by far the largest number of employees at the Fair were not actors or demonstrators but forces of crowd control.

Mechanistic crowd processing called for exhibits that everyone might understand and that most might enjoy instantly. The consequence was enforced glibness. The crowd process meanwhile left the individual no choice. He could not follow his own interest or loiter, as one should at a fair.

There was, to be sure, a professional competence. But the mechanization of the exhibits and the crowd control was a *tour de force* not only in technical wizardry, but in maintenance of wizardry from the faceless distance. After the exhibits were set into motion the professional could return to his home office, while his machine went on captivating all those people who stepped into the crowd process.

It seems that large societies, like large fairs, have a "critical mass" beyond which commercial exploitation of inane whims and fads is profitable. And in a society with the additional ingredients of instant communications, free time, freely expendable funds, an economic determination of social values, and active exploitive interests, nonsense has a way of becoming accredited within the whole society. If commercialism takes deep root in it, the nonsense becomes essential to the operation of the whole economy.

If the New York Fair foretells the wealth and leisure of the "Wonderful World of Tomorrow," the outlook is indeed melancholy.

5

Personality at Bay

The transformed environment of the individual—social immensity, big citizenship, technological virtuosity, dominant productiveness and consumptiveness, cultural professionalism, fractured interpersonal association—all this has made man a bewildered tenant in the house of his own making.

When the individual is viewed principally as a human resource, when his whole acculturation seeks to make him into a productive (and now consumptive) citizen, and when concern for his dissociation and breakdown seeks only to upright him into a productive posture again, we may expect that his humanity will break to the surface of society as inexplicable boils and ulcers that fester and rankle rather than as buds that flower, inspire, and excite.

In this chapter we shall look into a few of the consequences of the changed environment—the boils and ulcers. But we shall not be wholly pessimistic, for we shall also look into a few promising possibilities and set the stage for the remaining chapters, of which each takes up a new potential of humanity.

LOSS OF PERSON

The term "individual" refers to the distributive characteristic of millions of people that make up a society. It provides an abstract basis for discussing human rights, making social statistics meaningful, or studying physiology. By contrast, the term "person" refers to a finite and unique individual, compassionate and endowed with feelings and motives. It symbolizes the integrity of being human, fitting into a specific family or community, having a specific condition unlike any other person, and constituting a specific personality.

Primitive society scarcely needed to distinguish between "person" and "individual." But for modern societies, which rationalize, quantify, and generalize to accurately conceive of their universal problems and properly tackle them, the distinction is an important one, corresponding to private and public affairs. Efforts to comprehend broad social questions almost inevitably deal with people in discrete, autonomous terms and universal categories. It is natural that the Big Citizens work smoothly with the individual, but hardly know how to deal with the person. Consequently all industrial societies have experienced a deep loss of person in the way they organize political, economic, and social affairs.

The loss of person from normal society involves the loss of many intimate things: collective memory (we now must *read* stories to children from books), common locality (because of mobility, fewer people stay in one place for long), a common set of institutions (now they are infinite in number, size, and variety of special interest). But the most important losses to person may be a comforting perspective of life and drama of personality.

Man has always sought a view of life that maximized security and the egoistic value of existence. This interest helped shape the character of family, clan, tribe, community, kingdom, and nation, and it weighed heavily in the growth of religion and the arts. Comforting life views, unified into a social system and passed from generation to generation, were rarely in serious conflict with the necessary organization of ongoing affairs, of production or defense at the level of the village or small town. Rarely were there deep-rooted, psychically debilitating schisms of life of the sort that abound in modern, plural society. There was no science to question old ideas, even implicitly.

And early science was accommodating. Ptolemy in the second century confidently hypothesized that the earth was the center of the universe. His view was dominant for twelve centuries, until Copernicus theorized that the earth moved—and was not the center of the universe. Here was a world somehow more random, less purposive, less centered upon this earth and human life. From then on, science steadily invaded man's romantic convictions, pushing man out of the personal security of his myths or simple assumptions about life.

Scientific investigations slowly moved closer to the person himself as the biological and social sciences separated from philosophy. The more penetrating they became, the more they seemed to insult the person's physiological, psychological, and cultural foundations and shatter dearly held beliefs. Charles Darwin blasted the belief that man had a preordained place among living things, replacing it with the belief that man merely moved from an unknown past toward an unknown future amid a beastly struggle for "survival of the fittest." Man's existence would please or displease no one.

A half century later, Sigmund Freud struck directly into the individual psyche. His bold searches into the unconscious seemed to disrobe the soul itself. What he revealed or hypothesized seemed to make personality a fugitive from mysterious and evil worlds. Hardly could man's satisfying self-portrait have been more defaced than by the subconscious death wishes or libidinal drives Freud dredged to the surface.

Ostensibly seeking knowledge for its own sake, chilling scientific investigations contributed to a deeper disenchantment with life. But the philosophers were hardly more helpful in finding a place for person, except possibly in terms of political rights. Even J. S. Mill's argument for liberty lacked a suitable context in which the individual found his sense of being a person. Mill seemed to argue for a liberty that freed the individual from his communal origins merely for exposure to new forms of industrial serfdom. And to this day the philosophers have not matched their brilliant treatment of the rights of the abstract individual with an equally incandescent consideration of the intimate concept of person.

Even the very terms in which we perceive social life and analyze behavior tend to divert attention from a preeminence of person. They stress the use of numbers; only with numbers do we gain confidence in our observations. Numbers are scientific and science is our faith. Person, in all his uniqueness, tends to be incompletely knowable, and is excluded.

Our present lack of concern for person is also revealed in the different applications of statistics. In economics they are used as measures for movement "onward and upward." In social affairs they are primarily danger signals. On one side, pecuniary progress; on the other, social breakdown. Too often the "emergence" of a social problem means only that it has become statistically evident.

The alienation of man from the qualities of person is a consequence, not necessarily of the accomplishments of our age, but rather of our allowing the characteristic forms of our accomplishment to permeate all of our thinking. Because the discipline to work and the pressure to consume so completely dominate our thought and limit our experience to the external world, sentiments become less real and therefore less important—until they become disruptive.

The value a society places upon person can be roughly gauged by the intensity of social drama that celebrates it. Drama is to be found in the deeds of heroism; heroes have always had their myths, songs, and bal-lads. Drama is to be found in the soldier's pride in his own powers and those of his comrades, his fighting unit, and his people. Symbols of this pride were once found in flags, mermaid figureheads on ship prows, and garishly decorated weapons and shields. As brutal as conflict has always been, drama was once an integral part: fanciful uniforms, bugles and drums, grandiloquent gestures and chivalry.

But today where are the solacing mermaids on atomic submarines? What happened to the company buglers? At one time, war meant that men faced each other in deeply personal anger, fear and pain. Now machines kill men. What real *esprit de corps* can exist for a countdown?

The loss of person is plainly evident in the traditional professions (theology, law, medicine), which once were mentors of the individual, if not of his person. The family doctor was until recently an important tra-dition of American life. And in the Hippocratic oath, medicine has a pro-fessional philosophy that above all else defines and protects the relation-ship of the doctor and his patient. No other professional code states its objectives in such specific human terms. The one-to-one bond put forth between doctor and patient implies a high regard for person.

However, with the growth of specialization and the decline of the general practitioner, the doctor-patient relationship is becoming splin-tered. Under specialization a patient does not have a doctor; he func-tions within a referral system. For the doctor, of course, specialization affords higher status, higher income, greater control of practice, and in-creased freedom. But the patient—the person—is shunted from one spe-cialist to another. He cannot establish personal confidence; he must rely on referrals or rumors of reputation. Especially during serious health crises this is a crucial matter.

Specialization in medicine tends to devolve the profession into skilled vocations, for it undermines two characteristics that separate a profession from a merely skilled vocation: judgment and responsibility. Judgment of a patient's illness depends not only on knowledge of tests and treat-ments but on knowledge of the whole patient, his background and his temperament. That cannot happen when one doctor passes a patient on to another. Secondly, a division of responsibility reduces the personal interest of the doctor in the patient and tends to increase his interest in fees, special cases, and such desiderata as a smoothly flowing routine. Thus the face-to-face familiarity underlying responsibility steeply de-clines.

Once I drove a friend with a serious long-term ailment to a diagnostic conference with about fifteen doctors. The purpose was to examine a mass of tests and my friend's case history to decide on a course of treat-ment. We sat in a hallway and one by one the doctors passed us as they went to the conference room. None seemed to notice the patient they had come to serve; I assumed this was because most of them had never seen him before. After a short discussion, they called my friend into the conference room. When he was dismissed the doctors again filed past. But again not one of them noticed, said hello, or smiled. They were interested in the case, not in the person.

The basic human fact here is far more important than it may seem at first. In the end even high levels of skill may be worthless when the human relationship is lost. An unusual and brutal demonstration occurred at Auschwitz during the extermination of the Jews. One writer, Bruce Bettelheim, described how the doctors deluded themselves about what they were involved in by hiding behind the procedural formalities of their profession. There was a Dr. Mengele, an SS physician, who could maintain a "business-as-usual" attitude while treating patients just before their being sent to death. In one instance, "Dr. Mengele took all correct medical precautions during childbirth, rigorously observing all asceptic principles, cutting the umbilical cord with the greatest care, etc. But only a half an hour later, he sent mother and infant to be burned in the crematorium."

Another case demonstrated how a Jewish prisoner, Dr. Miklos Nyiszli, could be brought to the same frame of mind while acting as "research physician" at Auschwitz. "How Dr. Nyiszli fooled himself can be seen, for example, in the way he repeatedly referred to himself as a doctor, though he worked as the assistant of a criminal. He speaks of the Institute for Race, Biological, and Anthropological Investigation as 'one of the most qualified medical centers of the Third Reich.'" Bettelheim points out that Nyiszli was continually "taking pride in his professional skills, irrespective of the purpose they served. Again and again this pride in his professional skill permeates the story of his own and other prisoners' sufferings. . . . [Both Mengele and Nyiszli] had entered their profession before Hitler came to power. It was their peculiar pride in professional skill and knowledge, without regard for moral implications, which made them so dangerous. Although the concentration camps and crematoria are no longer here, this kind of pride still remains with us. It is a characteristic of a modern society oriented toward technical competence. Auschwitz is gone, but so long as this attitude persists, we shall not be safe from cruel indifference to life at the core." [1]

Another example illustrates the effects of an equally serious loss of person. At about 3:00 A.M., March 13, 1964, thirty-eight known witnesses saw or heard the events surrounding the murder of Catherine Genovese, 28, at Kew Gardens, Queens, New York. The murder took place in three separate knife attacks on an open street over a period of about 35 minutes. Not until after the tragedy was entirely over did anyone call the police.

Most of the witnesses were not ashamed or defiant about the fact that they did not respond to Miss Genovese's scream: "Oh my God, he stabbed me! Please help me! Please help me!" The most general attitude of the witnesses was that they did not want to get involved.

Apathy of one citizen about another, especially about the life or death of another, can occur only when a profound alienation penetrates the person-to-person associations (or contacts) between individuals. In normal times large numbers of persons interact smoothly together because they all happen to be "going the same way" (exchanging economic benefits). But there is little feeling between them. In the Big Society, organizations and consequently even individuals see everyone else as expendable or interchangeable. Where contacts of this sort predominate in a society, it is not surprising to find a profound loss of person.

The loss of life in the murder of Miss Genovese was but the final step in the social loss of person. Perhaps, however, the earlier, less dramatic steps of the loss of person—the loss of feeling, value, trust, and faith —were even more tragic, for they affect the essence of life in society.

DIMINISHED INTEGRITY

Respect for person is ultimately a concern for human integrity. There are two general sources for integrity: the individual's own behavior, and the society and its tradition. Although we normally assume that the individual is responsible for his own integrity, its roots are necessarily within the social processes that nurture his values, give or deny him opportunity for growth, and stimulate or constrict his behavior.

As part of the social basis for human integrity in recent centuries, no doubt the emergent political rights of life, liberty, and property—three critical foundations for democracy—stand out very favorably. But progress has its backwash. Since a superior education, for example, is now required for even minimal social opportunities, those who lack a secondary-school or college background suffer proportionately more than their barely literate grandparents did before education so decisively affected one's role in society. Today those with a second-class education are unacceptable to the advanced technological or bureaucratic system, and they fall into the human slag heap. Economically and socially banished, they have no response but bitterness and despondency.

In many primitive societies banishment was tantamount to death, since for one reason or another death generally resulted in such cases. Yet today in the Big Society whole groups and classes of workers are economically banished without cause, save economic obsolescence. Coal mining and farming are contemporary examples. Adjustments that eventually occur do not help the whole generations of people who have lost their social source of integrity, owing to the reckless workings of the economy.

The modern slums, in which most of the banished must live, are the root of social denial for each new generation. Even if officially the larger society offers a superior education to all, the slum-reared child suffers deeply conflicting social values, a denial of stimulation, a lack of guidance. Yet he faces equal competition with all others for grades, recommendations, college openings, and other social opportunities. Gradually we are realizing that even intelligence tests give the disadvantaged child bad marks for what his society does to him.

Delinquency and crime, especially in slum areas, are the natural product of systematic social denial. So we have a punk from Harlem standing before a judge to be condemned to death. In his way the punk may have maintained his personal integrity within the backwater code of his peers. And there is the judge with his impeccable career, his conscience, his advocacy of due process. Behind both men stands the impartial majesty of the courts. But was not society profoundly partial in its gifts? Does not the partiality of a lifetime make a mockery of the impartiality of the moment? This is the absence of social integrity.

Of course the events in the courtrooms are prefigured in the decades and the generations before. The persons involved are only specific actors who inherit roles they did not create. The society but judges itself and its own past when it passes sentence on its members. Each case is a defeat and a loss of basic social integrity that can only be reversed with a new start for the next generation. In large measure it is irrelevant whether the defendant, guilty or innocent, dies or goes free, for the real loss of life, feeling, and integrity was incurred long ago.

The problem of integrity, however, is not identical with that of justice. The social basis for integrity necessarily involves both positive and negative means, both opportunities and restraints. It must begin with orderly relationships. What is necessary for mature individual integrity is stability, coherence, opportunity, and grace in the social environment, on which basis the individual can build a parallel stability, coherence, opportunity, and grace within his own behavior. The reciprocity is direct and intimate.

This view rejects Hobbes' still common concept of social contract, in which ready-made individuals with mature minds came together and agreed to form society, in the same way a corporation is legally formed today. It follows more closely George Mead's description of the intimate mutuality of personality formation and social growth. That is, the human mind, through its relations with others, gradually learns to take the role of the "generalized other." Through the internalization of social responses society exerts itself "intimately and extensively over individual behavior." But, continues Mead, "social control, so far from tending to crush out the human individual or to obliterate his self-conscious individuality, is, on the contrary, actually constitutive of and inextricably associated with that individuality; for the individual is what he is, as a conscious and individual personality, just in as far as he is a member of society." [2]

The social foundation for integrity would seem to consist of at least three elements: (1) a reasonably unifying perception of life and its major values; (2) an integrating pattern of behavior in both the necessary and the selected pursuits of life, and (3) stable, compatible, and intimate associations. But attempts to realize these social objectives—which perhaps should be regarded as rights—face serious historic obstacles.

An industrial economy necessarily requires a mobile working population, a mass market, and huge cities. It differentiates the skilled and mobile workers with great articulation. Integration of resources, labor, production, and distribution takes place on the largest possible scale. We have seen how integration of production and distribution tends to fragment and dominate the behavior of workers and consumers. This minimizes the possibility of rebuilding a social unity about the individual, family, and community. In other words, there is a competition in society to determine whether the central forces of social organization will follow from industrial output or from social-psychological motives of men. The history of the past four or five centuries has been a clear and continuous shift in favor of output.

The shift has affected the individual in two ways. First, it has required him to make a major effort to acquire many arbitrary disciplines and to internalize a diverse conformity. Second, the crucial ligaments of organization having been monopolized by the requirements of functional performance, private life has been made secondary. Anonymity, mobility, and functional demand upon the individual have forestalled the evolution of effective associative traditions.

The force of disintegration is seen in the isolation and fragmentation of the community into its constituent elements: family, church, and economic organization. Of course, interpersonal involvements were fewer and simpler in the past. But more importantly, events in one area freely involved and flowed into the others. The community represented the totality of events, and the whole community was largely known to every individual. Even when ancient and early modern cities grew to a considerable size, their various sections often substantially retained this character—especially if both living and working were done in the same area and if the church, market, and square were in close proximity to each other. Some African cities retain such form to this day.

But as the cities grew and diversified, as commuting became general, and as the functions of the commanding institutions (especially the state and economic organization) became more complex and penetrating, the community waned. The organizational effects of the commanding institutions then became more divisive. The less influence the community exerted, the more the general organizational influences tended to become personally separate and socially irrelevant. The individual's life became a patchwork of separate institutional claims.

Automation is now being rapidly extended to all large-scale industries. There is no question of its long-term value for society; but the prospect in the short run is disruption and dislocation. The unions have partly succeeded in protecting large groups of persons in transition, but many others, especially in mining and agriculture, are being left high and dry. They are without work and income, without social status, and without encouraging prospects for adjustment. They constitute a significant part of the population. Yet they are so demoralized that they have no organization, voice, or pressure group to seek remedy—in a society that assumes all men will always vigorously represent their own interests.

Yet technical innovation will be supported with more conviction than remedies for the excesses resulting from the innovations. The social foundations for individual integrity have not yet become a part of the public dialogue, are not yet considered along with the requirements for production and the flow of goods and money. Of course, integrity is a many-faceted and elusive matter, we cannot calibrate it like a measure in economics without risking pitiable irony. Integrity must be defined by each society and by each individual; each generation must see its integrity anew in terms of its own circumstances and aspirations. Perhaps the defining process itself is the essential social requirement for broadening integrity.

In this brief review we have noted how a form of banishment strikes some members of the society and how the schismatic workings of the industrial society diminish the potential integrity of all of us. This challenges and tests the whole society. Paul Goodman, referring to youth and delinquency problems, argues that "the burden of proof, as to who is 'wrong,' does not rest with the young but always with the system of society. Some societies bear it easily; our society is not outrageously bad, but it is far from adequate, and it stands the test poorly." [3] This applies to the integrity of the individual and the whole social setting.

UNDERCURRENT OF DISORDER

The institutions that maintain the powerful initiative in society are those that enjoy a high degree of general understanding, a high-level integration of purpose, and, consequently, a high-level integration of functional operations. An outstanding example is our economic system. Its performance is closely monitored through a variety of statistical barometers, revealing in great detail its operating characteristics, trends, and potential pitfalls. Behind these barometers are very clear understandings or assumptions about positive goals, organizational methods, and operational practices.

The institutions that have the least initiative in society are those that are little understood, have a minimal integration of purpose, and have as a consequence little functional unity in their operations. They are, by and large, the institutions that directly serve the individual, especially his personal and social needs. Their barometers are essentially negative in character: they apply in the main to delinquency, crime, drunkenness, skid row, slums, relief burdens, mental disorders, school dropouts, friction between races, and the like. (Statistically evident progress in health and education is excluded here, because both support and results in these fields are deeply economic.)

High and low initiative, high and low integration, obviously reflect our deeper attitudes. The economic sphere we view in positive, progressive, and forceful terms. The social services we view in evasive and negative terms; their fragmentation, disarray, and level of support tell their own story.

This socially skewed behavior suggests another deep-seated attitude. Man himself is taken into account only as a "human resource" for economic or national power or as a defined problem for the large society, a drag on its smooth operation or a blemish on its glossy veneer. Little wonder that there is a pervading and overt cynicism among youth, a sneering at any belief beyond self-interest. Is not that the direction followed by the larger society as well, the twist of life that reduces form and drama to structured competitiveness for self-indulgence? Perhaps the cynicism is but the initial, honest reaction before the adult calculating lie converts it to mere callousness.

What we are saying to ourselves in the philosophical dialogue of our civilization in the twentieth century is that we shall create physical comforts, ostensibly for all, we shall focus our values, power, and initiative in huge organizations, and we shall expect man to learn to tolerate functional organization, economic and technological determinism, social disorganization, and personal dissociation. Only when the individual breaks down or becomes antisocial will we recognize him in a special way, by removing him or attempting to ameliorate the specific cause. We will do so only with localized remedies aimed at the individual, for our concern does not include reform of the social sources of maladjustment. Our remedies are designed to make him once again a "productive member of society." Then, as before, he will be expected to cope with the same situations again, and these will always press at the upper level of his tolerance.

Naturally, this powerful torque in society undermines organic interpersonal association and affronts personality at a cost of reaction, rebellion, breakdown, or escape. A less overt response may be simply cynicism, coldness, suspicion, or a sharper attitude of exploitiveness. But, in any case, the organization of society principally to serve aggrandizing institutions is not without profound consequences. The groundswell of inner despair comes to the surface of society in various disguises.

Numerous studies of delinquency, crime, neuroticism, alcoholism, extremism, the protesting beat generation and the hippies leave such behavior only partly explained. The studies only occasionally hint of causes within the deeper, broader social environment. General perspectives and correlations are rare. It will be worth our while to observe these several social aberrations or protest activities with a common, wide-angle lens and speculate about their relevance to our central question of social alienation of the individual.

If, for example, we look at delinquency and crime from a distance, they reveal an evident protest against society, however confused, tentative, and vacillating that protest might be: an external, action-oriented response to deprivations, conflicting value orientations, and sometimes brutal environmental pressures. If we look at neurotic behavior, we find a comparable, but internal and nonactive, protest against many comparable social circumstances: an inner escape from deprived interpersonal association, conflicting demands upon personality, or social pressures with personally meaningless rewards. Breakdown of normal behavior is a defeat for neurotic individuals, just as arrest and punishment are a defeat for the overt errant. Yet defeat in either case may come as actual relief from both inner and outer disquietude. Of course, action-oriented criminality is usually characteristic of men, whereas neuroticism is more characteristic of women, who too often "swallow" their frustrations.

Another protest against society is far more conscious, clear, and demonstrative: that of the bohemian, the beat, and now the hippie. From the roots of their behavior they loathe the ostentatious rigidities, functionalism, and even the affluence of middle-class life, viewing it as purposeless, meaningless, and lifeless. They emphatically reject not only bureaucratic organization, technological immensity, and colorless suburbia; they also openly eschew many basic traditional and Christian virtues: personal cleanliness; sanctity of sex, marriage, and the monogamous home; work and frugality; nationalism and ethnocentrism.

The beat/hippie movement is a basic but groping protest against all that the Big Citizens and Big Society stand for. It is a rebellion and, like most rebellions, stands out mostly for its excesses and numerous irrelevant trials and experiments. The beat/hippie behavior inclines toward garish demonstrations of art, folk music, bizarre poetry, nondescript dress, unusual interpersonal relations, and efforts to extract powerful emotional experience from themselves. Even the schisms, inconsistencies, and contradictions in the movement demonstrate the search for new social orientations that are at the base of rebellion.

The open ridicule expressed for "solid citizens" and the intense experimentation carried on at the simpler roots of life seems to say to workaday society: "Look, you social automatons, you have lost the worth of life; you have made the world compulsive, regimented, alienated; you have rid life of expression, feeling, and emotion."

And now the hippies have moved to center stage. Younger, more numerous, more culturally adventurous, the hippies reveal the beginnings of a forthright philosophy, something the more cynical beat progenitors failed to do. Showing tendencies toward communalism, true social egalitarianism, pacifism, and love (in all of its meanings), their experimental humanism is beginning to make more potent the protest against society. Although the hippie is still regarded as far out, he touches a chord of conscience in the solid citizen because he dares to devote his behavior to human virtues that most men thought were beyond normal social accomplishment.

Of course, there are numerous irrational qualities in the hippies' behavior, and serious consequences could arise from their use of LSD and other drugs. Nevertheless, there is a powerful point in the "irrational" character of the protest. First, the Big Society has preempted and construed the terms of rationality, so that the use of these terms would only submit the hippie to the value system of the Big Society. When that is done the prevailing values cannot be licked. The protest therefore must move outside the existing rationality.

Second, man is basically emotional and nonrational, especially at the motive roots of life. Rationality is a social imposition to make men orderly and to create a vast productive machine. But this orderliness serves economic and institutional purposes more than personal and inter-personal purposes. Thus the hippies seem to have said to themselves, in effect: "Let's go back to the emotional base of life, experiment with many forms of behavior, and then build a new social rationality based more closely upon human purpose."

Given the institutional expendability of persons and the bureaucratic bulldozing of personality in the advanced industrial countries, the call for a radically new start, now raised by the hippies, could hold a very great appeal for the oncoming generation. We should note with keen interest that the hippie is not evident in tribal, peasant, nonurban, and nonindustrial societies. He appears during the later stages of the industrial development process, just when bureaucracy and affluence reach a plateau—and when former challenges of development become monotonous career patterns.

We may find parallels with other forms of protest in habitual drinking—a commonly understood refuge from social conformity, individual dead ends, or *anomie*. Some persons turn this statement around and argue that the escape or protest is directed against the individual's own inadequacies (saying, in effect, that society may judge individuals, but the society itself is not to be judged). Either way, drinking still reflects the individual's context in society. Although he may first use liquor as a pump-primer for social conviviality, too often with a childish compulsive fetish, the chronic drinker ends by becoming a truly isolated individual. And this condition seems to arise most often in middle maturity after narrowly based career ambitions for wealth, power, or fame are dulled or evidently defeated. Drink is but a bitter solace to slowly lost life hope that was founded upon an emotionally shallow drive and a vocationally limited ethic.

Although thoughtful readers may balk at bringing such disparate behavior into a single perspective, observing that the muddy waters of the family wash don't all come from the same dirt, I nonetheless suggest that some aspects of extremism and certain elements of the automaton personality amount to protests or reactions of the same order.

Whereas the hippie remains aloof and is demonstrative in protest against society, the extremist is reactionary and turns upon it to remake it according to his own image. This image, unlike that of the hippie, requires more technology, more organization, more authority, more power, and even more denial of social diversity or deviation. We are told that the authoritarian is extremely insecure, especially in his interpersonal relations, and therefore puts forward a bold front and seeks compensatory security within steel-structured organizations, which attempt to force the whole society into the same frame, usually without serious regard for the means involved. Often extremists hold their views secretly, since they look upon society as essentially hostile.

The protest of the automaton, however, is an inner denial of spontaneity, rather than a bold outer reaction; it tends to close his world into a emotional clamshell. Evidently he feels that conformity will assure acceptance and fears that expressing his own individuality may bring rejection. The person of rigid mind accepts society as it is but responds primarily to its superficial aspects. Beliefs are maintained with a fastness that precludes fresh interpretation or even discussion. The automaton locks his personality into a few major perceptions of life purpose, such as the acquisition of money, the climbing of organizational hierarchies, or the narrow performance of thoroughly accepted practices. He cannot develop close, relaxed, or meaningful interpersonal relationships, though he may be a faithful if perfunctory parent or a member of service clubs. He may also be a candidate for extremist organizations when they become plausible in the public mind, for the calcification of feeling over a base of insecurity seems to be but one step from the condition in which extremism arises.

Although behavior fundamentally is structured by society, few studies of specific forms of aberrant behavior concern themselves with the cultural norms and broad social organization. One exception is the concept of delinquent subcultures whose values are "so continually at variance" with the larger groupings in society that conflicts created by these values considerably reduce the possibilities for eventual sound adjustments.[4] A more notable exception is the work of the sociologist Robert Merton, dating back to 1938, especially his description of the clear inconsistencies between cultural goals and institutional norms. "There may develop," Merton wrote, "a disproportionate, at times, a virtually exclusive, stress upon the value of specific goals, involving relatively slight concern with the institutionally appropriate modes of attaining these goals."[5]

Merton illustrated the importance of this relationship in a discussion of poverty and criminal behavior. "Poverty as such, and consequent limitation of opportunity, are not sufficient to induce a conspicuously high rate of criminal behavior. Even the often mentioned 'poverty in the midst of plenty' will not necessarily lead to this result. Only insofar as poverty and associated disadvantages in competition for the culture values approved for *all* members of the society is linked with the assimilation of a cultural emphasis on monetary accumulation as a symbol of success is antisocial conduct a 'normal' outcome. Thus, poverty is less highly correlated with crime in southeastern Europe than in the United States. The possibilities of vertical mobility in these European areas would seem to be fewer than in this country, so that neither poverty per se nor its association with limited opportunity is sufficient to account for the varying correlations. It is only when the full configuration is considered, poverty, limited opportunity and a commonly shared system of success symbols, that we can explain the higher association between poverty and crime in our society than in others where rigidified class structure is coupled with differential class symbols of achievement."[6]

Merton has thus incisively linked aspiration, limited opportunity, and poverty—three normal conditions in slums today—with "normal" antisocial behavior. And what could be argued as a social shortcoming in 1938 now seems to approach a social conspiracy. For the culturally deprived who live in the socially demented slums, the insecurity of employment, the continually threatening environment, and the absence of constructive challenge, opportunity, or career pursuits seem to bring only dilemmas and dead ends.

Even for those in the cultural mainstream, social formlessness combined with the bureaucratic order of behavior prompts a monotonous despair, with little hope for relief. Consider Paul Goodman's description of middle status organization men in the "apparently closed room": "They are aware that it is a rat race, their literature proclaims it. But they are afraid to jump off. Since they think it is a closed room, they think there is nowhere to go. And *in* the room, if they jump off, they fear they will be among the disqualified, they will be Bums. But besides, they are afraid *of* the disqualified, to mix with them, and this keeps them running." [7]

What is the meaning of all this? Can it be that opportunities and the rat race are normal; that the lack of opportunities and antisocial behavior are normal; that a general underlying despair is normal? Isn't there a clue in the organic foundations of society: the environment so superbly designed and maintained for the health of economic institutions, the Big Citizens, and the institutional environment so ineptly designed for men, principally to prevent the floodwaters of human resentment from bursting into the orderly processes of production and consumption?

Slums and denial of opportunities are in fact a part of the rat race. They exist in a wealthy society only because they reflect the mind of the majority, especially the leadership. Everyone must run the race, on terms set by the leadership, with whatever handicaps there might be. Every race must have its losers, and the mind of the loser is imposed upon those who live under squalid conditions.

Especially pertinent to the contemporary character of the rat race is the Negro Rights Movement. The Negro, as a slave, came into society as a loser; that was the law; and the Thirteenth, Fourteenth, and Fifteenth Amendments to the Constitution did not make him into a winner. Only now are we beginning to recognize the depth of the continuing schematic bias that kept him a loser. He suffered not only a special race prejudice but also the even more pervasive bias that assumed there must always be a large class of demoralized losers.

Negro leadership of the Rights Movement is coming to realize that it has not only stark racial prejudice to contend with, but also the larger problem of social poverty. The Negro has now achieved cohesiveness and has the support of a large part of the majority population. The wider significance of the Movement is that if its leadership is resolute and constructive it could become the nucleus for a larger movement to achieve a goal much beyond that which originally spurred the Negroes into action.

One of the Rights Movement leaders, Bayard Rustin, has publicly given voice to this larger problem and larger possibility. The success of the Movement, if it is really to attack the roots of the rat race, requires an inspiration toward profoundly liberalizing society as a whole, not just specific remedies in housing, education and employment. The long-term search for the Negro's rights reaches into the depths of economics, technology, and science and into the purposes of the city and of all institutions. This search goes far beyond any direct question of race at all, but may logically follow through from the force of the Rights Movement.

Certainly the Negro will not win his cause by achieving *de facto* equality. That will still leave him at the level of the loser in society, retaining the mind of the loser. He will only secure a full measure of social justice by helping to define a larger justice.

TYRANNY OF MASS SOCIETY

Emerging among the various social protests and afflictions, the authoritarian or extremist carries a direct ominous threat to plural institutions, human rights, social equality—the whole basis of freedom. Our century has already seen many advanced nations succumb to the attractions of the authoritarian; evidently the totalitarian form of tyranny is uniquely compelling in our age.

Our age is, of course, a product of the great burst of mind and body that took hold of man some centuries ago. That is what has made our age revolutionary. But, for most men, the revolution meant a puritanical reshaping for production via the Protestant ethic.

The social ideal in these centuries has been the self-reliant individual who dislodges himself from his restrictive past and plunges into exploration, science, trade, or manufacture. The more common case, however, is the bewildered rural migrant who becomes a manual worker in a large plant of a large city, forfeiting a socially comforting world while he gains very limited opportunities for a day wage and encounters a relentless social diversity and many conflicting modes of behavior.

But personal alienation is not limited to the first years of gross adjustment or to the generations that lack education. The sources of alienation exist in the forefront of the new life itself. The economics of life have been segregated from the social, religious, and cultural—just as economics has become a foundation for social, religious, and cultural membership in society. Producing has become almost totally separated from consuming; the easygoing rhythms and interinvolvements characterizing rural and small-town life have been replaced by hard and fast daily rotations of corporate production and private consumption. And work itself has been fragmented by the "rationalizing" of the means of production.

The segregation of behavior into specialized categories extends to the noneconomic life. Divisions among religious institutions, for example, become more blatant when at first contrasted in the close quarters of a city. Political parties and ideologies contend for acceptance. Class and educational rank sharply divide men.

Adjustments and accommodations go on as well, of course. But the accommodations that smooth over differences in the Big Society also blunt belief and diminish its meaning for the person. The distinctiveness that all institutions seek is worn down by constant abrasion. Consequently, most persons respond with more qualified commitments. First all beliefs are placed into a common social mosaic, and then slowly the mosaic is whitewashed, each part becoming more like the others in the mind's eye. Their sharp contrast is lost; strong personal identity is lost. The individual becomes less distinguishable in the mass, to himself as well as to others. Separate memberships and classifications remain, but increasingly they become equal, exchangeable, homogeneous.

And so the freedom, opportunity, diversity, and challenge of the new age and the city replace the formerly uncontested and unified world-view that once existed among most preindustrial peoples. But lost with the cast-off vision are a deeply personal security, understanding, place, character, and rhythm of life.

As with beliefs and behavior, so it is with the traditional institutions behind them. Dilution of belief leads to perfunctory participation and slow withering of organizational bonds in lodges, churches, even families. Though the institutions remain, sometimes even prospering outwardly, their emblems and oaths become, like their activities, less distinctive and more narrowly compartmentalized.

As the process of breaking old bonds continues, individuals become looser particles of the larger society. They become a mass of granules in which the only viable social container is the whole society. They become isolated from the small institutional groups that, in Robert Nisbet's terms, mediate between the individual and the larger society. The ominous importance of the masses is that when this process of loosening individuals from their vital moorings is well advanced, "half the work of the totalitarian leader has been done for him." [8]

"What is crucial in the formation of the masses," according to Nisbet, "is the atomization of all social and cultural relationships within which human beings gain their normal sense of membership in society. The mass is an aggregate of individuals who are insecure, basically lonely, and ground down, either through decree or historical circumstance, into mere particles of social dust." [9]

Nisbet tells us that in Russia up to World War I, "the ancient relationships of class, family, village, and association were nearly as strong as they had been in medieval times. Only in small areas of Russia were these relationships dissolving and the masses beginning to emerge. . . . It was necessary, as Stalin saw the problem, to accomplish in a short time the atomization and dislocation that had been proceeding in Western countries for generations. . . . For the new rulers of Russia realized that the kind of power requisite to the establishment of the Marxian order could not long exist if any competing associations and authorities were allowed to remain. The vast association of the nation, which Marx had prophesied, could come into being only through the most absolute and extensive central political power. And, for the establishment and maintenance of this power, the creation of the indifferentiated, unattached, atomized mass was indispensable." [10]

At root, Nisbet asserts, "we may regard totalitarianism as a process of the annihilation of individuality, but, in more fundamental terms, it is the annihilation, first, of those social relationships within which individuality develops." [11]

It is said that an army first "breaks" the civilian personality of a recruit and then develops a soldier out of him. Military life first denies a person his old habits, characteristic ways of behavior, and values, then supplies the ingredients and the setting for development of a new personality that is consistent with the necessities of being a soldier. First there is a denial, then a supplanting. Hence the existence of rootless masses largely fills the first requirement of social revolution; the only task remaining is the formation of an association of the whole, a centralization of belief and identity, an undiluted obedience to the will of the whole.

The means for achieving totalitarian control can be as varied as the sentiments that bring men to act. According to Nisbet they "can as well be racial equality as inequality, godly piety as atheism, labor as capital, Christian Brotherhood as the toiling masses." [12] But might not totalitarianism also vary as much in its basic forms? Might not tyrannies arise within the larger formal structure of democracy, as Tocqueville warned —tyrannies that accept legal and political rights along the grand avenues of life but deny men an essential social validity in the intimate alleys and doorways of behavior?

The West is now acutely aware of the evils of state totalitarianism. Because of the historic lesson of World War II, because there is more general wealth to conserve, and because of fears of thermonuclear war arising from aggression, the likelihood of simple and direct dictatorship has greatly diminished in the major industrial countries. But, quite as certainly, the underlying conditions of alienation continue to exist, and perhaps are growing. They tend to be both exploitable and exploitive. Particularly when the growth of advertising, public relations, and public opinion testing is combined with diverse corporate power and economic domination in life, there appears to be a new, more subtle potential for tyranny.

Until the sources of human alienation have been eliminated, therefore, we cannot trust that other kinds of tyranny will not arise. And so we shift our attention now to examine some affirmable possibilities.

QUALITY OF LIFE

During recent decades the term "Standard of Living" has become a household measure of economic progress. In the United States the term has also become a symbol of national pride.

Yet Standard of Living, because of the manner in which we conceive it, has also come to symbolize the uncritical acceptance of technological prerogatives, corporate values, and economic determinism in our lives. This is not to say that a quantified measure of wealth is not relevant. What we are questioning here is not obvious utility, but whether our aspirations are dominated by barren utility.

Of course, Standard of Living itself is only a measure of per capita flow of money. It is decidedly not a measure of social or cultural benefits, and it but crudely measures even our material benefits. This is evident in two respects.

First, the critics who have questioned Standard of Living as a measure of family income use the classical example of the housewife who is not included in income statistics. If she takes employment, however, and hires a housekeeper, both she and the housekeeper are included in the statistics. The fact that money changed hands in the one instance and not in the other was the sole basis for taking account of human labors as "income"—and altering the measured Standard of Living.

The second and more important limitation of the term lies in the built-in burdens associated with technology, large cities, and other conditions related to higher incomes. In the United States many expenditures are required beyond the traditional necessities of food and raiment, and these new necessities are a questionable contribution to a higher standard of living. As an example, consider the burden of an office worker who commutes to New York City from Long Island, Westchester County, or parts of New Jersey. Ordinarily he must own two automobiles—one for commuting (often merely to get to the train station), the other for family chauffeuring. At least three burdens deny the family the standard of living indicated by statistics. The first is the investment for the second and otherwise nonessential and nonpleasure-giving vehicle. The second involves recurring expenditures for vehicle operation, public transportation fares, and parking. The third typically involves three or four hours of daily travel to work and back, denying the commuter the free use and full benefits of his "high" Standard of Living. These burdens cannot be cast off easily: moving into the City is costly; car pools are difficult to organize and to keep organized.

But beyond its practical deficiencies, Standard of Living is not and cannot be a valid measure of progress toward the good life. In no way, for example, does it make our life more exciting or more worthy than that of the ancient Greeks. What was their Standard of Living? Probably lower than that of most of today's "underdeveloped" nations. Yet their style of life still challenges the best in the modern world.

Of course, modern society needs broad symbolic phrases to highlight its aspirations, to relate aspirations to changes taking place in life, and even to use in formulating broad social programs. If society's goals, self-image, and foundations for action are to be liberalized, then we need a new, more liberal symbolic foundation. A term with this promise has already achieved some currency: "Quality of Life." President Johnson used it, for example, in describing his program for the Great Society.

The term appears to have a number of virtues difficult to corrupt. First, "quality" does not easily allow any particular set of values to be scaled on one confining continuum. It invites *person* back into the individual, *character* back into society. "Standard" was inevitably reduced to mere counting and always called forth invidious comparisons. Second, "life" implies new meaning and range of varied but enduring values, whereas "living" seemed to stress the immediate and transitory. We inevitably associate Standard of Living with money and the economy. Quality of Life can more easily encompass the farthest reaches of human aspiration. Now that general wealth is foreseeable for all in the West and is even in prospect elsewhere, the broader goals of Quality of Life would seem to be in order.

A public concern for a Quality of Life should not rest on a single definition, certainly not a rigid one. Rather, it might better pass through a continual process of definition and evolution and involve many varying subjects. Even a renewed, less bullish concept of Standard of Living might be among them.

The discussion here should not be construed as a metaphysical exercise. Its concern is to broaden the popular dialogue about the conditions, motivations, and directions of human action. For example, we might list four possible dimensions along which a concept of a Quality of Life might evolve.

One quality might be the variety of paths of behavior open to the individual at his various ages or conditions of life. Broader opportunities might be offered to achieve either security or adventure, each in manifold varieties. Adventure might occasionally involve physical risk and be rewarded by public honor—a real moral equivalent to war. Perhaps we should declare our whole society to be a university, giving every individual all possible opportunities to develop his own interests and to find his own unique ways of contributing.

The quality of beauty is another and singularly rich concern for a dialogue about Quality of Life. For example, there might be a concern for beauty throughout our whole environment (both created and preserved), for linking both tradition and monument to beauty, and for reuniting beauty with emotion and with work, injecting it deeply within all activity. However, we must beware of confining beauty to formal art, for this would only stimulate artiness, a blind alley like our present concern for production and consumption. Perhaps we should declare our country a national park, every square mile of it, and see how this will influence our thinking about our environment.

Quality of association is another possible dimension of Quality of Life. It has been some time since society has given concerted attention to the simple goodness of interpersonal relations. Stress generally has been placed on a narrow ethic and rigid discipline, not on the innate values of nondirective human association.

Fourth, in a society of explosive variation and complexity, the evolution of equally varied economic, social, and cultural rights must be a part of any broadly based Quality of Life, amplifying the traditional political rights. If employment has become the primary source for social status and personal adjustment, this fact argues strongly for the establishment of a right, or equivalent right, to work. If education is the avenue to all fruits of life in a civilization, then a maximum, humane, flexible, and sympathetic education should not be denied to the least individual in society. Under an established right, ability to benefit from learning might be the only effective criterion for the extent, kind, and character of education and personal guidance each person should receive.

Our age has developed the technical and economic foundation for a Quality of Life, even while attention has centered upon the barren concept of Standard of Living. The present limitation is of outlook, not of means. But some elements of a broader Quality of Life do creep into the public purpose. Preservation of open space is one—and this is made urgent by the automobile. Higher education for larger parts of the population is another, although its value is limited by its utilitarian and specialized nature.

Among other elements creeping into the public dialogue is the architects' expression of "human scale." Here the architects refer to open or enclosed spaces, building masses or structures having a scale in proportion not only to the physical size of man, but to his vision, his foot movements, his sense of place, and perhaps even his feeling of the importance of human participation. Although human scale might mean one thing for a school and another for a residence, it helps remind the architect of the essentially intimate values most buildings might have for the individual.

Human scale is but a very small bit of what makes society *relevant* to the individual person. But as yet neither architects, nor sociologists, nor city planners have come to appreciate even in general terms the enormous *social* importance of physical design. The professional dialogue has little vocabulary and few active concepts. We have come to appreciate so dearly the prerogatives of power, money, organization, machine, technique, efficiency, and mass that we now assume all superlatives of yesterday must be surpassed today. But the central human fact remains: man himself simply cannot become a superlative. His sensibilities cannot become gargantuan to match his own accomplishments.

The first question we must always pose, then, in seeking a Quality of Life is *relevance* to man's own being—physical, psychological, social, political, economic, and cultural. Relevance is a question of what is real for man, what is real for his feelings, what is real for his purposes.

Whereas the architects in a very small way have openly begun to recognize a relevance of their craft to the individual, there seems to be only an uneasiness among contemporary economists. W. W. Rostow concludes his *Stages of Economic Growth* with the note that "man is a pluralistic being—a complex household, not a maximizing unit—and he has the right to live in a pluralistic society." He also quotes Lord Keynes' famous toast before the Royal Economic Society: "I give you," Keynes said, "the toast of the Royal Economic Society, of economics and economists, who are the trustees not of civilization, but of the possibility of civilization." [13] John Galbraith similarly quotes from Alfred Marshal at the outset of his book, *The Affluent Society*: "The economist, like everyone else, must concern himself with the ultimate aims of man." But Robert Brady in *Organization, Automation and Society* seems to speak for all contemporary economists in applying these maxims to plural society, to civilization, and to the ultimate aims of man when he says that cultural problems are of "such transcendent importance for both economics and all other social sciences," it is better that they "undergo more searching analysis later." [14]

As yet there is little to demonstrate that the economists have begun to feel out even the human scale of their subject. Only with a few exceptions, possibly John Galbraith and Kenneth Boulding, have they sought redress from the economic excesses burdening society, excesses that are legitimized in economic thought. The excesses first enter economic thought in the name of objectivity and then, by default, remain as valid expressions or purposes of the economic system.

The inarticulate uneasiness of contemporary economists—together with their general unwillingness to come to terms with human purposes—has antecedents in earlier and more brutal periods. Adam Smith, for example, seemed to pass off aloofly a similar uneasiness when he observed that there are "no acts of Parliament against combining to lower the price of work; but many against combining to raise it." [15] David Ricardo must have felt the same aloofness when he spelled out his famous iron law of wages: "Labour, like all other things which are purchased and sold, and which may be increased or diminished in quantity, has its natural and its market value. The natural price of labour is that price which is necessary to enable the labourers, one with another, to subsist and perpetuate the race, without either increase or diminution." [16]

The noneconomist, Paul Goodman, has raised the question of the human relevance of all professions, and also raised a central problem in evolving a broad-based humanely liberal Quality of Life, in observing that "there is no philosophy of medicine, no jurisprudence and no social theory of engineering. The social consequences are disastrous." [17]

PREEMINENCE OF PERSON

Occasionally one comes upon a beautiful example of the spirit of men who seek their own destiny. A particularly interesting case involved a person whose father had sent him to military preparatory school in the hopes that his son would follow him in his military career. When examinations for the military academy were given, the son managed to flunk them, but agreed to go on to an engineering school, the closest alternative to a military career. After a year in engineering he convinced his father that he should really be in architecture, a close cousin to engineering. Then, after another period of time, he shifted to another not-too-distant cousin: art. His father eventually succumbed to this choice as well.

Thus new realizations and new virtue may arise in every new generation. With the advent of automated production and the reduced burden upon each person of providing life's necessities, a truly fantastic new horizon of life is becoming evident. This open horizon is the frontier of human possibility. It makes all the more urgent the question that every new generation must ask: will we permit the old social exigencies, the old imperatives, and the accumulated limitations of the mind of the old production-bound and the more recent corporate-bounded generation to prevent us from seeking the full potential and the full virtue of the new freedom?

John Gardner has stressed that "the virtues which flower in any society are the virtues that the society nourishes. The qualities of mind and character which stamp a people are the qualities which that people honor, the qualities they celebrate, the qualities they recognize instantly and respect profoundly." [18] At no time in history has man had greater opportunity to cultivate virtue within himself, among his fellows, and about his institutions. But the real challenge of our age is to fully comprehend this inheritance and to conceive how it will contribute to what we want to be.

It would be a mistake to minimize the obstacles to a new, more human realization in society. Many are imbedded deeply even within our perceptions of progress and change. Few terms better reveal our basic misconceptions than "cultural lag." This apparently self-evident observation really highlights the *technological potential* and the *cultural inhibitions* of our time. The term expresses an oberved technological momentum, not a sense of social purpose. It evokes a vision of dynamic initiative in science and reactive backwardness in society. It therefore implies a determinism in the unleashing of nature's forces rather than a determination by men to direct the course of human life.

Moreover, cultural *lag* implies the peculiar view that culture adjusts to technology. Granting that adjustment between two things always requires a mutuality, shouldn't the main line of adjustment be in the opposite direction? Technology is nothing more than an exotic array of means, and these require adjustment to human ends. In the same vein we continue to believe that science can fully "solve" man's broad social problems. Science can contribute certain means to that end, but the solutions must be worked out by man. Finally, to solve "problems" is to focus on the elimination of impediments rather than on the positive and inspired goal-seeking that is the essence of a new civilization.

Many obstacles to a new realization are also imbedded in our perceptions and methods of organization, leading to a gigantic misdirection of effort. Socrates once said that "virtue in the state is not a matter of chance but the result of knowledge and purpose." In our age the state and all institutions emphasize knowledge and neglect purpose, and we segregate and splinter knowledge—losing sight of the individual in our very efforts to serve the individual. Oliver Carmichael has noted this in graduate education and research: "Pursuit of truth now becomes," he said, "too largely, pursuit of facts relevant to particular needs. . . . Filling the needs of society has apparently become more important than meeting the needs of the individual. It might be argued that the needs of society can in the long run best be met by providing for the needs of the individual. It is less certain that meeting the needs of society . . . will best provide for the long-range needs of either it or the individual." [19]

Of course, in abstract terms, the individual and society are the distributive and collective aspects of the same thing. But what we often forget, and what Socrates failed to tell the modern world, is that valid *purpose* must always rest with the individual.

6

Reconstitution of Community

Thus far we have considered how we systematically seek and largely achieve order and progress in terms of the large functional institutions—the Big Citizens—and how we just as systematically ignore the social setting of the individual and permit it to fall into psychic incoherence. There are many profiles of this social torque: the increasing number and articulation of corporate powers contrasted with the growing dependence of the individual; the urgency toward technological progress and apathy toward social results (as in the decline of agriculture); the rising ethic of consumption, revealing the same manipulation of men as the ethic of production; the jaundiced concern for human welfare, the purpose being to make human resources productive and the means being a tattered patchwork of social services; the splitting of life into the small conjugal family on the one side and mass cosmopolitanism on the other; the one-sided effects of science and the professions; and, not the least, the undercurrents of despair and disorder that rudely burst onto the social surface.

Each profile points to the same conclusion: that a major shift has occurred in the magnetic field that organizes the living environment of men and that this shift has responded not to men, but to the Big Citizens—a new sovereignty of immense will.

Future development, of course, may be structured by the forces that

105

organize society to remagnetize human sovereignty. Obviously it is neither desirable nor possible to eliminate the accomplishments of the drive to production. Therefore, the challenge for man is to devise strategies and tactics of development that will progressively remove the ordinary organization of production from the organization and behavior of men without undermining output potential. That is the promise of automation, but it is not the promise of the institutions that have developed such a powerful will in the drive to production—the institutions that now organize automated production.

This and the following six chapters will illustrate some possibilities for remagnetizing *human* social organization in the coming decades of development: community and community development, industry, the city, institutional ethics, education, and planning.

We shall start with a concept of community, an institution that by its nature facilitates a quality, depth, and character of human response in interpersonal association. Except in tiny fragments, community does not now exist with the metropolitan masses—and so we must consciously plan and build community, just as we must conceive and organize other kinds of modern institutions.

A reconstitution of community in the twentieth century should reaffirm the preeminence of human interpersonal association in the structure of human organization. In contrast to bureaucratic forms of organization, which serve isolated functional needs of men and tend to deny meaningful interpersonal relationships, community should reassert the continuity, context, and integrity of *personal* membership in group life.

This view of community implies an articulation of the physical and social environment of human behavior with great concern and thoroughness. In a world in which institutions are predominantly self-assertive, competitive, and expansive, surviving and prospering only with the help of powerful internal defenses or outside defenders, community will reemerge only when society sustains it by conscious social intent, purposeful planning, and adequate means.

BASIS FOR COMMUNITY

When we speak of community we speak of a social organization wholly reflecting man as a social being. Community may be thought of as a social matrix with a comprehensibility, wholeness, and immediate relevance to the emotional realities of being human. For the person, community should present a sense of social identity, promote a sense of self-sufficiency, and therefore prompt greater personal integrity.

The need for community is essentially man's inherent need for character-making association. And the association we speak of is deeply interpersonal. Neither the person nor the setting can be generalized, abstracted, or standardized. The parties to an association cannot be interchanged; nor can their responses of friendship be borne by tape, wire, or photo, except as vestiges of past associations. Especially, association cannot consist of merely functional contacts not elaborated by personal mutuality, dialogue, choice, leisure.

Modern man crucially needs a valid middle range of human association, the range largely displaced during the last two centuries' drive to production. Western man has retained in the family a reasonably viable, intimate, and private level of association, despite great vicissitudes. At the other end of the social spectrum Western man has created a new cosmopolitan level of essentially anonymous behavior, including not only bureaucratic organization of business and government, but also cultural and educational activities, based largely upon specialization and professionalism.

The challenge of community is to reestablish a worthy intermediate or "public" range of association of individuals, between the complete intimacy and protection of the family and the awesome anonymity and performance-governed behavior of the cosmopolitan society.

The full range of human association may then be divided into three quite distinct parts: the family, which is *private;* the community, which is *public;* and the cosmopolitan society, which is *anonymous.* In broad characterization, the family is naturally intimate and wholly communal. Community is largely interpersonal and familiar, and the individual is freely and widely participative, mostly as an amateur. The cosmopolitan life is impersonal and corporate, and the individual there tends to be either a passive layman or a productive professional.

In no inherent way should a full and stimulating life in one area exclude or contradict a rich life in the other two. The individual, according to his inclination, might direct his behavior toward one, or two, or balance it in all three. But there must be a valid institutional or environmental framework supporting all three before the individual can have a real choice. Here, it seems, may be a fundamental basis for *individual* freedom, for *individual* challenge and opportunity, and consequently a foundation for meaningful individualism.

If we were to speak of checks and balances, as we do in politics, then the three independently valid arenas of behavior offer a significant measure of protection and relief against the social tyrannies that afflict almost every individual at various times in his life. Any social arena can produce a social tyrant. A family can brutally impose its will and deny personal growth to the individual; the corporate world can chuck any formal career aside in its ruthless trading in individual expendability;

indeed, community can ostracize or coerce deeply. But none can be as monolithic if other valid options of association are open to the individual. Three well-developed arenas of social behavior would open up acceptable retreats and alternatives.

Community has a potentially vital bearing upon the generation and transfer of social ideals, and the eclipse of community in the West may help explain a growing cynicism about expressions of altruism. When the roots of an ideal have developed between persons in an interpersonal atmosphere of growing confidence, they can be transferred to the larger realm of society. Very significantly the ideals of the larger society rest on ideals and ethics founded at the interpersonal levels of behavior, as abstractions of concrete face-to-face confidence between persons. On man's finite scale of being, it seems, abstract ideals must arise within the most finite and concrete personal experience. Then they can be transferred to the larger world by definite stages. This foundation for a wider morality might be expressed roughly in the algebraic concept that two elements equal to the same thing are equal to each other.

It is elemental that a Boy Scout cannot be a "brother to every other Scout" until his interpersonal experience gives him an intimate sense of what other Scouts are likely to be. A poignant demonstration of how a transfer of intimate ideals can take place occurred in Japan in the first days of the Allied occupation in 1945. A young lady walked around a narrow intersection of a city and there suddenly faced in terror the first American soldier she had ever seen. War propaganda had taught her to expect only rape and murder from the Americans. In one horrible moment she felt confronted by such a fate. The soldier realized the girl's shock, and wanting to correct matters, showed her a picture of his wife and two young children. In one instant he dissolved her fears by identifying himself with the universal and intimate ideals of family life. The profound common values from each of their experiences of family created a mutual understanding between them, namely that humanity would prevail.

Conversely, a specific inability to maintain a sense of interpersonal cohesiveness in a time of trial was demonstrated by American prisoners under Chinese "brainwashing" during the Korean War. Under the Chinese, the American prisoners failed to organize the "buddy system" and a system of internal justice, which they had normally done in foreign military prisons before. Interpersonal *esprit* was broken down by the Chinese tactics of selectively giving privileges for accepting desired attitudes and assisting in the "reeducation" of others. Every man became alienated from every other; the will to resist and to keep faith was lost.

An extremely high death rate of 45 percent among the American prisoners was in part attributed to their serious demoralization, for the physical treatment and living conditions were reportedly no worse than American prisoners had experienced in other wars. In one case a man who had vomited and was lying on the floor of a prison barrack was thrown out into freezing weather to die by another soldier who could not stand the stench. Although there are always individuals willing to carry out such acts, what is telling is that many other men who witnessed the incident refused to follow even the lowest basic moral of collective behavior, the common preservation of human life. The Chinese chief of intelligence in Korea could very well ascribe to these Americans, then, a "weak loyalty to his family, his community, his country, his religion, and to his fellow-soldier."

On the other hand, all 229 Turks who were captured in Korea marched back through Panmunjom. ". . . [T]hese Turks survived," reported an American psychiatrist, "very largely on the basis of an exercise of the most devoted kind of love among themselves. When a Turk was really sick, other Turks bathed and fed him and washed his clothes and lay beside him to keep him warm and in general just let that Turk know that he wouldn't die. He was a Turk and they were going to take care of him." [1]

The loyalty between individuals, and the group spirit underlying larger cultural ideals, can be exerted in times of trial only to the extent they are deeply ingrained in the behavior and belief of men in normal life. Ability to perform together in a military bureaucratic regime is not enough: that is hollow, and most of it is provided externally. When the bureaucratic machinery is whisked away after the men are captured, all they have left is their deeper devotion to each other, which is founded upon the depth of devotion they experienced and matured upon in the society from which they came.

Responses in times of trial are not unrelated to responses in normal times. The kind of personality one develops is ultimately a matter of the kind of associations one has. This is why function-dominated organizations foster function-dominated "organization" men. This is why corporate organizations created to serve as specialized means tend to specialize not only men's skills but their personalities as well. And this is why the material and functional means of life are taking on the character of the ends of life.

The American social philosopher George Mead described the genesis of this relationship as the human individual's ability to take the role of others into himself. Only by "meaningful communication" is self-consciousness attainable. "It is through taking the role of the other that he is able to come back on himself and so direct his own process of communication. . . . And thus it is that social control, as operating in terms of self-criticism, exerts itself so intimately and extensively over individual behavior or conduct, serving to integrate the individual behavior or conduct. . . ." [2]

"It is the unity of the whole social process that is the unity of the individual. . . ." Here Mead suggests the immense directive influence particular forms of society have in shaping the emergence of each new generation. He further stresses that "in so far as the individual can take those organized responses over into his own nature, and call them out by means of the symbol in the social response, he has a mind . . . whose inner structure he has taken from the community to which he belongs." [3]

In his book, *The Quest for Community*, Robert Nisbet observes: "What is involved most deeply in our problem is the diminishing capacity of organized traditional relationships for holding a position of moral and psychological centrality in the individual's life. Interpersonal relationships doubtless exist as abundantly in our age as in any other. But it is becoming apparent that for more and more people such relationships are morally empty and psychologically baffling. It is not simply that old relationships have waned in psychological influence; it is that new forms of primary relationships show, with rare exceptions, little evidence of offering even as much psychological and moral meaning for the individual as do the old ones. For more and more individuals the primary social relationships have lost much of their historic function of mediation between man and the larger ends of our civilization." [4]

"There must be," writes Nisbet in a later passage, "in any stable culture, in any civilization that prizes its integrity, functionally significant and psychologically meaningful groups and associations lying intermediate to the individual and the larger values and purposes of his society. For these are the small areas of association within which alone such values and purposes can take on clear meaning in personal life and become the vital roots of the large culture. It is, I believe, the problem of intermediate association that is fundamental at the present time." [5]

If a modern, renewed community is to mediate the immensities of modern society for the individual, it will have to strengthen and unify the local institutional setting of ordinary daily and seasonal activities. If it is to prompt social ideals within him, it must focus upon the intimate and familiar setting in which ideals can attain their psychic and social importance.

ECLIPSE OF COMMUNITY

Since community has declined decisively over the past centuries in the West, and now declines rapidly elsewhere, after serving as a virtually universal form of human organization, it becomes important for us to know why it declined. At the same time we must ask how community can be nourished in the technological and urban society.

It is indeed strange that anything but the inclination should be required for man to form stable common association in community. Alexis de Tocqueville attested to the effectiveness of this inclination in America over a century ago, observing that the village community was "the only association . . . so perfectly natural that wherever a number of men are collected it seems to constitute itself." [6] Lewis Mumford has concurred, saying that communities were "so spontaneous, so unartful that they seemed the products of nature rather than deliberate associations evoked by human need." [7] Yet today the classical small rural community rapidly dwindles in social importance. Only bare fragments of community exist within cities. The decline everywhere parallels the sweeping changes associated with industrialization and urbanization. "These elementary groups," Mumford laments, "were fated to be swallowed up by the spawning of mass civilizations before their absence was missed or their positive functions—above all, their educative and man-molding functions—were evaluated." [8]

The first seeds of the decline of community probably lie in the great awakening of the Renaissance and in the restlessness emerging with the growing plurality of religious and intellectual life. Trade expanded and the pace of life quickened. Growing rural and urban productivity began to be felt: first a rural labor surplus began to build up; some individuals drifted to the towns. Later the towns added more positive opportunities for those who had become ambitious for a "better life." A subtle shift took place away from sentiments sustaining inherited values, in Robert Park's terms, to interest in ends not present. [9] Ultimately, both the "push" and the "pull" of the blunt economics behind urbanization became more powerful. For the less certain rural migrant there was little hope of returning to his village, which chronically had more workers than the land—and later the economy—could support.

The restlessness as well as changing economics amounted to an attack upon community. The emerging spirit of science and intellectual exploration contributed to the attack: unrestricted investigation, impartial research, and boundless theories ran counter to the mood and comfortable social order of the medieval community. Eventually libertarian and egalitarian philosophies combined with the new importance of employment and production to undermine the traditional role and status of communal life.

Community itself consisted mostly of intangible qualities, connections rather than substances. These made for an inherent lack of hard institutional defenses. In village form, community naturally bridged the political, economic, and religious activities, and could not be distinguished from them. But, unlike the economy, the government, the church, or even the family, community had no built-in interest group to defend it. Community was, in effect, the sum of them all.

Most of these institutions eventually vacated their role in community, or so diversified and expanded that they became irrelevant to it. More than that, kings and rising industrialists hardly required prophets to tell them that "the traditional primary relationships of man" became, as Nisbet stressed, "functionally irrelevant" to the state and economy.[10] To the extent community held sway in the individual's deeper seat of belief, such a belief had to be subdued to permit initiative and growth for state and industrial interests.

The story of the eclipse of community, then, is one in which the functions supporting community migrated to the larger society. Expanding trade, factory manufacturing, and cash-crop agriculture made the village more dependent, the town larger. Political power centralized more distinctly in the national capitals. Expansiveness was rewarded for its own sake, whatever it applied to. Nearly all that took place in the new urban centers made community less possible: the masses of people and workers, the growing economic determination of social organization, and sharper class distinctions of wealth, education and privilege.

Yet there is little evidence that man rejected community. Community merely became irrelevant to the exciting or powerful new political, economic, and intellectual conditions of life. Subtle needs for psychic and social integrity in social organization could have little bearing when expansiveness of life beckoned with such promise. If man left community it was because of a bribe of modernity. He left it for the same inexplicable reasons that today make him insensitive to the ugliness of his urban environment or hypnotized to the loss of life that follows from commuting four hours daily.

CONTEMPORARY CONTEXT

Can community be recreated in a society that is almost totally urban and industrial? A first question involves the conflict between traditional and modern ethics. In classical community there usually existed an intimate economic cooperation in which the fate of an individual was shared with that of an extended family, clan, or whole village. This cooperation and sharing comes into conflict with the ethic of business and government, which is based on strict impersonal organizational accountability and objectively evaluated performance—"without regard for persons." Transferred to the modern society the old ethic is condemned as nepotism or worse.

The conflict represented a transition between two opposed kinds of economic system. Friction arose specifically because one kind of economic security (group sharing) declined before others (such as social security measures) were adopted or adequately supported. Thus, if economic security is ample and assured in the future, there is little likelihood that this conflict could become significant again. Consequently the question need not affect a new role for community.

Nevertheless, community is still sometimes considered to be in implacable contradiction to industrial society. Such an attitude overlooks the dynamic changes and accommodations society demonstrates anew each generation, and merely places the old and the new in awkward juxtaposition. The potential of community should be considered, rather, as an essential counterpoint to industrialism and the immensities of the Big Society. Isn't there a telling need for a counterpoint to social mass, economic giantism, bureaucratic rigidity, or the economic expendability of the individual? Might not community be a mediator between the *means* and the *ends* of society?

Community potentially gives modern society a new measure of pluralism. If life is open and competitive it can also be intimate and comforting; if it can give opportunity to worldly aggressive instincts, it can also allow for spirited local traditions. Mumford well expresses the significance of community as a social counterpoint: "The more readily we conceive the planet as a single unit and move about it freely on missions of study and work, the more necessary it is to establish such a home base, such an intimate psychological core, with visible landmarks and cherished personalities." [11]

Certainly a modern role for community should not and cannot follow the closed model of the medieval village; nor is the nineteenth-century New England town a practical model for our day. The eclipse of meaningful community among men has always been connected with the rise of urban, industrial, and mass society. If a new community is to appear, it must achieve a sound social pattern within that basic framework, within the larger worlds of universal knowledge, travel, and communication. Most centrally, community must become an agent to socially integrate the chaotic physical and social environment of cities. Therefore, before it can be realized in practice, a reconstituted community requires a new form with a new purpose and a new spirit.

Lawrence Haworth has astutely assessed the bearing of community upon contemporary life. The measure of our times, he asserts, is the *opportunity* that has arisen through differentiation and specialization, and the *community* that has dissolved as a result. He judges both opportunity and community to be equally important and possible in our society. "Taking our clue not from history but from the individual and his sense of his own well being," Haworth would "accept the challenge of molding an urban environment in which community and opportunity are both ingredients." [12] And, in these times of tenuous position of personality, the reemergence of community may well constitute a new dimension of *social* opportunity as well.

But how is community possible in practical terms? Certainly contemporary community can no longer come about by inclination alone, any more than government, corporations, education, or good health can come about by inclination alone. Like all institutions, communities must be "deliberate associations evoked by human need."

Today man easily controls his physical environment, and he is slowly learning to control the complex urban environment of his own making. He is learning some physical design requirements to achieve specific social objectives. He is also learning to be purposeful at a level to match his larger undertakings; the wider portents of what technology is doing, what corporations are doing, what is happening to cities, and what is happening to the individual are slowly entering the parliaments of social decision. National development plans in the developing countries are examples of a broader concern, though they have far to evolve. Larger meanings are beginning to be widely understood. Political action is beginning to be taken to assure more thoroughly positive results from the diverse interaction of environment, institutions, and individuals.

CONTEMPORARY FORM

If we consider community worthwhile, then our task is to consciously model its basic form and establish the conditions for its reemergence among urbanized men.

And if community is valid for mankind as a whole, it should be valid in some form for man in his various conditions—advanced or developing, wealthy or poor, urban or rural—though not necessarily for all individuals. Man's varied conditions and motives call for a variety of community, just as government, family, and church vary in their different environments. The essential community should be a simple and flexible instrument integrating men's social purposes, precisely as the stock corporation is an inherently simple but infinitely flexible instrument mobilizing men's economic forces.

If community is to become worthwhile, its bare roots will probably resemble those of the small classic community, though its character will necessarily differ greatly. Robert Redfield assigned to the classic community four attributes:

(1) Distinctive: "Where the community begins and where it ends is apparent."
(2) Small: It is "so small that either it itself is the unit of personal observation or else, being somewhat larger and yet homogeneous, it provides in some part of it a unit of personal observation representative of the whole."
(3) Homogeneous: "Activities and states of mind are much alike. . . . So understood, homogeneous is equivalent to 'slow changing.'"
(4) Self-sufficient: It "provides for all or most of the activities and needs of the people in it." [13]

Notably, each of Redfield's last three attributes—smallness, homogeneity and self-sufficiency—contributes in its own way to the first, distinctiveness. In an urban society, then, the most important characteristic of the classic community is the integrity and unity of its whole form and function, and the integration of the physical, economic, political, and social elements of individual group life regularly involved with it. The central ingredient, distinctiveness, is as attainable in our contemporary setting as it is in a folk setting. We do, after all, attain clear distinctiveness in the very complex forms and functions of government, business, and transporation.

What distinctiveness is possible for a modern community? What can make it psychologically relevant to the individual person? What is the possible counterpoint to unlimited bigness and unbounded complexity, to infinite expansions of man's means, to functional subordination of man's behavior?

The essential framework for modern community, following from this analysis, might consist of the following: *a people, a locality, a set of institutions, a variety of activities, and a body of understandings that form a related and meaningful whole for the individual.* Community should create a social structure that enlarges the human significance of interpersonal association.

This definition of community envisages a social *unity* for the individual based upon his roles and interests. At the same time it adds a new dimension to social *diversity* by providing a third major realm for the individual's life career, alongside the family and participation in the cosmopolitan society.

There is no inherent reason why a modern community should cramp, directly or implicitly, the worldly role of the individual. Community should in no way hinder progress in science and technology, aggressive life ambitions, increasing productivity and corporate expansion, world travel and a breadth of outlook, cultural excellence and opportunity, or emotional depth and intellectual maturity. In contrast to the classical community, which was isolated from the large society and monolithic for the person, modern community—under conditions of modern mobility—could not conceivably withdraw into a new social isolation or spawn a narrow world outlook.

The important applications of community will be within cities, or within closely interrelated urban regions. Community constitutes a principle for molding the human environment and all the activities that contribute to the vitality of the individual person. These are differentiated according to human social and psychological requirements. An urban community would then encompass a limited number of inhabitants in a limited area with a distinctive and unified physical design, in contiguity with other communities, and have easy access to the major cosmopolitan institutions of the metropolis or region.

The possibility of giving physical integrity to community within the mass environment of cities owes much to Clarence Perry and his "neighborhood unit" plan of 1929. Perry defined the boundary of the neighborhood with major traffic arteries and natural features of the topography, giving it the "distinctiveness" noted by Redfield. Perry also defined a neighborhood center with an elementary school and park, but left the marketing functions to the periphery. However, to Mumford, the "social core is more significant than any particular manifestation, for here ideal human purposes prevail over the preparatory agents and means." [14] This clearly implies a more comprehensive range of behavior at the center for all ages and interests and all times of the day and week. Thus, the urban community has (1) a clear boundary with an identity and integrity of what each community consists, and (2) a vigorous center with functions that permit common forms of association to evolve toward their ideal.

Unlike most present urban living areas, which are largely barren of varied institutional activities, community must incorporate a wide range of governmental, social, and economic functions—beyond those of the family but less than those of the massive endeavors of the large society. "In any society, the concrete loyalties and devotions of individuals," writes Nisbet, "tend to become directed toward the associations and patterns of leadership that in the long run have the greatest perceptible significance in the maintenance of life." [15] Although modern community cannot expect to reclaim the activities that once supported life, it must nonetheless serve numerous important activities. It can and should seek to attract or develop institutions that will have special social significance after industrial automation has displaced man from basic production. Then a new wider range of the arts, with stimulating involvements of family, church, market, school, and a rich variety of individual endeavors, can well spawn an equivalent to the "maintenance of life" in the new community.

Unquestionably some of the most important functions to return to community are political and governmental, for communities require these to manage their own affairs and to determine in some measure their own destiny. This may seem a backward step to those who now struggle to consolidate chaotic metropolitan government. But perhaps both goals are connected. In the principle of federation exists both a unity of the whole metropolis and a unity of the parts, of which the community is the most significant. Many important municipal functions, such as major elements of education, recreation, and health, but also fire, police, and local public works, can be effectively managed at a community level. And, very probably, if meaningful powers were granted to localities within metropolitan areas, there would be a greater popular willingness to accept metropolitan consolidation.

What is important is the completeness with which any valid human community must be conceived—specifically the thoroughness with which economic and political life, as well as the social, religious, and family life, must be integrated with community.

Fundamentally, community is a principle of organization rather than a unitary organization itself. Its mode and its means are participative and integrative rather than operative and proprietary. This participative principle means that community is host to the active organizations serving men in their local environment. Conversely, the organizations that form a coherent environment for the finite individual help constitute a community. Organizations give substance to community; community gives them human relevance. Community is a limited diversity, rich but not bewildering. It is host to organizations that arise among or serve its members, but it responds to the needs of people rather than those of organizations. The participative principle thus promotes a *local* and *social* plurality while maintaining basic social coherence and simplicity.

SPAN OF COMMUNITY

The size of community must be limited to what is socially and psychically comprehensible to the individual. The area and population will determine, in effect, whether or not community actually exists. Business and government are by nature expansive, but the distinctiveness of community is related very closely to a restraint of its size. In this it is more akin to the self-discipline and completeness demonstrated in the mature human body. Too large a population and too large an area eventually defeat the purpose.

A modern community needs to be small enough that an individual can know about all of its organized activities and have at least a casual acquaintance with a significant proportion of its inhabitants. It should be large enough to support most of the normal range of voluntary associations, as well as commercial, professional, and governmental services. In balance, the community should be of a size to be varied and stimulating, yet such that the individual can feel himself intimately a part of the whole community and always feel his role to be both personally satisfying and in some way important.

Considering these factors, the most advantageous level for population in community seems to be between four and eight thousand inhabitants. This range concurs with that used by many physical planners of residential communities, but is larger than that used by others who base population on the service area of one elementary school. Assumed here are two or three elementary schools and one small junior-senior secondary school, the latter greatly adding vitality and diversity to community functions.

But the community of from four to eight thousand people cannot be the sole fulcrum of organization, and two other levels of community participation invite consideration. One is a neighborhood cluster, or microneighborhood, involving perhaps as few as ten families or as many as one hundred, and a population of from thirty to four hundred individuals. The cluster would stimulate association between families and prompt activities centering about very young children. Within the cluster might be a small common or green associated with facilities attractive to collective use: small play yard, preschool room, outdoor fireplace and patio, swimming pool, garden furniture and decorative fixtures. Interior pathways might lead to the community center. Beyond basic design and assurance of space, improvement might normally be left to the residents to develop and manage themselves.

The other level, larger than community, inviting consideration is the district. Incorporating between ten and fifteen communities, its population might range from fifty to one hundred and twenty thousand people. The district would provide services too large or specialized to be in community: a college or branch of a university, large-scale retailing and general wholesaling, metropolitan administrative divisions, industrial centers not identifiable with individual communities, reserve facilities (such as fire-fighting equipment) and advisory services (such as police records and coordination). The character of participation would be partly cosmopolitan, but the boundaries would be definite to encourage a common perspective about responsibilities and problems.

However, the primary focus of concern should remain with the community, which maintains both a limited diversity and a social coherence in group life for the individual. For this reason the neighborhood cluster should not be more than a tenth of community and the district should not consist of less than ten communities. At closer relative sizes there would be a tendency for a confused competition to arise; there is no purpose in having competition between various levels of organization; competition would only dissipate the distinctiveness so crucial to community. Both the cluster and the district have valuable services to provide, and one of the most important is to contribute to the vitality and integrity of community.

Community would be the center of participation, the common meeting ground affording the deep richness of interpersonal association and also wide opportunities for local institutional participation. Formal and informal behavior would mingle by easy degrees from one to the other. The stiff character of local business and government would be softened by close association with their constituents. Breaking the rigid segregation of specialized function would tend to dull the calculating and exploitive contests of money and power. Special interests would blend, in part at least, and result in a larger interest of the whole. Art might not be so rigidly separated from commerce; commerce might not be so rigidly separated from education; and education might not be so isolated from the home.

But setting a norm for community should not preclude, in particular circumstances, a special composition. In a large metropolis a given community might, for example, consist substantially of people in the arts and entertainment field, and this would certainly bear upon its form and character. Another, more rural community might reflect the activities of people working in lumbering, supplemented by a number of retired people. Sometimes particular conditions of tradition, topography, or consensus may warrant a community with a larger or smaller population than normal.

The importance of variations of community is that, while there may be a norm reflecting an ideal, the variations that lend distinctiveness and promote character are themselves important aspects of the ideal of community, as they are of personality. Community will again be real for people when they seek to find one having a bearing on their own personality and interests, as they now seek a house—in socially barren surroundings—with a given number of rooms at the price they can afford. The variations of community should still reflect the ideal of community.

The range of alternatives in community offers the individual a number of ways of relating to it. He might be fully involved, including employment, or participate only slightly, or not even associate at all, if he chooses.

We might, however, expect a natural course for individual behavior in community. At birth and for about two years a child's world is quite completely circumscribed by home and family. Gradually it might expand to the neighborhood cluster. Then, when school and related activities take on importance, the whole community might become a significant fulcrum of activity, continuing in varying forms through secondary school. In college the young person's interest might expand to the district, metropolis, and world. At marriage, the role of community might again reassert itself, and be reinforced as the next generation began its excursions beyond the house. Finally, in old age, the community may offer not only assistance and leisure activities, but perhaps personal consolation at the loss of a loved one.

Seen in this way, community might be considered as a social framework and cultural resource for the individual, and as a means to personally experience many intimate excitements of civilization, complemented on the one hand by the family and on the other by the cosmopolitan society. Excitement evokes the best in men and brings forth the most worthy elements of civilization.

UNIVERSALITY OF COMMUNITY

Robert Redfield emphasized the slowness of change in classical community. Although a similar stability and continuity would also be necessary in the modern community, it need not apply to all residents. The speed with which modern man becomes acquainted and involved in groups new to him suggests that a certain mobility would not be detrimental to the role of community as a whole. Greater stress probably should be placed upon the framework in which mobile people can quickly orient themselves to a new social environment.

A man who travels widely, or deals with problems of great abstraction, or holds a unique specialization, may find in community much-needed relief from these preoccupations. In a modern context, community is not a sanctuary for parochialism; it is a home port for the individual *as a person*. It is a finite station for the finite individual. Unless associative life is reasonably satisfying and creates a sense of human purpose—which can arise only from close interpersonal experience—there is then little meaning to great exertions for the welfare or advancement of mankind as a whole.

If man is to increase his capacity for universal brotherhood he must nourish healthy roots of personality, based upon the satisfactions of face-to-face trust, mutual devotion and love. Only when personality is anchored in durable interpersonal experience is there a reasonable basis for extending good will to other peoples and enlarging it to an abstract ideal of human brotherhood. Such also is the foundation for strength of character, and for defense of one's beliefs without falling into vengeance. Society thus needs to give credence to the ego and its ethnic foundations before the individual can be expected to acquire a more universal faith.

And as we might begin with the intimate relationships of family that nourish healthy personality, we might also find easy stages by which attachments and understandings may be enriched and expanded to the larger society. A valid association of people in their community, a "public" association of the kind flourishing in Athens in its greatest period, offers a crucial intermediate setting for the peaceful and fruitful association that all men must find together. George Mead has stressed "the implicit universality of the highly developed, highly organized community." Not only are the achievements of community potentially universal, as are the drama, art, and philosophy of Athens, but the molding of men of great breadth and strength may be the most significant of all contributions to universality. Mead considered that even the existence of community held a universal potential: "To the degree that any achievement of organization of a community is successful it is universal, and makes possible a larger community." [16]

And it was in Athens that community and city brought a balanced provocative influence to bear upon the behavior of men. Athens in the fifth century before Christ had many characteristics like those here ascribed to community. Since it was far from the largest of ancient cities, varied and intense participation of most of its citizens in most public affairs was the rule (though slaves and women were excluded). There was a delicate interlacing of the diversity, stimulation, and aggressiveness representative of the city and the humane understanding, pride, devotion, affection, and vital commitment more closely akin to community. What resulted was not only a new level of humanism but unprecedented advances in philosophy as well. Moreover, Greek science arose out of a setting that today would seem parochial and constricted. Something of the same provocative urban/community environment also existed in renaissance Italy, Elizabethan England, and Revolutionary America.

Two characteristics seem to be associated with the emergence of new levels of creativity and maturity in each of these ages: (1) there had been a growing but still very moderate level of urbanization; and (2) the men were of wide rather than specialized accomplishment. City populations were usually less than one hundred thousand. Specialization had only a minor effect on men's careers. In such an atmosphere the universal genius da Vinci emerged, as did the English writers, philosophers, and scientists born between 1560 and 1642 (Shakespeare, Bacon, Hobbes, Locke, Newton) and Jefferson in America a century later.

Community in our age of giant urbanism would seem to have a comparable but opposite role to that of the city in ages past. While early cities fanned fresh air through small constricted communal beehives of men, community can now offer salutary shelter for the socially wind-burned personality of urban masses of men. Together, community and city might bring man to a new expanse of humanism, one that industrial abundance promises to make universally possible but one that is also obstructed by the bureaucratic reaches of industrial organization.

HEART OF COMMUNITY

The ideal of community will be most deeply expressed in its center. Here will be found the diverse interests and yet the casual famil-iarity that promotes excitement. Here many regular activities and cele-brations may be carried on among, by, and for essentially the same per-sons. Here may be the common involvement and easy exchange between the active and passive, festive and functional, governmental and private, sacred and secular, adult and youth, maker and seller.

The essential functions and organization of the center of community will follow from the roles and inclinations of the individual, rather than from the needs for specialized products and services. Unlike the centers of cities today, the center of community will be highly heterogeneous: commercial activity will be a part, but not a dominating one.

Relaxing the boundaries between governmental and private affairs, or between utilitarian and nonutilitarian behavior, need not blur the legal or administrative distinctiveness of any particular institution; but it does suggest closer levels of cooperation, more involvement in general affairs, and less domination by special interests. Therefore, a government agency or private business may be expected to be a vital foundation for com-munity life, even as it is now an organization with a specialized service to perform.

The physical design of the community center will be formed for the man afoot, for the intermingling of diversity, for environmental grace, for interpersonal association at ease, and for gaiety and festivity. It might involve a number of interwoven functions that now tend to be segregated: (1) municipal, including administrative functions, fire and police protection; (2) commercial, involving retail shops, restaurants, and professional offices; (3) education, including primary, secondary, and diverse adult community programs; (4) health, tying together hospi-tal, clinic, and convalescent or rest-home services; (5) cultural, library, recreation, and athletic programs; (6) membership organizations, includ-ing churches, lodges, voluntary associations, and youth groups; (7) pri-vate schools for music, art, drama, dance, writing, and so on; (8) repair, maintenance, and storage activities; and (9) a number of small "creative industrial" shops.

So much for the inventory. What may seem eclectic actually brings together a broad range of activities highly relevant to the interests of the individual. During the whole of the day and evening they are easily accessible to him and to each other, stimulating a varied interplay. Their physical coherence establishes a basis for vigorous *common* dialogue, consensus, and leadership initiative on all matters of importance and interest.

Two characteristics will be especially important in composing and enriching the unity of the center. The first is the multipurpose use of as many facilities as can be conveniently managed. Economy of investment and operation will be a significant benefit, but the primary value will be the effect in weaving diverse activities into an interconnected pattern, facilitating many kinds of freely initiated cooperation.

For example, an annual festival, including performing and visual arts, debates, athletics, dances, and banquets, might jointly use gyms, auditoriums, plaza, shops, restaurants, and even the hospital and municipal meeting rooms. If these facilities were all within a compact community center—from which the automobile with its space demands and physical divisiveness would be excluded—the whole center might easily participate in the celebration. Indeed, the center should stimulate and mobilize the many possibilities for man to celebrate life, as well as perform more prosaic functions.

In day-to-day affairs, the combining of municipal and secondary-school library resources might not only afford both groups better book services but also assist the library's evolution into musical services, local history promotion, serious discussion activities, and the like. School shops and classrooms, too, now underutilized and often forbiddingly sterile, might be made fully usable for all the people. The reason for today's poor use of public facilities is partly historic, partly the chaotic misform of cities, partly rigid jurisdictional prejudice and budgetary purity. But the reason lies also in the absence of positive conceptions to make costly facilities fully beneficial. The integration of the secondary school within the larger mosaic of the center of community would be especially stimulating.

Perhaps the most important potential multipurpose facility is one that is now generally scanty and unimaginatively developed: the community center building. If it were conceived as a home for the entire range of private voluntary associations—and as a means to promote their formation—it might well become the community's own "clubhouse." Equipped and regarded with all of the pride of private clubs, it might include meeting rooms, club office rooms, lounges, garden, kitchen, special activity rooms, and at least one large multipurpose room. It might well have its own staff to service private organizations and perhaps to manage certain activities in its own right.

The second characteristic serving to unify the center of community is the formal relation and integration of services. Two examples illustrate how the integration might work.

Consider first a combined hospital, convalescent center, and clinic that is integrally a part of the community center. The major principle is that the sick remain within their community to the extent their condition permits. A healthy community should offer a healthy social atmosphere to encourage recovery, including a limited number of mental patients. (How grievous is society's treatment of those who break under the strains society imposes, separating them from all normal interpersonal association.) Being in the community center, many patients can readily stroll to the plaza, greet passers-by, even enter into some activities, while perhaps only a hundred-yard wheelchair ride from the hospital door.

The second example pertains to education. In the past century most of the expansion of learning has been directed to making man more externally useful, not giving him greater satisfaction from the act of learning. Essentially, education has become the means to internalize the drive to production. Didn't the business philosopher Peter Drucker recently call education the only real form of capital formation?

But if we perceive community as it might evolve, education may show a considerable part of its worth for men in the depth of interest an individual acquires in making creative contributions to others. Central to creativity will be many formal, informal, and casual means of discovery and learning. Human growth of this kind will not flow from an atrophied night school, but from a widely based program, sensitively mingling education with action, private with public means, organized and not-so-organized approaches, secluded and popular endeavor, individual and group participation, and many kinds of compensation, rewards, and acclaim.

The role of education will be most important when new communities are created. The inhabitants will be new to each other; the institutions and facilities will be new, unfinished, or undeveloped. Through many kinds of special classes and conferences, the people will be able to form a common image both of what they are and what they can be. They will need to lay the intellectual foundations for action to complete their facilities, organize their full range of institutions, resolve major questions of precedent, stimulate a pattern of festivities—in short, create the organic form of their community behavior, and define their tradition. These founding steps can take place under the auspices of an adaptive and wide-ranging educational effort.

A rich and responsive education in the community will best show up in the wide variety and invigorating depth with which individuals and groups challenge themselves and each other, particularly as free time expands. Courses could be focused for such groups as an Undersea Exploration Society, a Local History Society, a Landscape Art Club, or a Biblical Archaeology Society. Besides operating their own community education, perhaps the schools might sponsor diverse private teachers and schools in whatever field there is initiative.

The elementary and secondary schools might benefit greatly from varied ongoing involvements with the larger community. Often a course of instruction built around an intellectually challenging community activity would have far greater depth of meaning and relevance for a young student than an isolated classroom effort could ever have. A student's formal period of schooling might be further integrated into activities of community if a number of leading citizens taught part time and if students could fulfill specific educational objectives by participating in adult community education.

Education should blend with all activities in which creativity, knowledge, and judgment play a role. It may thus contribute to a social coherence and an organic flow of events in the whole community. Social coherence lies in the connections that give meaning and continuity to ordinary events and life cycles of the individual, not to those of his organizations and anonymous functions. Social coherence is not found in the separation of behavior into discrete boxes of behavior: family, education, entertainment, sickness, job, vacation, profession, usefulness, youth, retirement. These may each be real, but separated they are the dismembered body of the individual's existence.

AMATEUR SPIRIT

The community center and its activities will not achieve distinctiveness or vigor without a distinctive kind of leadership. The unique qualities of the amateur appear to have this potential.

If the specialized professional illustrates the functional separation of behavior, the amateur equally epitomizes the social unities and continuities of behavior. The professional is a highly trained and socially disciplined member of a group with a claim to monopoly over some area of endeavor. The growing universality of professionalism and its preeminent position in social affairs has tended to make a man a specialist first and a person afterwards.

But the amateur, mostly self-disciplined and largely motivated in the content and character of his activities by his inner interests, tends to conceive his own particular behavior in a freer personal and social context, for he is not dependent on a strict institutionalized performance. The amateur's potential role is flexible and freely inventive on the one hand, and likely to be more closely involved with immediate human affairs on the other. The word "potential" is used advisedly: today's stress on the coherence of specialized functional performance and upon the type of institutions that organize them pushes the role of the amateur toward a certain character of specialization as well.

The skill and discipline of the professional are for sale, and this places a pecuniary linkage between individuals. What gifts he makes to others or to society tend to be either money or specialized skill. The amateur, however, gives of himself; and it does not matter greatly whether the form of the gift is related to what he does best. Moreover, the amateur is more likely to give, for he follows his activities out of varied motivations, rather than the thought of gain. For the same reason the amateur is likely to find greater satisfaction in his community. He is not as likely to pit himself in a strict competitive stance. More likely, he will seek a social setting in which his contributions will be appreciated and his efforts honored.

In community there will always be the professional. This is not to be disparaged. What is important is that every individual have many available avenues for personal expression characterized by the broad personal commitment of the amateur. In community, at least, the vital spirit of the amateur should normally override the cold precision of the professional. The professional's supremacy rests with his skill, the amateur's with his spirit, and community is preeminently the place for expressions of the human spirit.

Just as the attitude of the professional now radiates to the amateur, it is possible that the spirit of the amateur may one day enliven that of the professional—at least in community.

In 1946 Granville Hicks wrote a thoughtful little book entitled *Small Town*. He described his experience and observations as an intellectual who lived for a number of years in an old rural community in the eastern United States. Several of his observations on the behavior of the townspeople suggest qualities of life that community might restore.

The first quality is the sense of character that permeates social behavior. Hicks noted it in this way: "I do not pretend that I like everyone in town. There are a few persons I like very much indeed, some I strongly dislike, some of whom I disapprove, and many toward whom I have no particular feeling. But there is no one—well, to be exact, almost no one—who is a blank, who exists for me merely as a function or a type. Good, bad, or indifferent they are there—forces, dynamos, or, more accurately, entities, organisms, or, to be quite clear, human beings." [17] Plainly there is little terror of anonymity.

The second quality is the character of understanding, interest, and tolerance that is enlarged by a breadth of association: "I am quite convinced," says Hicks, "that the more perceptive and thoughtful of my neighbors have a better grasp of human realities than most of the intellectuals. They know so many more kinds of people, and they know them in so many more ways. . . . The tradition of rural shrewdness is not a myth." [18] In another passage Hicks suggests that "the practice of tolerance goes hand in hand with rapt interest. Births, marriages, deaths, fights, arrests, new jobs, and similar events receive appropriate attention." [19]

The third quality is found in the lively and profound sense of the past. According to Hicks, "the significant thing about the natives is the way they think about the past—not merely the individual past but the community past . . . real talents as a conversationalist display themselves only when some occurrence has touched upon memory." The people of the town are "loquacious and dramatic and very funny on the subject of the past." [20]

Conversely, the contemporary urban resident lives for the future, and is a creature of it. His present is consumed in a ladder-climbing routine. His past, seen as a series of errors and successes, has little personal interest for him and is a lost dimension of experience. It is not relived; it is not funny or sad, dramatic or profound; nor does it involve a sharing, or have a distinct character that grows with group memory. The present is raced through in the hope of a tomorrow; therefore, the course of urban life is more episodic than organic, and the urbanite tries to evaluate each episode for the future.

It is natural that intense interest in the past by the people in a small town should be associated with an equally keen interest in the drama of ordinary affairs, the variations of individual character, the changes of scene, the incidents of grave or humorous portent—and the weaving of all these with tall stories, exaggeration, and wit. The interest in persons is not a form of meddling, as the urbanite may see it, but a mark of the high esteem placed on people. The continuous and common exchanges of individuals who meet in varied roles creates the foundation for interpersonal understanding, then for a trust based upon understanding. And it is this foundation that best nourishes within the individual an ability to care—not as a formal altruist, but with the simple conscience and self-respect that cannot "look into the bloodshot eyes" of someone he knows without active concern.

One should not mistake the growth of a collective conscience in the public life of community for a utopian love among citizens. Friction, disputes, antagonisms, and feuds are apparently a part of man; community may even etch them more clearly. Yet the form of community affords an excellent means for personal cooperation, trust, and love to evolve between those who are so inclined.

When we think of contemporary community, we think of the development of men more than of institutions. Institutions are appropriate in community only insofar as they contribute to the social development of the individual and make him essentially comfortable in his social environment.

Community is therefore a means to shift the center of gravity in the organized life of society back to the person. During World War II Lewis Mumford suggested the essence of what that should mean: "The task for our age is to decentralize power in all its manifestations and to build up balanced personalities, capable of utilizing all our immense resources of energy, knowledge, and wealth without being demoralized by them. Our job is to repair the mistakes of a one-sided specialization that has disintegrated the human personality, and of a pursuit of power and material wealth that has crippled Western man's capacity for life-fulfillment. We must provide an environment and a routine in which the inner life can flourish, no less than outer life; in which fantasies will not be wholly dependent upon the film, in which the need for song will not depend wholly upon the radio or the gramophone; in which men and women will have a going personal life that is central to all their associated activities. We must create conditions of living in which the life of a parent will be as momentous and as full of interest and as valid as any other sphere of activity: a life with its own center of gravity. We must offer more physical outlets, not merely for aimless play, but for sober manual activities: the work of the gardener, smith, carpenter, weaver, no less than potter, painter, sculptor. Ironically, the introduction of these salutary arts is now delayed until a neurosis appears; whereas in a well-balanced life they are ways of guarding against a breakdown." [21]

Repetition of a few points may prevent possible misconceptions about a reconstitution of community: (1) Though community would involve patterning men's organizations, it would not organize life *for* the individual. On the contrary, it is a structure that should enlarge the alternatives open to the individual. (2) Community is not a monolithic definition for utopia. It is simply a society's *social* structure aimed at giving preeminence to the individual. (3) The existence of community should not hinder a worldly outlook or a role in the advanced economy or science. Men would move freely, and modern communications would prevent isolation.

Many objections to community are focused upon the conditions with which community has been identified in the past: physical isolation, lack of diversity, lack of stimulation. However, present problems more often arise from the opposite conditions: contacts without meaning, social variation without relevance, stimulation without focus, worldliness without roots.

Community should be considered as a context and continuity in which the whole experience of man is related to the personality of the individual. It should be prized as the middle range of social behavior in which mature individuality can be nurtured and the sense of freedom can find its most real expressions for the individual.

7

Community and
Development

In 1948 in England a conference on mass education in the developing countries used the term "community development" to describe a comprehensive approach to programs of economic and social improvement of peoples in their local setting. That term has since been applied to many national programs, to a new profession, and increasingly to varied and long-standing social service programs in the industrialized countries.

In the emerging nations community development has been undertaken to speed economic development. One official report put it this way: "The development and mobilization of human resources is central to the concept of community development." A "mobilization" clearly infers a decline of community, not its development, and "human resources" is clearly in the Western tradition of reducing men to the purposes of industrial development.

By contrast, in the economically advanced countries where the decline of community has been a fact for two centuries, community development now largely aims to recover the social casualties of industrial development and to ameliorate its results by making the individual economically viable once again. One American program director said that his purpose was "to salvage and improve human resources." Once again the basic economic intent is revealed by the similar industrial terminology.

In this chapter we shall examine the two forms of community development and show that both purposes of community development will be better served if the primary objective is centered upon a renewal of community. Some requirements will be considered that may help adapt community to industrialism and urbanism while preserving, if not expanding, personal freedom.

PROMOTING DEVELOPMENT

The idea of community development in the developing countries is deeply embedded in the notion of program comprehensiveness. Before World War II the typical programs of rural improvement sought only specific objectives and emphasized technical and specialized approaches. If a government wanted to assist farmers, it aimed for specific improvements only in farm practices. If it wanted to stimulate a local economy, it might either help organize cooperatives or improve transportation.

With the economically motivated peoples of the West such approaches worked reasonably well. If you show a man an improved practice, usually he will follow it. But as they were introduced to the peoples of traditional—not yet "developing"—societies encrusted in thousands of years of custom, such programs regularly failed. This was the tendency in all of the developing countries. New sanitation facilities might be left completely unused. A water agency might report it had successfully drilled fifty wells, but a year later only three or five might be in use. Farmers would revert to old practices the moment extension workers moved on. Thousands of such efforts had very little effect. Consternation and bafflement were the reactions of conscientious program directors.

One early comprehensive experiment, called the "Gurgaon Scheme" [1] after the district involved, was carried out in the Punjab in India in the late 1920's and early 1930's by F. L. Brayne, an English civil servant. Brayne summarized his broad span of interest under seven headings: (1) institutional work, (2) rural sanitation, (3) agricultural development, (4) education, (5) cooperation, (6) social reforms, and (7) coordination and publicity.

The comprehensiveness illustrates Brayne's evident concern for the interlocking nature of improvement in rural life. Yet even this approach was rudimentary and incomplete, as Brayne acknowledged in commenting upon the immediate results of his scheme: "This work is not being done by villagers determined to live a better life but by villagers determined to please their District Officers." A later observer noted that Brayne used high-pressure methods and sought rapid results. In any case, very little of this work was evident a few years after Brayne left Gurgaon.

After World War II an American architect and city planner, Albert Mayer, was instrumental in initiating and guiding the now classical Pilot Project, Etawah, from 1948–1954. In this experiment community development took its present most characteristic form. Mayer stressed a synthesis of various concepts for a more comprehensive and coherent approach based on mutual efforts of both the people and government.

To accomplish an awakening it was necessary to establish an entirely new relationship between government workers and the people. Specifically, there could be no aloofness; close involvement with and confidence of the people was required; authoritarian orders from the top had no place if the people were themselves to become deeply involved in their new endeavors. This Mayer called "inner democratization."

To Mayer "the single lobe [the single-purpose project], the outside gift, the unprepared general atmosphere—these are a fatal combination." [2] While his concern centered upon the growth of the people themselves, all steps were taken with a methodological rigor and followed with critical examination. Especially three criteria were applied to projects in Etawah: felt need, confidence building and know-how.[3] The first sought initial involvement, the second and third, a personal and social growth based on a successful experience. Ultimately the real success would be a new confidence and initiative in further endeavors.

Thus, a successful strategy required not only a coordination among the agriculturists, cooperative organizers, health officers, and educators, but a direct and paramount concern for the behavior of the people themselves, their beliefs, organizations, and concerns—in short, their community. This was the basic requirement for working with traditional peoples. And it was the foundation upon which the principles of community development evolved.

Thus, community development ideally became a comprehensive program to promote balanced continuous improvement of all people in a community or local area through unified efforts and according to a general philosophy of objectives and a pragmatism of method.

Out of the experience of the decades following World War II many working principles and practices have been put forward, tried, selected, and modified. Together they form an inspiring and liberal chapter in the recent inventiveness of man:

(1) *The Primacy of People.* The programs must center upon the people because in the long run there is no other kind of development;

growth will not take place without their complete involvement. The programs must begin where the people are—their community, their practices, their beliefs, their aspirations, their prejudices and fears—and remain relevant to them as changes occur. The important changes are those that occur within people themselves; the external physical changes are but symbolic artifacts to the inner growth.

(2) *Self-help.* The observable material progress in community development occurs as individuals and the community learn to take the initiative to help themselves. Special importance has always been given to self-help, and some persons narrowly equate self-help with community development. Self-help is one of those earthly simple practices, age-old like seed propagation, that has recently achieved a hybrid potential. The hybrid potential is derived from a strategy of external assistance. However, even the best seeds will have no value if we merely give them to the earth without controlling the essential environment and without applying exacting measures to assure their regeneration. Self-help assistance is most successful when it gives a man permanent new capacity to act. Premium is put on the efforts of the assisted, not the assistance; upon this point turn the strategy and tactics of giving for self-help.

All self-help projects, if they are to gain and maintain acceptance and confidence and to enlarge the sense of equality and freedom, must be voluntary. Initially, at least, projects must be wanted strongly, close to home, and highly "observable" in effect. The variations of self-help assistance are enormous. In arrangement, they may be provocative ("Here, try this"), mandatory ("We will, when you do"), or permissive ("Now, with this, you can go ahead"). In effectiveness, a project may be a catalyst for a chain of events, may stimulate skills growth, trigger organization, spur ideas, radiate these ideas to others, and even have direct material benefits—though the record has always been humble.

(3) *General and Coordinated Approach.* All efforts for community improvement need to be seen and carried through as a part of a whole. Long preparations may be necessary before projects can be properly or successfully initiated or carried out. Coordination and staging assume the establishment of long-term objectives through planning, but planning with a flexibility.

(4) *Tactical Introductions of New Practices.* All innovations should be organized and presented, first of all, to widen the horizons of the people. Technical training and the making of physical improvements are secondary. Most efforts must be organized to reflect the villagers' felt needs as they are and as they evolve. The complexities of social and technical progress require many carefully planned field pilot projects and evaluations. Very astute criteria of measuring progress in social, institutional, educational, and economic areas must underlie all plans and evaluations.

COMMUNITY AND DEVELOPMENT

(5) *Village-level General-purpose Workers.* Sometimes called community development worker, promoter, animator, or friend of the village, the local worker is the primary agent through whom change is initiated in the community. His responsibility is usually limited to as few villages as possible to emphasize personal relations as a trusted friend—since village people have not yet learned to transfer their trust to outsiders merely on the basis of qualifications or assignment. The workers are supported by specialists in such areas as agriculture, health, and cooperatives.

(6) *Institution Building.* Most efforts seek directly or indirectly to create or strengthen local institutions and build local leadership. The most regularly sought institutions are village councils (political development based as much as possible on traditional leadership, such as the village Panchayats in India); cooperatives; and men's, women's, and youth groups for discussions, training, special projects, and recreation.

(7) *Training.* Varied training plays increasingly important roles in most community development programs. These efforts occasionally take on the character of complete educational systems—dealing with a whole population—sometimes as intermittent classes by a village-level worker or specialist, sometimes as concentrated one- or two-week programs by traveling teams, and sometimes as longer courses at some distant location for local leaders. They are, however, related to what is currently important in the community—such as a major agricultural self-help project, the formation of a cooperative or village council, or a campaign against intestinal parasites.

Community development programs are carefully integrated to achieve both special and general results. For example, a village-level worker in his first year may establish a rapport within a village by giving first aid, loaning various tools, stimulating a clean-up campaign, and organizing a self-help effort to build a much-desired foot bridge over a small river. Meanwhile the worker may convince the people of the benefits of forming a village agricultural marketing cooperative, one of the alternatives of a general community development strategy. During the second year the main effort shifts to this task, assisted by the cooperative department. Membership is recruited, leaders are chosen, and a one-week training program is held on all phases of cooperation. Later a self-help project is undertaken to build a simple cooperative storeroom. Eventually agricultural extension workers give demonstrations on improving rice production. Many specific joint efforts may be initiated to follow up these early projects.

Community development is rarely this effective in practice because the hurdles are many and difficult: lack of qualified and vigorous staff personnel to carry projects through the terribly long process to completion—or to the time when they may become reasonably independent local functions; schisms between competing local leadership, between the conservatives and progressives, or between those who might achieve a disproportionate advantage in a particular project; or the loss of enthusiasm by volunteers because of reneging or slowness of results. But perhaps the most serious hurdle is in the application of specialized governmental services to general-purpose community development, to which we will soon turn.

We have said that the principles underlying community development form a liberal chapter in man's recent inventiveness. But this is not the whole story. For the first time in recent history technological specialists have met significant defeat in their efforts to promote their specializations onto people. Simple villagers in their humble setting of community have made the specialists pull back and seriously reevaluate their position vis-à-vis the individual and the customary social groups. These people have forced the ruling powers in the larger society to develop a concern for people in their ordinary social setting. This is one of the few significant victories over crude technical "progress" since the utilitarians began to grasp the initiative several centuries ago.

But the "liberal" victory may be short-lived. Among the principles espoused in many community development programs and by many authors there is little mention of *community* as a continuing value, little emphasis upon its merits or its integrity as a principle of social organization. "Community" is still a meaningful word, carrying with it a vague acceptance, and, when combined with the word "development," is popular with many governments. Community development is important as a term, but community itself remains as a tool for development, not as an object for development.

Contemporary community development, therefore, frequently seems to be little more than technology and bureaucracy dressed in social armor, seeking to create the harsh accouterments of development at the same cost in personality-sustaining associations that accompanied industrialization in past centuries. And if community development is but a subtle means to break the individual loose from his social moorings for the barren sake of industrialization—to destroy rather than modernize community—then the liberal potential of the tactical victory of the rural villagers is lost for them as surely as it is for their counterparts in the "advanced" countries.

If organized community development disregards the larger implications of the peasants' "silent revolution," its leaders merely serve the crude objectives of economic development and the game of power behind it. The social scientists who contribute to its techniques are but little removed from their brethren who have subverted knowledge of man and the integrity of science to the purposes of advertising or industrial organization theory.

Yet regardless of the philosophy of its leaders, community development at present must face profound political, economic, and organizational hostility to its object of reorienting and modernizing community. This new field of endeavor is being tolerated by the main political and administrative forces of governments only insofar as it continues to open up communities to other programs, other kinds of development. The continually precarious political position of most programs and their regular difficulties within administrative hierarchies offers a constant reminder of this fact.

Many of the administrative and at least some of the political problems of community development have to do with the general purposes and comprehensive approaches inherent in this new field. It requires a *social* integration of methods, and it assumes a subordination of specialized programs, at least at the village level. Thus it poses a direct challenge to the traditions of the various autonomous and specialized branches of contemporary governmental administration.

Agriculturists or health officers (or their departments) hardly relish having their work integrated with that of other agencies in a local development program, even though they may have a voice in its formulation. Their custom is founded upon a closed hierarchy leading directly into the national cabinet. The specialized identity is sanctified by long precedent.

What usually occurs in practice is a *modus vivendi* in which specialized departments continue their traditional programs in the villages. Community development amounts to an added activity, not a restructuring of government operations. Specialists cooperate with community development where expedient, but programs to assure coordination and incorporate principles of community development over the whole range of governmental action affecting local areas remain largely on paper. The conflict stiffens at budget time. Actual coordination often involves a sharing of the budget of community development, leaving unaffected that of the specialized departments.

Some of the implications of this situation are discernible. In some cases the community development programs will be terminated, as was Pakistan's in 1961. Many programs will be robbed of their potential effectiveness by successive budgetary and programmatic restrictions. In the long run they will be narrowed to a small part of their original scope, becoming in effect specialized agencies themselves. Many of their officers will actually welcome this outcome, because it will remove them from much political attack. They will rationalize their motives by declaring that they can do much more effective work in just a few activities. In the end the breaking of the individual from community will proceed apace, aided by the effective use of certain community development principles.

The dominance of specialist interests will assure that the most promising and worthy ends of community development will be defeated. Once again knowledge about man will be used more to control man than to enlarge his personal and social well being.

AMELIORATING DEVELOPMENT

Unlike that of the developing countries today development in the West came about largely as an unconscious drive and inner movement. Governments did not play a central role; hardly even an active one, and were not expected to do so. The West's industrial revolution came about as a mutation of cultural genes, really a series of mutations compounding their effects each generation. Historically the personal manifestations of growth were suddenly there—worldliness, individualism, inventiveness, asceticism, will. But, like many other social phenomena, why they did not appear earlier, later, elsewhere, or differently cannot be fully explained.

There were, of course, various kinds of informal indigenous community development. Craft guilds certainly served this purpose, lasting in modified forms through the eighteenth century. Cooperative barn "raisings" on the American frontier sometimes supplemented individual initiative or resources. In a sense the family enterprise served as a nodule of development. Even the initial joint stock corporation might be included. Only in the backwaters of development in the West would the provocative role and external self-help assistance of community development have been important.

What is today coming to be called community development in the West is really a reaction against the unbecoming results or side effects of development: unemployment, migration and transiency adjustments, slums and bad living conditions, family disturbances and dissolutions, bad sanitation and poor health, dissociated individuals (especially youth), meaningless and rootless patterns of routine, and maldeviant behavior (crime, alcoholism, drug addiction, homosexuality). Even "our 'welfare state' is," according to the philosopher Charles Frankel, "the bandage we wear as the sign of past wounds. . . . [Dressing the wounds] reflect[s] a view of human welfare, and of the conditions of its pursuit, which is as warped as the view of a convalescent about the energies of the human body." [4]

Moreover, the work of many social agencies has merely taken over many of the welfare functions once part of the extended family and community. The social agencies attempt to perform the specific services once arising informally out of the whole social unity of the community, but they lack the personal values that have always been a part of community. That is, the social services are by and large separated and anonymous. Partly this is determined by the present physical, economic, and social pattern; partly it is our characteristic specialized response. It is what might be called ameliorative community development.

Very significantly, the diverse services now called community development in the West seek to smooth over the effects of the tumultuous changes brought upon us. They are a system of social retrieval, symbolically not very different from the gathering of scrap, tailings, and other waste materials for conversion to useful by-products. Note the wording concerning one of the most liberal contemporary endeavors in a Ford Foundation pamphlet entitled *American Community Development:* ". . . the Foundation developed a program of large-scale grants to help selected cities mount a coordinated attack on all aspects of deprivation, including jobs, education, housing, planning, and recreation. The purpose is to help local-government and private organizations confront the human problems of slums and 'gray areas'—changing neighborhoods characterized by family breakdown, low-income residents, and newly arrived groups from rural areas." [5]

If Western community development were not predominantly a simple retrieval of human resources, it would not be so peripheral to the main events of society nor so absent from the central order of social structure and decision-making. The social services otherwise would undoubtedly establish more basic solutions for the individual within the social setting, and not merely give first aid to the social wounds. As Richard Lichtman has pointed out in another connection, "community is not a corrective but a constructive system of human existence." [6] That is hardly the function of today's community development in America.

Let us look at a few of the diverse elements of community development in the industrialized society. Agricultural extension is often included, but it is really a technical service aimed at the industrialization of agriculture; therefore we shall by-pass it.

The cooperatives movement, sometimes now associated with community development, was originally founded in England in the 1820's to form comprehensive communities, not simply economic enterprises. This reflected the strong utopian influence of Robert Owen, who stressed the formation of human character. But the social and communal influence soon waned, although for many decades education continued to play an important role. Cooperatives, in North America at least, grew most vigorously among peoples in the stagnant backwaters of the economy, usually in the rural areas. The most dramatic example was the Antigonish Movement in the Canadian Maritimes, which greatly helped those people out of the fierce straits of the Great Depression.

The cooperative movement, therefore, carries with it a certain sense of social retrieval. Its future appears destined to be ever more economic in the rural areas as food production is further increased in scale and mechanized. The growing preponderance of specialized cooperatives—credit unions, mutual insurance, health plans—suggest the same future for the cooperatives movement in urban areas. Only housing and consumer cooperatives seem to hold a wider potential, and these tendencies are meeting stiff resistance. The trend is clearly utilitarian. Economic competition requires economic terms of performance, and this tends to eliminate any other role for cooperatives.

The American Grange could also be linked with community development. It combines certain aspects of a labor union, a fraternal order, and a community center, and in many localities it has been associated with cooperatives. Its peak of influence was in the 1870's, shortly after its founding, and the technological transformation of farming now foreshadows further decline. Interestingly, however, a 1938 prize-winning definition of the Grange reads like a preamble of community: "The Grange is a great farm fraternity: building character; developing leadership; encouraging education; promoting community betterment; instilling an appreciation of high ideals; teaching through work and play the value of cooperation and service in the attainment of happiness."

Of course many other organizations can be classified within community development—such as the Red Cross, Boy and Girl Scouts, YMCA and YWCA, Boys Clubs, and the Salvation Army, to name a few. In one way or another they contribute to the well-being of almost every family.

Without question, however, the institution that most nearly approaches the character of a community development in America consists of the settlements, neighborhood houses, and community centers. The concern of these centers is a whole neighborhood, although the cluster of services they provide is still considerably less than comprehensive, and though normally they do not serve a neighborhood of any cohesive nature.

The settlements (their original name) were created in the 1880's to deal with what one neighborhood house (as many have come to be known) now calls the "many faces of trouble" of the disadvantaged. Nevertheless, according to Mumford they established in some degree a "social nucleus." In its ideal "the community center was a place for discussion and debate and co-operative action, on all public issues: its purpose was to restore initiative, self-consciousness, and self-direction to the local group: a challenge to partisan loyalties, one-sided decisions and remote control. Once established, the community center might launch out in many directions, as Toynbee Hall [in England] and Hull House had, fostering participation in amateur theatricals, the practice of the arts and crafts, forming a center for the spiritual and cultural life of the neighborhood, as the church had once done." [7]

Yet, for all their promising beginnings in the 1880's, the settlements, neighborhood houses, and community centers never exceeded more than a few hundred reasonably vigorous centers. Always seriously handicapped by a shortage of funds, they seemed to lose some of their promise about the nineteen-twenties.

Perhaps the orientation to the "many faces of trouble" limited the overall effective potential of the movement. Even when all its energies were focused on the problems of the "downrodden," of course, a woeful burden remained unmet. Yet there might have been a better overall service, even to the disadvantaged, if the community center concept had been expanded to the whole of society.

The close identification of the neighborhood houses with delinquents and broken families implies that "healthy" neighborhood areas have no need for them. Probably this image has been damaging to the whole movement. As it is, a neighborhood house or community center implies that the area it ser/es is not healthy, is declining or a downright slum.

And by focusing on the negative side of social life the neighborhood houses have likely foregone much financial support. Today, too many people, money given solely for work in the slums appears to be poured down the drain. Slums seem hopeless and degenerative, unconnected with middle-class motives, morals, and striving. The most effective appeals for popular support can be made when donations will be returned in part to the donor in his own social setting. A movement that is solely identified with slums cannot do this.

Also of major importance here are long-range basic improvements in the physical and institutional environment. Although long-range institution-building by settlement houses has not been missing, emphasis has always been given to resolving the problems of immediate human urgency. Once again this reflects the directness of compassion, and cannot be slighted. But it does not build a social setting that will progressively diminish the source of so many social ills. To use business terms, there must be long-range capital investment as well as current expenditure if there is to be growth and development.

A more comprehensive social development philosophy, then, rather than a philosophy of ameliorative services, might have made the community center movement a greater over-all force in the society. Still, the movement has given us a good tradition, small and dedicated, and worthy to build upon.

It was not accidental that Clarence Perry, who defined the neighborhood unit plan, was also active in the settlement movement. He foresaw a role for the unified community center in his unified neighborhood. But the concept of an integrated physical environment joined with a unified pattern of institutions and services never matured or developed. Community development thus continues to be fragmented at its core.

The course of American community development has taken a self-conscious turn since about 1960. Numerous universities, for example, now have teaching programs under the heading of community development. Some are oriented toward sociology and others toward social welfare, and one at least toward local administrative problems.

Other important examples of the new self-consciousness of community development are the large programs supported by the Ford Foundation in Boston, New Haven, Philadelphia, Oakland, and North Carolina, mostly through private organizations. Although the organizations themselves are supported by large outside grants and by some federal money, most of the organizations are not themselves operational. They usually maintain staff only for planning, research, and coordination. Most of their funds are granted in turn to a variety of other organizations, such as neighborhood houses or school systems, to carry out specific tasks. As noted earlier, the program is described as an "integrated attack on all aspects of deprivation" and seeks "the causes of poverty and human deterioration rather than the symptoms." A heavy emphasis is given to education.

Like community development in the developing countries, the Ford projects approach a comprehensiveness. But the stress is upon education and the aim is pointedly economic. The emphasis on education implies that skills, attitudes, and perhaps initiative of the individual are the critical factors in breaking the vicious cycle of poverty and deprivation.

If one judges the American mind correctly, we may expect the economic motive to prevail as the decisive criterion of success. The programs will be considered successful when the people concerned are on their feet and back in circulation again. The root of the problem as seen in ameliorative community development is to make the individual once again viable in the society. This must show up economically—in a job. Then, according to the prevailing attitude, the social solutions will follow as a matter of course.

This follows from our deeper views of society. We see the negative effects as *social disturbances,* and we see the positive solutions as *economic progress.* The economic goals are clear and the social goals are unclear—and so our solutions must follow from our most positive objectives. This is another way of saying that organization of society *shall* follow from economic determinants, not from social or humanistic ideals.

The corollary is that we see basic economic solutions largely in institutional terms and we see social solutions mostly in individual terms. We are willing to organize or adjust the *structure* of the Big Society to facilitate a vigorous and growing economy. We are not willing to organize the society in anything like comparable terms to create a setting for individual well-being. In this the society is set and largely unchangeable; the full burden of adjustment and conformity falls on the individual. We press upon him to make arbitrary adjustments and conformities in an essentially uncongenial and rigid environment. The stress on education represents this corollary in the Ford program. Education aims the adjustment requirements at the individual. It cannot affect the structure or character of the society that the individual must endure.

American community development, if such a diversity deserves a coherent term, is a special-purpose humanism—to assure economic viability. Its methods and programs are still uncoordinated in their effect upon the individual; therefore, it cannot claim a humanism of method. It still views services primarily as number, kind, and quality to achieve specific results—not pattern, system, or relevance to attain a wholesome and conducive social setting. Its social goals are lost in economic and large organizational prerogatives; so neither can it claim a humanism of relevant social purpose. That is, its goals aim to achieve external adjustment by the individual and ignore internal contentment or satisfaction.

Americans are pragmatic rather than idealistic regarding collective social goals. They hold social ideals as individuals, though they have lost to the larger corporate entities of society the ability to act upon social ideals. This pragmatism leads Americans to react to social *problems,* rather than to seek to seek out social *opportunities.* In contrast to economics, where more collective idealism is practiced, the contemporary processes of community development are essentially negative, whatever the motive spirit. So long as community development remains founded on these pragmatic and negative foundations, its work will be limited to the few, its widest results to nondisintegration, and its broadest goals to the economics of living.

DEVELOPING COMMUNITY

This chapter has discussed the two major branches of community development. First, in the developing countries, the paramount aim either avowedly or implicitly has been the promotion of economic development. Second, at least in North America, the purpose pervading community development efforts has been to ameliorate the adverse effects of economic development and to make the individual viable in the economy.

It would seem, however, that the vital center of community development in either the advanced or newly developing countries is absent when it fails to seek a social setting more basically congenial to the individual. Economic advancement and the amelioration of the human blight arising from industrial development are both ultimately empty of value as central goals for community development, for they are not associated with intimate human purpose. Indeed, an intimate social context is necessary for human values to arise, expand, and evolve to a constantly fresh maturity. A rich and diverse spirit within the individual will most probably arise only with profound personal meaning in group life.

The bewildering diversity and scale of contemporary life now demands that the social foundations for individual values be structured, stabilized, and protected at the human scale. When the prevailing results of development are becoming more atomistic and personally disenchanting, the development of value-giving personally coherent institutions must take precedence to give the economic and technical forces of development the meaning they are assumed to have. Community, as a structure nurturing human value—especially in a program conceived as *community* development—must be ultimately superior to economic objectives, as many leading economists admit. Community is closer to the ends of life, and can give emotional shape and character to the means of life.

If the re-creation of community is accepted as the central organizing objective of community development, each activity and project will be measured for the long-term development of community, as well as for its economic development or its ameliorative benefits. In this same way a corporation judges each decision in relation to long-range institutional development objectives as well as short-term profits. Some circumstances may require temporary diversions; perhaps some specific long-range goals will change. But the efforts of community development, like those of a corporation, must nevertheless be continuously focused upon central objectives.

If community development is to seek a modern form of community capable of creating a congenial social setting for the individual, it might include three major components, either in the newly developing or the industrialized countries. The first is environmental design. To assure physical coherence in the face of the city's infinite atomism, we need a clear definition of where the community begins and where it ends. This will be the first step toward the distinctiveness described by Robert Redfield. The boundary will guard against the intrusion of activities disruptive to the purposes of community. (Didn't Max Weber suggest that when the citizens fail to "man the walls," the city ceases to exist?)

The finite area of community and its integrity are relatively simple to achieve. A greater challenge lies in physical design, to create an overall internal unity and social coherence. The sense of social unity will be derived, as previously suggested, mostly in the center of community, and it will greatly depend on the humanism that can be infused into the whole layout of the center and the architecture of each part. The center needs many attractive and varied activities, spaces, and objects, a free-flowing movement, and a commonality to draw people not only for their daily functions but for their intense interest in associating with the central life of the community. Finally, each community requires its own small Forum or Acropolis.

Of course, there are special planning and architectural challenges in schools, parks, housing, and other elements. What is crucial is the preservation or creation of a diverse, unique, and revered beauty in every part of the community. Whether landscape, sculpture, or structure, the portent of beauty is that it engenders varieties of love and honor. For this reason the most endearing forms of beauty should also be associated with the community's most honored traditions and memories.

The second major component, after physical design, involves the many external institutions that bear upon the community and help shape it. A government's community development program itself is one example; so are all other governmental and institutional services having a local importance; so are commerical and professional services. It is important that their structure, character, and performance fit within and strengthen the community with the same coherence that should exist in the physical layout.

Externally provided services enhancing the integrity of a community can be described in terms of certain characteristics: (1) the degree to which the community is the unit for the organization of each service, (2) the relative stability of personnel assignments in a given community, (3) residence in the community where feasible for those employed there, and (4) the degree to which local interests and conditions influence the character of management of each service. In effect, each level of metropolitan government and each corporation or professional service represented will contribute to a unity to the extent each adjusts its policies to the community's ideal pattern. Metropolitan administration might be organized at that level and a policeman, fireman, or librarian assigned on a permanent basis within one community; they should not be randomly rotated among a number of communities. Similarly, commercial retail outlets might be organized to serve one community; they should not be designed with the hope of attracting substantial business from neighboring communities. And considering even single professionals, a medical doctor with a general practice in one community contributes to community while a specialist serving several does not.

On the other hand, the community system in most cases will establish an efficient framework for administrative and distributive services, probably more than the present mixed pattern of locations and boundaries.

The third major component of community development consists of the organizations and activities arising and serving entirely within the community. Here the very existence of varied internal institutions and traditional activities organized on a common basis is an indication of virility in community. Whereas physical design is largely preparatory for community development and certain external organizations are necessary to help initiate and serve community, the existence of many internal participative organizations may be considered as a fruition of community development. This, of course, is especially true for new communities.

A certain commonality of outlook and activity probably cannot evolve without some structure of federation among both internally and externally based organizations, including official and nonofficial, commercial and noncommercial. A coalescing of interest and a joining of all organizations in community activities is necessary to give the individual a sense of social wholeness with which he can identify himself.

Local government is unquestionably the most important internal institution. And this, too, requires municipal federation in metropolitan areas or regions to avoid chaos. The community needs a local authority that can respond flexibly to unique local interests.

One of the most valuable responses of local government in the community may well be the provision of public support for many creative activities organized under various auspices. For example, grass-roots drama/music/arts programs could expect to prosper only if the facilities and part of the operating expenses were independent of the proceeds. Most localities could not obtain such resources except from government. Responsible *local* government could best justify, manage, and account for such support.

Now, how will community of this character contribute to economic growth in the newly developing countries? Community is, first of all, a rational recognition of the reality of being a person in human society. To the extent society can respond to this reality in life it may expect the individual to respond more rationally to the needs and opportunities for economic growth. Community offers an intimate foundation for the individual to understand the society's struggles and aspirations—and to identify himself with them. So far in the first decades of development much attention has been given to motivating people for specific development purposes, but precious little to evoking in them a wider and deeper development *esprit*. Community should establish a basis for a development *esprit* to arise.

On a more practical level, community establishes a rational basis for planning the physical form of the city, creating not only a social setting but a clear and common framework for organizing and relating all forms of municipal, commercial, and professional services, simplifying even the collection of census data and relating it accurately to recurring public and commercial information. Especially in lands undergoing rapid urbanization, urban community can fulfill a valuable role in receiving and orienting rural migrants to urban living and in giving them a framework of interpersonal response akin to that which they left in the village. Community should be, therefore, an effective fulcrum for all urban community development activities.

And how will community help ameliorate the adverse effects of development? If community is a vital force in development—in peoples' lives—it will probably have eliminated many of the sources of adversity. Its significant service, therefore, should be constructive and preventive. But community also presents a social basis for taking early note of the remaining "faces of trouble" and ameliorating them in the most complete and humane way.

Such an expanded concept of community development must also be appreciated at the national level. As presently constituted, national development planning is focused almost entirely on the technical and economic objectives of change. Vigorous community is not likely to arise under the domination of this objective. At present, education, health, and community development receive allocations in the five-year plans only insofar as they demonstrate a vital connection to the goals of economic growth—in this case as manpower development or human-resource development. They are merely supporting elements of the economic infrastructure. They are clearly subordinate, having no independent claim of their own.

To bring the broad development objectives into better balance, national development planning might consider incorporating a dual theme into development. One theme, of course, would focus on economic development, as at present. The primary vehicle for advancement here would be industrial technology and corporate bureaucracy, and the gauge of progress would be the standard of living.

The other theme would focus upon the well-being of the individual—that is, upon qualitative changes in life. The primary frame of reference for affecting these changes would be community development. Although the two themes could not be separated precisely within many specific programs and projects, their appearance together as twin objectives and counterpoints in plans, formulas, conferences, and negotiations would tend to create a closer scrutiny of ends and provoke a constant referral to the deeper human motives of all development efforts.

Each theme also requires a quite different theoretical approach, or series of approaches. While economic planning offers a broad mode of integrating the processes of agricultural development and industrialization, community development offers a means to integrate social development—and to give it a purpose independent of and ultimately superior to naked economic growth.

If man is to find his fullest potential *as man,* that potential will likely be found in the institutions giving most complete attention to man's own worth, wholeness, and growth. In so doing, these institutions probably will also contribute most to man's external capacities—promoting development in its gross economic dimensions. They will ameliorate the negative results of economic development almost as a matter of course. Certainly this approach offers greater hope, not only for special-purpose humanism or a humanism of method, but for the broader humanism of the ends of life as well. Thus the development of community may give a broader and deeper philosophic value to the larger struggle for development by all peoples on all parts of the earth.

8

Magnificent Decline
of Industry

In 1955 *Fortune* magazine published a buoyant article entitled "The Magnificent Decline of U.S. Farming." [1] The author proudly reflected upon massive advances in productivity per capita and yields per acre. He duly noted accompanying declines in acres, farms, and farmers. This was, of course, a triumph of the American economic system—whatever it might be for the American rural way of life. And the profound changes continue. In the ten years after 1955 production per man almost doubled again, and the decline in farming followed apace.

The decline in agriculture foretells a similar decline in all fields of production. Indeed the decline is already underway in industrial production and is in prospect for office employment. In 1959 for the first time in history the number of people employed in the United States in producing goods (including food) dropped below those employed in services.

This decline offers a magnificent potential for society—freeing man not so much from arduous labor or general tedium as from the pervasive invasions of all behavior and understanding of life by economic and institutional purposes.

Perhaps we may begin to judge our economy as we now judge individual machines—the less attention they require the better. The less the economic burden interferes with our lives, the greater is our individual freedom and inner potential. But, considering the present grasp of economics on our lives, new modes of production will not necessarily yield this new freedom.

Of course, the world's poor are still a generation or more removed from problems of abundance. But the problems of scarcity have been the subject of literally thousands of books, while few have broached the frontier questions of the abundance already facing hundreds of millions of people in Europe and America. Moreover, the struggle to overcome scarcity in the developing countries should be enlightened by a knowledge of the emerging possibilities of abundance, as well as some of the peculiar inversions of human intent and awkward traps carried with it.

Somehow, the speed with which modern society comes to its most important achievements seems to assure that those achievements will be grasped with zestful ignorance. That at least seems to be the case with the emergence of general affluence in the United States. A. N. Whitehead, one of the most farsighted men of this century, as late as the 1930s could not even envisage such a possibility as general wealth: "You may, perhaps, by some great reforms," he said, "obviate the worst kind of sweated labor and the insecurity of unemployment. But you can never greatly increase average incomes. On that side all hope of Utopia is closed to you." [2] History's quick proof of Whitehead's monumental error has not prompted society to question deeply its ignorance of the implications of affluence. And so now we stand with these triumphant human capacities, but do not know how to direct them to effectively serve human aspirations—or, more importantly, to broaden human aspirations.

The long historic struggle for individual worth has had to cope, first, with man's limited capacity to act and, second, with his inability to grasp and govern the capacities he has achieved. The latter is the major problem in the advanced economies today. In but a few generations man's capacities to act have multiplied, creating in society an awesome complexity once attributable only to nature. The new, more complex and powerful capacities seem to be creating new human possibilities while simultaneously preventing their realization—an ironic impasse of history.

Arthur Clarke, who often allows his mind to leap "lightly across some centuries of intensive development and discovery," figures that the problems of production and distribution will one day be completely solved by what he calls a "replicator." And, with the coming of the replicator, Mr. Clarke wistfully hopes that "our age of roaring factories and bulging warehouses will pass away, as the spinning wheel and the home loom and the butter churn passed before them. And then our descendants

. . . will remember what many of us have forgotten—that the only things in the world that really matter are such imponderables as beauty and wisdom, laughter and love." [3]

But should society defer its hopes to such a millennium? Though our immediate possibilities are incomplete and imperfect, does not automated production, operating with fewer and fewer people, announce that we can now put our factories and counting houses farther and farther into the social background? Even now we may turn some of our attention to the broader human aspirations that strive for "beauty and wisdom, laughter and love."

RAMPANT PRODUCTIVITY

The vast current impact of industrial change does not necessarily excite mankind. Indeed, amid so much change a boredom about change has set in, together with an unconcern about the deeper meanings of the change. As with the decline of agriculture, we accept technical virtuosity and economic power while largely ignoring their human repercussions.

Yet, one can hardly conceive a transition with greater implication for altering man's conduct of life. And changes in the future may be expected to come faster, hit harder, and ramify further. The momentum of scientific discovery assures a long continuum of shocks in the industrial countries, creating ever larger pushes toward social instability.

Automation is, of course, the contemporary frontier symbol for the revolution in science and industry. The computer is its primary instrument. Astonishingly, it is both relieving man of his most stupefying factory and office tedium and assisting the probing of his most perplexing theoretical problems in science.

Among the professions, medicine is using the computer to monitor patients in surgery. Sweden has begun to develop techniques for comprehensive and detailed health examinations for whole populations. In law, computers are being applied to criminal records, statistics, and analyses. Computerized instruction, with audio-visual devices and team teaching, will have profound results in education.

With trepidation we may see mechanization in retailing, restaurant and hotel services, resort and amusement activities. And in the home, thermostats and automatic washers are unquestionably a prelude to automatic cooking and cleaning. Hopefully, mechanization will not penetrate the symbolic and cultural heart of society, as it did a bit when Barry Goldwater automated his flagpole.

Not too far in the future the advanced techniques of chemical analysis, power application, and computer control may comprehensively process sea water for its varied store of minerals, its fresh water, and perhaps its algae production. Similarly, comprehensive mining may extract all useful minerals from the ground, not just a few high-grade ores. In some cases this may be combined with the upgrading of soils for increased agricultural productivity.

About a more diversified use of automation we may make four general observations that are relevant here:

(1) Inescapably there will be a trend to larger organizations. Small organizations will increasingly become irrelevant to the centralized, high-volume, international production that is now emerging and inevitable. In some cases single industrial plants or complexes will be able to produce all of a given product for all the world's population. This is already feasible for many products, such as jet transports. Already the onset of supersonic transports will apparently reduce the aircraft producers to three —one each in the United States, U.S.S.R., and Western Europe. This is another way in which man's wealth is steadily becoming more collective: in resources, production, corporate control, and in the imperatives of distributing the manufactured abundance.

(2) Flexibility in industrial organization and plant location will continue to increase. Old locational requirements of materials, markets, and labor will be weakened, particularly as labor requirements are reduced. Even the need to be near management activities will be reduced as the computer and remote controls become more effective. The obvious potential emerging from these new conditions is that factors other than calculated economics *can* play a larger role in the organization and location of industrial enterprises—most notably in the formation of cities.

(3) Where once only the ruling elites could refrain from production, we are now approaching a time when at least the necessities and many of the amenities of living will be produced by an extremely small fraction of the "labor force." Possibly only the "elites" will then inherit the role of production.

(4) The prospect of virtually unlimited abundance makes paramount the reexamination of not only our economy but our assumptions of man's economic and social existence. This revolutionary change will require a new value structure in society and poses numerous questions for *all* social traditions.

This review is not intended to present a rosy picture of a scientifically based "wonderful world of tomorrow," a view all too prevalent, and prompted by the promotional system of enterprise and a faith in uncharted innovation. Considering our present awesome technological momentum, there are unusual dangers in uncritical views, and these extend to the highest levels of social analysis.

For example, in 1963 a study entitled *Resources in America's Future* projected population, production, and resources needed to the year 2000. In estimating automobile ownership the study noted that "the most likely rate of growth is . . . 300 percent." The study predicted annual purchases of 28.8 million cars that year (the "high" projection was 73.7 million!) and a total ownership of 243 million cars—compared with production of 7 million and an ownership of 59 million in 1960. "As a minimum," the report states, there will be "a car for every .94 adults," compared with one for every 1.9 adults in 1960.[4]

These predictions—which were made without qualification or critical comment—illustrate one pitfall of specialized interest. What is involved are mathematically produced estimates based on trends that do not take estimable consequences into account, let alone social purposes or needs. They do not consider the possibility that even our present transportation system may be badly unbalanced and misconceived, requiring complete redress long before 2000. When such specialized studies do not account for the implications of their assumptions, their extrapolations too often become nonsense. Are projections of future output based on the assumption that the country will produce what is best for it? Then the estimate implies that 243 million automobiles will make a better America than 59 million.

This is intellectually mischievous. Do we also build four additional interstate highway systems, and multiply the congestion and dispersion of our cities? Is more than one car per adult reasonable as a personal, social, or cultural ideal? Can this much automobility be defended as transportation, or even as an outlet for vanity? What happens to those who can't (or don't want to) drive in such a mobile world? Will individuals have a choice of movement in a society built to the specifications of three hundred horsepower? What are the resulting imperatives governing the form and simple livability of our cities? What is the effect upon health of physical immobility imposed by the driver's seat?

A society that develops the capacity to manage 243 million automobiles can hardly be expected to retain a concern for much else. Yet if the pervasive power and monolithic interest of the industrialist is effective, with an intellectual assist from "objective" scientific analyses, that will be our destiny. Shouldn't such a quadrupling of our automobile population be avoided for the same human reason that India should avoid a population of a billion human beings? Clearly, if endless gluttonous production is to be the result of the revolution of science and industry, a truly agonizing reappraisal of industrial society and science is in order.

REDUNDANT ECONOMY

Man has always striven for abundance. But abundance has usually carried with it problems that man has not always cared to admit or face. The development of the earliest cities required a rural food surplus. Commanding this surplus, the cities then created the special forms of abundance that were the ancient civilizations. But the rise of abundance was at the same time associated with man's first general and systematic means for one man to subvert and use another. Only by a despotic centralization of wealth could the ancient civilizations have arisen. The urban division of labor created not only wealth but also the diverse cultural amenities that made wealth supremely attractive—and attainable for the few. The division of labor made wealth more collective in society by requiring commercial exchanges, and the accumulation of money and property favored private hoarding.

But the wealth of the past was relative and only highlighted the more general scarcity. Only since World War II (the same period in which development has been initiated everywhere) has productivity in some countries risen to a point where scarcity is not the pervasive driving force for the majority of the people. With the coming of automation the problem today very nearly reverses that of the earliest emergence of abundance in society. Then the ruling elites sought to bring ever larger numbers of people together to render to themselves all "surplus" energies, skills, and materials. But today we must find means to more effectively disperse the increasing abundance created by ever fewer workers. The distribution of abundance is important merely to keep the economy in proper working order. Yet the deep rut of our thinking still argues that all men must produce during their full mature lives if they are to consume at a reasonable level of life.

A growing abundance and the volatile nature of a more monetized economy open the door to rapid vacillation in consumption levels and the plague of depressions. Although there is a growing consensus that society is learning to avoid the severe forms of depression, numerous observers have lately been seriously concerned about the high level of unemployment persisting despite steady increases in national income. Productivity per capita increases more easily than does individual consumption, and so increased productivity disemploys people, casting aside many who cannot share the abundance and leaving the productive capacity underemployed.

In a special way the economy partly overcomes both the overproduction and unemployment. A combination of enterprise incentive and great wealth has produced an essentially nonfunctional redundant economy, a parasitic growth on the central economy, unrelated to the necessities and amenities of the "good life."

The redundant economy, which is extremely varied, tends to arise (1) when one product prompts the need for more of the same or for other products; (2) when general wealth and gross profit margins permit use of a variety of measures to synthetically expand the market of a product or make it more costly; (3) when products or services arise from special manipulation of the economy or from special appeals to personal security or vanity; and (4) when international conditions create various forms of national competitiveness.

Any specific economic redundancy may involve more than one of these factors. Most redundancies have at least some footing in a necessity or a genuinely sought product or service, and, conversely, most industries today carry with them at least a small degree of redundancy.

Unquestionably the automobile is the most penetrating and illuminating example of redundancy, which it reveals in three separate ways. First, by excess power and unusable bulk, by impractical gadgeteering, by style flourishes that each fall rival those of Paris, and by controlled obsolescence, Detroit has shifted interest from transportation to profitable crude consumption. Second, the industry is one of the largest users of another, far more obviously redundant industry: advertising. Third, by a variety of stratagems and circumstances the auto industry has largely defeated other modes of passenger transportation except air; the automobile has at the same time remade the city upon its own scale and made itself indispensable and in effect self-multiplying. Secondary but important redundant industries have then arisen to build Chinese walls in the form of freeways in town and country and massive parking structures in downtown areas, not to speak of bureaucracies that manage them. The result is an industry of outwardly incontestable necessity, but with an inner social destructiveness. It epitomizes one major strategy Big Citizens use to enhance their sovereignty.

Redundancy also occurs in the way certain activities are carried out. If the purpose of insurance, for example, is to "spread the risk," then many of the 1,200,000-odd American insurance employees are redundant to the basic service. That is, much of the cost of service, sometimes a major part, is applied to selling and advertising, premium collection and processing, claim investigation and litigation, and high profits of the insurance companies. Some 4800 companies are sustained merely by the "paper passing" that spreads the risk in this profitable enterprise.

Similarly, there is much redundancy in the shadows of the central economy, featuring meaningless product differentiation, costly styling, and gaudy packaging as well as much of what is performed by personnel and public relations offices. Even decision-making and R & D have developed toward ritual and job-security evasiveness—assisted by committees, conferences, scholarly papers, training, consultants, and subcontracting.

The most powerful force underlying economic redundancy is the fifteen-billion-dollar advertising industry, discussed in Chapter 3. Its very theme calls for redundancy: to promote higher levels of consumption regardless of the need or the merits of the end use.

But probably the most perfect example of parasitic economics is that of trading stamps. Not only do they add a higher overhead to merchandising while adding no intrinsic value to the goods whatsoever; they also compel the consumer to conform to a special behavior to attain a value less than he should have received for his expenditure in the first place. The stamps create an illusion of higher value while actually creating a superfluous secondary marketing system with an extraordinarily high overhead.

Space exploration, supersonic transports, and like programs, when motivated by world competition and carried out in crash programs, also produce a species of redundancy. They make little economic sense, no social sense. Yet they deprive more economic programs (such as public urban transportation) and worthy social programs (urban renewal, poverty) of vital funding. This is the tragic pity of the redundant economy as a whole, for economic redundancy distorts public and institutional purpose. It is simply that mechanism in society which increases measurable output more in response to the power and benefit of institutions than to the needs and desires of people.

The redundant economy reveals a fundamental paradox. On the one side the economy seeks to maximize production and improve efficiency by raising output while reducing input, especially labor. On the other side, the economy has created a new make-work economy epitomizing the unimaginative uses of wealth. The economy, by creating a wide variety of redundancies, turns out to be its own consumer for an increasing part of its output. It has created an elaborate system closely approximating the squirrel wheel described by Galbraith.

If depressions plagued the early stages of productive abundance, the rise of redundancy may equally well inhibit progress at the later stages of productive abundance. But this is a question still awaiting a proper formulation.

REVOLUTION OF ABUNDANCE

Withal the excesses of the redundant economy, the additions it makes to employment do not fully compensate for the reduction in manpower attributable to advancing automation. Means to save labor have recently become so spectacularly successful that they seem to fore-close the traditionally conceived balances of supply and demand for labor. Production historically limited human consumption; now the effort to raise consumption to meet productive capacity through the redundant economy is becoming incestuous and simply wrong.

Traditionally conceived, full employment therefore is no longer tenable as a legitimate social goal. The dilemma facing us in employment is perhaps best stated by Gerard Piel: "No reasonably predictable rate of growth in the productive sectors of the economy seems equal to overtaking the current rate of technological disemployment. . . . Even an expanding economy must employ progressively fewer workers in its productive sectors. . . . Even at the present level of opulence, the consumer economy shows signs of surfeit. . . ." [5]

Yet the dilemma facing us is more profound than resolving unemployment. The imperatives of emerging levels of productivity are more deeply revolutionary. Fortunately the challenge is a promising one for man—if it can be seen in its positive humane terms. As of now, we are woefully unprepared to meet the revolution we are creating.

I have suggested how we perceive our common goals predominantly in economic terms. These economic goals are positive and precise, though limited in scope. By well-developed methods they are translated into highly organized and sophisticated means of action. Conversely, I have suggested that the broader social goals are secondary, less well defined, and frequently negative in character. Predominantly they bind up the social wounds. Their methods are less comprehensive and less penetrating.

As our economic goals rapidly tend toward fulfillment, they already show signs of losing their challenge for men. "We have sensed," says Galbraith, "though we have not recognized the declining importance of goods." [6] But the economic establishment now pressures people to expand their consumption of an ever widening range of goods for a narrowing of life interests. Society is prodded into running faster after the old goals precisely when those goals have dwindled in value. This merely mechanizes Galbraith's squirrel wheel. Thus Galbraith notes that much of the economy is "geared to the least urgent set of human wants. It would be far more secure if it were based on the whole range of need." [7]

The general absence of broader goals for the economy has been observed by many social critics. Philosopher Charles Frankel suggests that "our very success over the past generation may itself be one of the present obstacles in the way of doing the jobs that now need to be done. The pace of events has left us a little breathless and our progress a little tired. Our affluence seems to have stunned rather than stimulated us." [8] Gerard Piel, publisher of Scientific American, believes that "in the long run, larger questions must be asked and answered" in connection with abundance.[9] David Bazelon says that "there is probably no more profound personal issue that any of us will have to face than this one." He asks, "Can we stand prosperity? Can we give up the Scarcity idea?" [10]

W. H. Ferry, Vice Presient of the Center for the Study of Democratic Institutions, states the problem more succinctly within the framework in which solutions must be derived: "New theories and new institutions are called for, not more modifications or touch-ups of the old. . . . Socialist incantations, like capitalist incantations, are largely directed to vanished circumstances." [11] In the view of Herbert Gans, "Social planning and social research must begin to find ways of revising the institutional arrangements and beliefs that provide social and personal worth." [12]

Yet the current flow of concern is not matched by theories and proposed solutions that might grasp the full human promise. A "Marxian pall" seems to have been cast over social inventiveness, and a millstone of "scientific objectivity" appears to weight against any social proposition that is not a simple projection of historic facts. Unfortunately, we are left with an empty granary of socially debated propositions and a starved idealism just at the juncture of history when a humanely directed revolution is most nearly possible.

Moreover, contemporary concern still predominantly revolves about economic potential or economic problems, whereas the theories that are direly needed are social. Such theories must incorporate and assume the production of wealth. Most of all, the missing social goals must be formulated to replace today's vague and negative goals. Diverse, open, and challenging rather than rigid and restrictive, the theories must create avenues of meaningful choice for the person to establish his own integrity and worth. A highly productive economy must underlie the new goals but not dominate them. That is the logical result of the shift from an economy of scarcity to an economy of abundance.

Another problem is posed by larger physical capacities. Magnified just as much as the positive human possibilities are man's individual and collective capacity to disrupt, to exploit, and to destroy. Less and less order is imposed by nature. Social order now must be imposed from within, where the new power resides. Society's achievement of a new self-discipline to maintain social order may very well become a central issue arising from our new powers and opulence.

CONSTRUCTIVE ABUNDANCE

The negative and inept way in which man has approached abundance in recent history—the nineteenth-century failure to recognize the productive implications of widespread increases in purchasing power, the doctrinaire refusal of governments to take countermeasures against depressions until the nineteen-thirties, and our current acquiescence to the destructive forces of the redundant economy—are suggestive of man's failure to understand the larger social potential of wealth. This is an astounding shortcoming, like that of a rich miser. We have only faintly realized that contemporary national abundance is enlarged by its use, founded on the *momentum of productivity*, in contrast to the static traditional wealth that lay largely in nonproductive or marginally productive *property*.

Only slowly did the American industrial elite learn that increasing the purchasing power of workers was the most powerful way to create wealth for themselves. In no other way could the fortunes of the Carnegies, Rockefellers, and Fords have arisen—though the understanding came after it was largely demonstrated in fact. And today we are learning to understand the potential of our farm surplus. Surpluses once undoubtedly contributed to the depressions we have suffered. But in the 1950s this abundance was put to work as a vehicle for development abroad. The results are now becoming increasingly beneficial to all concerned.

We are gradually realizing that similar benefits may arise from imaginative use of other forms of abundance. There is no greater form of abundance, no greater human potential, than well-trained people. And this abundance, too, is enlarged by the services it provides to others—individually, nationally, and internationally, through such programs as the Peace Corps. Indeed the unfolding lessons from inspired uses of abundance reveal that new and more varied abundance is usually generated.

There is something of a paradox about wealth, especially the wealth of a whole society: it seems to be created by its use. Perhaps that paradox is implicit in the goal Herbert Gans has suggested for the society: "The ideal target is a society in which non-work institutions are more important than work, and in which the departure from the labor market is anticipated rather than feared." [13] In the past this has been achieved only by the idle rich at the expense of the remainder of the population. But the paradox is this: it was such "idleness" that led to mathematics, science, fine arts, and speculative thought. And it was this diversion from work that ultimately led to the productive system whose benefits we must now learn to reap.

Neolithic man began formulating our contemporary definition of work when he first began to tame animals and till fields. That is, every man must produce his own because in conditions of basic scarcity no man can supply the needs for others. Only later did the elites slightly modify this definition for their own benefit. The notion has thus come down to us that a man without productive work is unworthy or unfit. This attitude weathered even the Great Depression, though the problem of the depression had very little to do with the willingness of man to work and very much to do with the uses of productive wealth. Simply put, the problem was this: wealth was lost because wealth could not be used, not because it was not there. Productive wealth was idle and many suffered because of it.

Still we have inherited an overpowering edict to make work, to organize society about a goal of full employment. With the new devices of production coming into use within vast organizations, full employment is capable of producing fantastic surpluses of our traditional material needs, and a lot of foolish side production as well. Yet individuals remain rigidly bound to a miserly ideology of work, and an immense amount of energy still centers on the problems that surpluses create. This approach keeps us from achieving other, enormously more worthy objects of civilization.

The positive abundance we have created is not material, ultimately, for men have astonishingly little use for material surpluses. The real potential arising from high productivity is a new worthiness in man. The only ultimate value of abundance is the abundance of life, not of goods.

Our concept of work and its social equivalent in full employment becomes less useful each year in achieving any sound social purpose. Indeed, past conceptions of work are steadily becoming a negative, even deadly, impediment to whatever social or individual ends we might strive to secure. Of all the specific impediments to opening new human possibilities in society, none appears to hold the logjam in place more firmly than full employment.

In recognition of this contradictory behavior, a number of recent economic proposals anticipate the time when income will not necessarily be related to work. Galbraith has suggested that unemployment compensation should be raised to a level approaching an employed wage and be available on a long-term basis. In times of high unemployment the level of unemployment compensation would rise; at times of low unemployment the compensation would be lowered. Control of the level of compensation, according to Galbraith, could yield a balance of incentives based on the need for labor, an increasing support for consumption in times of decreasing demand, and a counter to inflation in times of expansion.

Other persons have made proposals with longer-range implications. These, often called "income grants," assume that jobs will continue to decline and that the grants would one day become general. Herbert Gans visualizes "a future era in which all members of society will be eligible for such a grant." [14] Everyone, regardless of his financial condition, would receive it as an irrevocable right. A committee of economists and writers regard the right to an income "as the only policy by which the quarter of the nation now dispossessed and soon-to-be dispossessed by the lack of employment can be brought within the abundant society." [15]

A fair judgment of the potential for income grants is not possible if they are considered under our traditional bearish attitudes of welfare. If the grants are not at least conceived in positive terms, if they are merely considered as a laggard's byway, then their possibilities cannot be fairly evaluated. The onset of abundance is revolutionary in the most radical way, and the revolution is already becoming a primary fact of the advanced industrial society. Whatever actions are proposed, especially those capable of a central creative solution, must be judged with a wide new vision of possibilities—and necessities.

In patchwork fashion we have been slowly evolving toward income grants. Present unemployment compensation is a limited element, as are retirement programs and old-age assistance. One might include scholarships and all forms of educational subsidies to students old enough for employment. Even vacation and sick-leave pay are of this nature, if we include all income received for time not spent at income-producing work.

A superficial alternative to income grants exists in a shorter work week, work month, and work year, early retirement, and work sabatticals. Undoubtedly a continued shortening of the work life will take place in some fashion, but this will not in itself open the new possibilities raised by abundance. It will not resolve residual unemployment or even technological unemployment over the short span, only help keep it within the bounds we are accustomed to tolerating. More significantly the simple reduction of one's work life does not in itself help redefine work toward the attainment of richer and more worthy individual careers. Life remains divided into rigorous educational preparation, then frenzied productive work, and then idle retirement. We still lack a reasonable social unity for the individual—work continues to be separated from family, social participation, and, consequently, from an atmosphere in which personal ideals are generated and become real.

Most significantly, a mere shortening of work life leaves the emotional and social make-up of the individual in the hands of economic organization, whether in private or public employment. The institutional power remains to coercively manipulate personality with the threat of denying him career, income, social status, personal challenge, and retirement. This is a potential tyranny of the most exploitive nature, an unanswered question of industrial democracy. Whatever alternatives relating to abundance are considered, a prime question concerns the means to increase the significant choices for the individual.

Income grants, although they can be extremely varied in the way they are made, might eventually be adjusted to provide what is considered in each period a minimum adequate standard of living. This leaves a man free to follow other pursuits, with or without additional income. It allows him freedom to follow a career of his own will and his own making. The exact definition of "minimum" might shift according to the variables noted by Galbraith, but presumably they would never need to drop to hardship levels.

Incentives to provide public services and attend to the automated production processes might be based first on the general desire to have more income than provided by a living grant. As I shall soon suggest, the diversity of response by the individual and the cultural advantages that may accrue to society as a result are immense. Second, observation of motivation patterns in different societies shows that our system of social motivations can itself be widened, deepened, and presumably oriented by ethical affirmations. Career motivations might then be oriented to the more intrinsic values of society—beauty, knowledge, good works—especially to unique forms of contribution.

But what will motivate persons to undertake many years of training to manage and advance our productive system? Two things: first, adjustment of the level of wages for work, as at present; second, the challenges inherently taken up by man. The most dedicated persons in history rarely had a pecuniary motivation. What will be of greater social consequence is an *esprit*—call it a social myth—a system of values and rewards *meaningful in their time* for a man to serve his society. It is noteworthy that in Turkey, where women carried the brunt of working the fields, men took over when the prestigeful and fascinating tractors made their entry. Then farming became *man's* work.

As the head of a slave-labor camp might be dubious about free labor, so others are dubious about free labor unmotivated by a subsistence wage. Enslavement and subsistence wages are but two of many possible ways to motivate people. Both are negative and coercive, and both deny the growth of person, of integrity, of individual worth. Our thought has been steadily reduced to the judgment that dollars equal motivation. This is dismal and demoralizing. For this reason we have lost sight of other motivations, other forms of *esprit*.

The meaning of income grants is difficult to understand because it involves a new kind of social purpose. Heretofore most benefits of increased productivity have been applied to increasing material abundance, some to reducing working hours and providing fringe benefits, some to allowing early retirement by the well-to-do (though surprisingly few have done so). The powerful new purpose promised through income grants is the freeing of man as much as possible from the productive system itself, from external discipline over the whole human career. The meaning of income grants is therefore a new horizon for human freedom.

RECONSTRUCTING CAREERS

Yet income grants are strictly an economic solution. As long as the questions and their solutions remain largely economic, the higher positive values of abundance cannot be attained. If abundance only makes a man idle, the individual will certainly develop the same sense of personal inadequacy and social uselessness that dominated him throughout the Great Depression. If traditional attitudes toward work are maintained, and assuredly they would be without new kinds of challenges, the man without a traditional *job* would experience social rejection, individual disenchantment, and a cultural purposelessness. Thus, income grants might well leave a personal, social, and cultural vacuum.

What is concurrently required is a new conception of the purpose, role, and orientation of work and of the whole human career, a redefinition that will conceive a greater fulfillment for the person and more diversified contributions by individuals to society.

Adding this dimension to income grants brings us to the heart of the issue of abundance. No question of human good takes precedence over how man conceives and organizes the basic course of his behavior throughout his life. Again we must acknowledge that the important problem is one of conception, not of capacities or human abilities.

Let us now consider some fairly specific possibilities in connection with two aspects of community: creative industry and public service.

In the general composition of community the proposal for creative industry is based on a person's desire to be creative and productive and on the joy a person receives from working with his hands—that is, from articulating his mind and body. It is also based on the value of beholding in one's home familiar objects made by known persons, the value of the simple connection between a possession and an association. It derives from the meaning to a craftsman who follows a whole process through from raw material and conception through creation, exchange, and use. It also derives from the personal sense of being a unique part of an indigenous creative tradition within a vigorous social tradition. The proposal assumes that the desires for craftmanship and its products will persist, whatever the abundance we have through automated production.

Creative industry based on personal craftsmanship becomes fully viable (1) within the context of community and (2) with the support of income grants. Of course, few men today can be self-sustaining solely by making ceramic ware, furniture, or metal art objects by hand, especially if each item is created with a pride of craftsmanship. But given an income grant that sustains a basic living level, and given a desire to seek creative uniqueness within a familiar setting, a great variety of small independent craftsmen could establish markets for their wares and derive a good supplemental income. Part of their production might be purchased locally in the community, part sold through "export" outside the community.

What is implied is that the economy of the future would consist of two parts. One would be that of the Big Society—highly capitalized, automated, mass-distributed. This economy would be the great institutional dynamo for man, but would fade into the background of his *more important social and cultural affairs*. The other economy—creative industry—would be varied, personal, and deeply merged into these social and cultural affairs, as it has been since antiquity.

Some persons may suspect that creative industry represents a wholesale retrogression to the middle ages. There are a number of reasons why it does not. First, only a relatively small part of the active population might pursue these endeavors. Nevertheless, craftsmanship represents a real choice for those who would elect a nonautomated role in production and a personally creative interest in materials, design, and the skills that bring them together. Second, in an age of technology and bureaucracy, small workshops offer an avenue for individual initiative and choice relating to personal routine, kind of product, and style of design—qualities now both scarce and deeply necessary. Third, the potential range of products of the contemporary craftsman is immensely larger than when he was the sole means of production. Lastly, modern man has virtually eliminated a personal response to the ordinary materials of the earth, and he must now find relief from synthetic anonymity. We profoundly need to maintain viable contacts with wood, metal, and fabric (just as we do with the soil, open spaces, and seasons).

Other considerations are also important. It was the durable virtues of the independent yeoman farmer that sustained Thomas Jefferson's confidence in the democratic system. We may recall also the humble pursuits that have sustained remarkable men, such as the Dutch philosopher Baruch Spinoza who was a lens polisher, or David Thoreau who was a pencil maker. Today the outstanding author Eric Hoffer is a retired San Francisco longshoreman. Perhaps a devotion to the arts and letters might even be associated with a craft tradition within community, possibly as a free counterbalance to the professionalized, disciplined intelligence of our universities.

Perhaps Gandhi was right, at least in part, in urging India to stress its cottage industries. After more than a decade of rejecting his proposal, I am now convinced that these industries have a role to play—right in the center of the advanced economy—and that they are also close to the center of a virtuous society, as Gandhi believed.

The second aspect of community important for the redefinition of careers is service. Fortunately in America there is a solid public consciousness of humanitarian and public causes. But the individual finds few ways to become fruitfully involved when he has a full-time employment. The good cause of volunteer service has never had a firm and general foundation, except among a very few exceptional and wealthy individuals. When the emerging abundance is converted into a freedom from economic necessity, a new and broader tradition of service to humanity can arise and take hold. This freedom will allow the mind to focus beyond family maintenance, will tend to reduce covetous attitudes by diverting the mainstream of education and effort away from material acquisition, and will make more time available for liberating pursuits.

As a first step, service might become part of a person's normal range of activities, not as a *burdensome offering* but as a *rich involvement*. Next, an organized structure for service may beckon the individual, place him in a useful and congenial setting, and offer him appropriate challenge. Third, a new and varied range of incentives might be offered to inspire humanitarian service (as we now inspire military service), which in turn would be honored by an array of profoundly respected rewards and medals (as we now honor military valor).

Again, the most important possibilities for service lie within community. Service to teaching, health, the arts, youth, and the festivities and celebrations of life may gain a new richness when offered among those who might one day reciprocate or within a setting that reflects the knowledge of good deeds back to the doer or those close to him.

Living grants would make service possible at the level once attained by Greek citizens (with the support of slaves). Education, health, and other vital services have been arbitrarily isolated from normal citizen participation by professionalization and specialization. High levels of performance in many of these services do not require complete isolation from normal social intercourse. Indeed, especially in education and health, wider participation might bring highly beneficial improvements.

Few persons have realized the revolutionary potential for service represented in the inspired example of the Peace Corps. Here is demonstrated a *publicly organized* means for service by volunteers. *Partial pay* eliminates the steep sacrifice that the majority could not afford to make. *Selectivity* and *training* of the volunteers gives the service a status and proficiency. An administrative arm provides *direction* so that the volunteers may be promptly assigned and made effective.

For many persons, a paid, part-time, "selected volunteer" service,

assisted by income grants, would also permit ample time for free participation in other activities such as theater, youth programs, festival
arrangements, community politics, and any activity that imagination and
interest might create. Work, service, and social participation might then
imperceptively intermingle, each thereby becoming more wholesome and
beneficial.

The person who chooses to be an exception may do nothing or may
follow a solitary interest not related to the ongoing activities in the community, perhaps as a composer, artist, author, or absorbed hobbyist. A
writer under these circumstances would be freer in his choice of subjects
and perhaps more honest (objective) in his point of view; if he were independent of salaries and subsidies from various institutions, he might
escape a sense of obligation to substantiate the institution's position. An
income grant as an established right would powerfully stimulate the expansion of these liberties.

The entire question of enlarging the means for an individual to define
the kind and character of his "work" is vitally related to the expansion of
human liberty. Liberties exist insofar as significant alternatives are available that are both accepted *and* provided for in the society. Full liberty
calls for positive opportunities as well as safeguards.

These remarks concerning creative industry and public service can do
no more than suggest a redefinition of work and career. A more thorough-
going investigation might analyze conceptions of the generalist and specialist, the whole range of means for creating human satisfaction and
fulfillment (along with provoking spirit and excitement), and the recon-
ciliation of the individual's inner well-being and external adjustment.
Less rigid lines demarcating the beginning and ending of a career would
be worthy of consideration. Most importantly, a new definition of work
might consider shifting some of the emphasis from what work produces
to what satisfactions it will give.

The real importance of material abundance is the new *human* abundance it may afford. This is an opportunity that is historically unprecedented.

DISENGAGING THE ECONOMY

The decline of property as a life motive throughout society is
now almost as inevitable as was the end of the American frontier toward
the end of the nineteenth century. Even though remnants of pioneering
remained after 1890—new lands to be developed, new towns to be
built—the old open frontier with its stolid isolation and hard-fisted
struggle with nature rapidly diminished. The old ethic had to be con-

verted to something new, for it no longer held the same challenge or promised the same self-satisfying reward.

Long before the end of the frontier, however, industrial development had begun to capture the imaginations of those with a "pioneering" spirit, and indeed it was part of the same tradition. This is the spirit that today stands so flush with success.

As property and production lose their grip on human motives, the crucial question is the degree to which a moral equivalent can arise to fully and profoundly challenge men. What can replace the struggle for abundance that few people imagined could ever be won? Such a possibility never figured at all in the utopian and revolutionary terms of Marx.

The mammoth proportions of this problem are suggested by the centuries the West required to attain its commercial and productive ethic and organization. The depth to which the decaying ethic penetrates our behavior and patterns of thought is revealed by the grasp it has on our cities; the domination it has over the content and character of our education; the importance it plays in government programs and decisions; the extent to which it influences human relationships (consider the role of money); the supremacy it holds over the selection, location, and course of careers; the conception it has lent to land and property; the direction it has given to science; the creation of a specious redundant economy largely superfluous to human welfare; the power it exhibits over the arts; and the tenuous state to which it has brought organizations that do not contribute appreciably to economic ends (compare, for example, the rise of universities with the decline of community). Today all of these easily observed extensions of the economic ethic penetrate the only condition of life we know. They seem natural, even necessary. But they have not been either natural or necessary to most other societies, and until one or two generations ago they did not even penetrate deeply our own rural past.

The practical problem facing all Western society in the coming generation is to disengage the economy from the deeper pursuits of life, and to give those pursuits independent strength and freshness.

In one sense the disengagement of society from industry and commerce, anticipated in the basic disengagement from agriculture and the pastoral life, is but a new stage in the long process of liberating man from unhuman tasks. But the new stage will require a reversal of many attributes of organized existence now considered essential and basic.

The decline of industry now in its initial stages is a transition without a direction. The ethic is beginning to decline, but there is no moral equivalent arising to challenge more than a small part of the population. Old traditions of community and the diverse excellence of civic life have been submerged in the drive to production. The arts and sciences are active, but they hardly present an adequate theme by themselves to offer the whole society.

Perhaps more than at any time in our history we require the conscious creation of a new central ethic. Some of the areas that must be affected by it are plainly evident. The redefinition of work just discussed is one. The redundant economy is another. The purposes of education must be reformulated to elevate the person, not merely his usefulness. A socially differentiated urban environment of livable, vital communities must be defined to resurrect the city from its industrial debris. But a central new ethic first requires a powerful dialogue that will cut through massive layers of bureaucratic pragmatism and penetrate the problem of the rising social sovereignty of corporate institutions. Such a dialogue is not clearly audible.

9

Human Image of the City

Cities are the chief artifact of a civilization. The modern city reveals a civilization devoted, not to gathering places for human drama, worship, and civic affairs, but to workplaces for making and to arterials for moving. This is as true for the center of cities as it is for their inner and outer suburbs.

Drama, worship, and civic affairs reflect a civilization focused upon social relationships, whereas making and moving focus upon machines and economics. And economic affairs have become predominantly the bailiwick of large bureaucratic institutions.

Physically, the consequences are profound: a scale of construction adjusted to the capacities of machines and institutions; a scale of population advantageous to labor markets and mass retailing; an urban structure advantageous to economic penetration and exploitation; and on the other hand a disarray of the facilities and institutions that respond to psychic, social, and cultural aspiration.

Cities also reflect the leading essence of a civilization. Thus the results of human development—the honorable, the brilliant, and also the despicable—have always been magnified in cities. But man's past always remained largely rural, and the effects of urbanism remained partial and incomplete for most people. Inevitably the future of development will be increasingly urban.

169

The life of cities has always been relatively unstable, being especially susceptible to the ravages of war and disease and to degenerate or despotic rule. In the past during times of misfortune cities could draw new vitality from or fall back upon the durable strength of the far larger population of the countryside. This was shown even during World War II when the population of many cities in Europe and Asia dropped by more than half through death and dispersion. But today the city everywhere grows rapidly, encompassing more men, more of man's behavior, and more continental space. The contrast and interplay of urban and rural life will surely diminish and may disappear.

Years ago someone observed that cities were once set up by the rural areas to do the things not possible in the countryside. Now, as others have pointed out, the countryside has become a creature of the city. In the more advanced economies few aspects of life in the countryside remain without urban domination, even where the landscape might superficially suggest that rural life is distinct from that of the city.

Yet despite the prevalence and power of the modern city, its role in the vital contemporary development of society, in both advanced and newly developing countries, is surprisingly passive—it is merely a container and not an active instrument. The city is understood largely as a corollary to the directive and motive economic forces of development. It does not enter into the councils of decision along with calculations of capital accumulation, gross product, or standard of living. Attention is directed to all of the things that compose a city but not to the city itself. The city is mostly conceived as an indifferent *adjunct* of change rather than a useful *tool* or a valued *objective* of development, especially in the newer countries.

That is the way we conceive of the modern city. Yet the character of the city—its beauty, vitality, and simple livability—naturally reflects the manner in which it is conceived. Thus, if the city itself is not an objective of development, it will be a doubtful environment in which to achieve a quality of life. More significantly, the city will not become an environment to inspire and nurture community, social variety, and cultural opportunity—the ultimate pleasures of being human. Only economic opportunity will be afforded.

Being only a corollary of development—perhaps but a function of production, distribution, and consumption—the contemporary city seems to require large new capacities to overcome the mountainous burdens of society left by the chaotic energies of technical and economic capacities, the energies that disrupt society's own best functioning and place barricades against its best inner development.

We might wonder, for example, what anthills would be like if ants had cars. Even without cars, anthills present an unbearable complexity.

Should the ants desire such innovations, their antlanes would stretch out interminably. An anthill would no longer be an anthill, but rather a dispersion agglomerated along antlanes. The dispersion of functions would but magnify congestion of movement. The ants would no longer form an ant society; that is, traffic would become their primary mode of interaction. The ants could no longer walk the long distances, nor be safe; movement and safety would always require cars.

Now, if we should ask what would happen if while the ant population doubled the automobile population multiplied six or eight times, then it is beyond comprehension to understand how ant civilization could continue. Action would be reduced to movement; movement would be reduced to friction and congestion. Yet perhaps the industrious ants, not knowing this, would somehow find a way to maintain their cars and still survive under increasing burdens of life.

So far, however, the ants have not accepted such burdens upon their living arrangements. But man has.

Nowhere is there a more profound urgency in the age of development than to elevate the purpose of the city. What is critical to acknowledge, as did the Greeks and Romans, is that the city itself is a singular object of civilization, and that it is also instrumental for all other modes of excellence, greatness, and humanity.

URBANIZING WORLD

Two dimensions of contemporary urbanization stand above all others: (1) the immense population growth of the world's cities, and (2) the geographic expanses that are beginning to be consumed by cities. Both point to vast unprecedented scales of urbanism: the first to a time when the world's population may become totally urbanized, the second to a time when all inhabitable land will be subject to some form of urbanism. At present the population potential is best illustrated in the developing countries, the consumption of space in the advanced.

Urban population is an approximate barometer of economic development. While less than 5 percent of the persons in some of the least developed countries live in urban places, more than 80 percent are urban in several of the most developed countries. Urban growth reflects the growth of the total population and the proportion of the population that shifts to urban places.

The United Nations estimated the world population to be 2,990,-000,000 in 1960. This was an increase of almost 473 million in ten years, or two thirds of the whole world population in the year 1650. The U.N. medium prediction world population for the year 2000 is 5,965,000,

000, or virtually double the 1960 figure. The bulk of the population growth will take place in countries that are presently less developed— and less urbanized.

In 1960 roughly one fifth of the world's population, or 600,000,000, were living in cities and large towns. If development moves at an orderly pace, we may expect that as many as half of the world's people will be living in cities by the year 2000. This is a very short time, of course—just enough for a person born in 1960 to reach his middle span of years. Yet by 2000 over three billion persons many inhabit the cities and metropolises of that time. Whereas the total world population is likely to double, the total urban population could well grow fivefold.

Some persons may argue that such predictions are too high. Perhaps they are. But our concern should be with the upper possibilities of urbanization, especially with the requiremerÙts to meet such a growth. Also 50 percent is an average: in Europe and North America the level of urbanization may well reach 90 percent, whereas in many countries of Africa and Asia it may still be 30 or 40 percent. Further, economic development and urbanization might proceed more rapidly than presently expected, owing to a gathering momentum. Relatively modest current campaigns for health, food, and education could well be replaced in twenty or thirty years by massive surges of economic growth. Thus, a fivefold growth of urban population appears to be both possible and crucially important to prepare for, if not in the year 2000, then perhaps by 2010.

The fivefold estimate is reinforced by the increasing propensity of developing peoples to migrate to cities in relatively early stages of economic development. Students of contemporary urban and industrial growth have noted increasing tendencies for urban migrations to seriously overstep increases in both agricultural productivity and urban employment. Historically, European and North American cities evolved upon a relative balance between growing rural productivity and increasing demand for urban labor, except during periods of economic depression. The present problem of excessive urban growth is undoubtedly related in part to rural overpopulation. Both rural unemployment and underemployment are merely shifted to the cities. In a certain respect, then, urbanization is not a symbol of economic development, but its converse. Both the traditional "push" from the rural areas and the "pull" to the cities, which once were positive, have now become partly negative in character.

If one looks at Latin America, for example, he will find an astonishing phenomenon in the creation of shacktowns or *favelas* around the larger cities. In 1954 at Lima, Peru, 10,000 persons took possession of state land overnight. Within days the population reached 25,000, and within a few months, 50,000. A similar area of Santiago, Chile, grew from 65,000 in 1940 to 145,000 in 1950. In 1953 it was estimated that 311,000 or 38 percent of the population of Caracas, Venezuela, lived in slums, mostly on steep mountain slopes or along ravines. In the late 1950s in Mexico City, 993,000 persons or one third of the city's population lived in one-room apartments; another 315,000 lived in shack houses; and 420,000 lived in *colonias proletarias*, settlements on state lands that had been unoccupied in 1940. Many of the *barrios clandestinos* in the cities of Colombia have reasonably well-built structures, but are built on land unsuitable for development and lack running water, electricity, and sewerage.

All of these conditions are symptomatic of premature migration. They add a heavy burden to the process of economic growth. The excessive urban populations without effective incomes aggravate the problems of providing not only food but also a higher level of services than is required in the villages, such as police, sanitary protection, water supply, housing, education.

This view is contested by many economists and some urban planners. But it cannot be contested, I believe, that the painfully heavy investments made in conjunction with the heaping of people together in unprecedented masses are resulting in simply miserable cities. This enormously reduces the possibility of establishing a minimally worthy city for future generations and of achieving a congenial physical environment (which must surely be a major objective of economic development)—that is, of creating the physical medium for the growth of civilization. Moreover, it makes mandatory a future urban-renewal struggle that may well challenge all progress in economic development.

Excessive migration to cities would therefore seem to have the same general significance in retarding development as explosive population growth. If a rural person is underemployed but requires very little in paid "services" he is not much of a burden on the resources applicable to development. But if he migrates to a city and is unemployed there, where he must be sustained by more complete and sophisticated services, he becomes a heavier drain upon the small and struggling modern sector of the economy. Thus a man "out of place" is a burden upon the economy in about the same way as a newborn child throughout its years of growth and education.

Still, whatever man does, cities as we know them are likely to grow to a completely new scale. In 1800 not one city had reached a million inhabitants. By 1955 some 96 metropolitan areas throughout the world had passed this mark. Moreover, New York, London, and Tokyo had each passed the ten-million mark.

Kingsley Davis, an urban sociologist, has estimated that, without intercession by government, the population of the City of Calcutta will grow to at least 36 million and possibly as high as 66 million by the year 2000. If such a city seems improbable, we may note that the 66 million residents of Calcutta would still be only 6.6 percent of India's estimated population of one billion human beings in the year 2000,[1] whereas about 8.5 percent of the U.S. population lived in the New York metropolitan area in 1960. Yet even the lower projection of 36 million for Calcutta is more than double the present size of metropolitan New York and almost seven times its own 1960 size. There is clear evidence, then, that the new scale of cities in the coming decades will rise to the order of 30 to 50 million human beings.

A terribly important question is thus raised: How can man conceive and plan for cities of this magnitude? How can they be made worthy of the kind of life man hopes to achieve by development? We may have learned to achieve a functional framework for a population of fifteen million. But we have yet to learn to make a city of even a hundred thousand that is socially congenial to the individual person. This question has hardly been formulated in terms in which solutions might be sought.

The scale of urban population growth in our age and the startling possibilities for the future are compounded by the second vast dimension of urbanization, which is simply that the urban consumption of land is increasing much more rapidly than the population. This phenomenon is particularly evident in the United States. Many elements are contributory: larger home lots, one-story factories, larger airports, wider highways and larger parking spaces, and the tendency to indiscriminately disperse and by-pass large quantities of land.

In the United States the automobile is both the voracious claimant of vast expanses of land and the chief means to make the land exploitable to urbanism. It tends both to generate its own need for land and to provide the means to fulfill that need. Here is revealed a most astonishing and unique role for a product, comparable only to narcotics for the whole society. And like narcotics, which dominate an individual's perception of life, the automobile dominates the structuring of the urban environment.

The automobile already occupies up to four-fifths of the land in shopping centers, up to one-half at manufacturing plants and research parks, from fifteen to thirty acres per mile for freeways (plus interchanges requiring up to forty acres), and up to 10 percent of each urban lot, as well as land for service stations and dealers in new and used automobiles. City streets typically occupy between 25 and 40 percent of a city's developed land area. The car's powerful grip on high-valued commercial property is so great it has now increased its occupancy of land in downtown Los Angeles to about 60 percent.

Perhaps the more significant aspect of urban consumption of land made possible by the automobile is the by-passing of land in the accelerated outward expansion. There is hardly a major city in the United States that does not have scattered urban developments extending twenty, thirty, and sometimes sixty miles from its center. The growing impunity of distance is now pressing the rings of expansion of Philadephia into the orbit of New York, and Baltimore into that of Washington. Along the entire four hundred miles from Boston to Washington commuting orbits are now interlocking and forming the celebrated American Megalopolis. Perhaps a few decades will see this axis rotate and vastly expand, with New York and Chicago as the major anchors, creating an urban conurbation measuring one thousand by five hundred miles. Even now one may ask what habitable and accessible square mile of New Jersey or Connecticut, or of Pennsylvania and Ohio, is not already subject to the random location of an industrial plant, a scattering of houses, or a regional shopping center.

The lesson of increasing mobility and of limitless areal expansion of the city is not lost to the brokers of land resources, who promote the best of both "town and country" by locating major developments midway between two cities. These projects take advantage of lower land values, two labor markets, and access to the benefits of either center. The Great Southwest industrial district between Dallas and Fort Worth in Texas and the Research Triangle between Durham, Raleigh, and Chapel Hill in North Carolina involve several thousand acres each and have together established a major prototype now followed widely.

The disunited metropolis and the emerging intermetropolis are not all that confront the new order of urbanism. The western states have witnessed the sale of large desert spaces for urban estates. An area larger than Massachusetts or Israel in Southern California's Mojave Desert has been occupied by more than 250,000 randomly scattered persons. While these people live in an area a hundred times larger than a traditional city of that many people, they move about the whole area in a cobweb pattern of commuting, shopping, recreation, and wholesaling distribution movements. The number of subdivided lots is of the order of ten times as many as are in use, and this leaves but a ghostly suggestion of urbanism over many thousands of square miles. Any rational pattern for future utilization is thus preempted.

The implications are profound. A mammoth new consumption of America's land resources equal to the area of Rhode Island is taken up by the urban bulldozer each year. But this is the less important fact. An ultimate dispersion—that of randomly urbanizing an entire continent—raises a specter for the industrial society that is equaled only by the specter of the population explosion in the nonindustrial countries. This momentum toward social tragedy is most clearly foreseen in the application of wealth and mobility to the dividing and peddling of land in the desert of Southern California. And besides the loss of resources involved, the dispersion undermines centuries of evolved local government practices and destroys any remaining civic coherence.

The precedents now firmly established presage a new continental distribution of population, unlike anything of the past. Already the terms "urban" and "rural" are largely meaningless. The main virtue of land is steadily being reduced to availability—not soil, water, or climate, as in agriculture, and not strategic location, transportation, and accumulated services, as in the traditional cities. These are still talking points, but they are increasingly irrelevant to the formation of habitational patterns.

At the level of their capacities, the emerging countries also reveal an indiscriminate and persistent land consumption. Most Asian or African cities have their own strips of urbanism on the few roads leading to their centers, as well as nondescript congregations of houses widely scattered about their periphery. The principal difference exists in the limited means that they can focus to break the severe bounds that defined all urban location, size, and form in the past.

Population and area, then, are the two major dimensions appearing in contemporary urbanization. They depict a vast population intake and an unprecedented territorial outburst. They are forming a mountainous groundswell of man's earthly community. In themselves, they tell little of specific effects upon the individual, though they obviously place a gigantic new frame about him and pose a major question about the future course of collective life.

URBAN MISFORTUNES

The significance of cities is that, in building them, man has accepted a more complete responsibility for shaping his own environment. That responsibility increases with the capacity to build. Since economic capacities for shaping the environment have so radically increased in scale in the present era, along with the population intake and territorial outburst, society's responsibility must now be extended even to protecting all prized features of the natural environment from the reckless destructiveness accompanying the new capacities. An initial recognition is found in the urban-inspired programs of acquiring land for permanent open space at the local, state, and federal levels of government. When he must protect what he so long struggled to overcome, man's capacity for shaping the environment has reached a new and ominous comprehensiveness. The responsibility of man to his environment is now also approaching an absolute. So far, however, city-making still appears to be following the biological mistake of the dinosaur.

The contemporary American city is an inheritance from the exuberant era that found unlimited space, proclaimed continuous progress, and believed that the city was a center for endless opportunities. And so it was built. Uniform rectangular streets and blocks provided for all apparent opportunities. Any function might occupy any tract or parcel. Any vehicle might move on any street and have equal access to any lot. Any city might expand to any population level and outwardly any distance. The free market applied to land as readily as to goods. Provisions that might have given shape to growth, whatever their character or purpose, were fought to a standstill and countered by many measures of indiscriminate promotion.

The location of industrial, commercial, and residential functions resulted from bidding on the price of land. Business functions bid highest and dominated the growth pattern. Housing overflowed into the areas between and beyond. Hence, the city became commercial in both form and purpose.

The city grew and partly differentiated itself, but the various residential areas never achieved full integrity because the growth of industry and commerce demanded an internal migration as well as outward expansion. A physically sound living area might become mixed with workshops and garages in two decades, and then become completely commercial in two more. Most areas rapidly deteriorated from the impact.

In such residual living areas, nodes of neighborhood activities and services had little opportunity to combine into general functioning centers. Residents had little basis for a sense of identity and common unity, which would help them understand their urban interests or to defend them. Lines of daily activity, and therefore lines of interest, interlaced indiscriminately throughout all residential areas, drawn merely according to the value and availability of land. The most meaningful line of interest to the man was to his job, the woman to her shopping, the child to his school, the family to its church. Rarely did enough lines of interest focus at a single center to develop a common understanding of local affairs. Thus, the city was endless in commercial opportunity but atomistic in its effect upon group life.

Up to modern times the city was always bound to a relatively confined point of geographic space, a point of exchange, wealth, intellect, power. Today the spatial bonds have been broken by modern transportation. The attendant territorial outburst of the city reflects, first, this power to disperse and, second, dissatisfaction with the city as it has been shaped by transportation, production, commerce, and land marketing. These conditions exert a new kind of antiurban "push" and "pull," completely the reverse of initial urbanization. The push is away from the unbecoming city and the pull is toward the open and serene countryside. But the result is not the creation of the best of two worlds, but a running from one and a destruction of the other.

The misfortunes of the American city seem peculiarly bound up with the wealth we apply to waste and destruction. This is evident in the profuse trash we scatter about, which requires fantastic programs of refuse collection and disposal. Automobile graveyards symbolize a more serious blight. Both show that increasing society's capacity to produce increases its capacity to waste—and to clutter lives and make the environment inhospitable.

As yet we have hardly begun to discover the depths of our ability to waste: we have such wealth that we are able to waste—and to escape from—the city itself. With wealth we escape from the city that was created to produce wealth, when both the city and wealth might have together created a more wholesome habitat for man. What other interpretation can be given to the abandonment of large sections of every city by the wealthy and middle class to slumlords? What other interpretation can be given to subsidies of slums brought about through lower evaluations and lower taxes for deteriorated structures that violate health and building codes? What other interpretation can be given to federal and banking loan prejudices strongly favoring new single-family suburban housing? What other interpretation can be given to heavy expenditures for highways while public transit deteriorates?

The resulting waste of our cities is waste of our chief asset of civilization. The waste is systematic. It is an epochal pity because it wastes human sensibilities, even human life.

On the other hand, the American ideal of achieving the benefits of both "town and country" at the scattered fringes of cities is now being overtaken by the gigantic paradox it entails.

Any people who interact as a whole, as they do within a city, must expend proportionately more energy in movement as their numbers increase. That is, a city of one million people engages in more than ten times as much total mobility as a city of one hundred thousand. Commuters in larger cities spend more time traveling. Proportionately more resources must be invested in transportation.

When the automobile plays a paramount role in urban mobility, or even a significant role, there is inevitable congestion because the ground space required for parking and moving a car is between fifty and one hundred times as great as that required for a pedestrian. The passenger capacity per lane of public transit, and therefore its efficiency of space utilization, is about twenty-five times as great as the best performance by a lane of auto traffic. Automobility, therefore, is inherently inefficient mobility. Although it may be flexible for the individual, its movement and storage in large numbers is extremely difficult to rationalize. Automobiles simply contest for the same spaces, until congestion like that in Manhattan forces a recession in the face of complete stagnation. From then on the margin of congestion remains just slightly under the point of municipal futility.

While the car is the biggest factor in creating central-city congestion, its decisive role exists in giving visible but mistaken relief from congestion to those who relocate at the periphery of the city. And at this point the automobile drastically alters the natural history of city-making. By leaving the relatively compact center of the city for the periphery, a business removes itself from the only rational focus of public transit (and even from the confluence of major streets). Joining other emigres at the urban periphery, each business multiplies its occupancy of ground space. Overall travel distances are increased. There is then further reliance upon the automobile; therefore more space and money must be allocated to parking lots, street widening, and traffic regulation. Ultimately there comes a new congestion involving more cars with fewer passengers driving longer distances in more directions.

Thus congestion becomes associated with the consumption of larger urban spaces, not with the compactness of urban development. Even the illusory sense of spaciousness in suburban land developments is lost as arterials become hopelessly congested. The value of a city, which is simple contiguity, is dissipated. After all, a great city, someone once said, is but the quantity, quality, variety, and intensity of services closely related to each other. As the city is made over in the image of the automobile, the determination of behavior passes from man to his transportation capacities. And, when man becomes as bound to it as are the people of Los Angeles, automobility becomes the civic passion. Someone has also said that men make cities and cities make men. Now it appears that men make cars and cars make both cities and men. The city that elevates its scale of behavior from man to the automobile necessarily must concentrate its chief abilities upon mobility. Thus the arterial system dominates the city plan.

Moreover, concern for mobility itself is incomplete unless there is equal attention given to the problems of coming to a stop. Thus terminal points of transportation at home, at work, at shopping, at the stadium and civic hall, at high schools and colleges, all have their site plans dominated by the requirements—and the new scale—of the automobile. Clark Kerr once noted at Berkeley how a parking crisis is the one problem most likely to draw a vigorous response from the faculty.

When the future of the city is dominated by efforts to overcome the weight of its transportation system, especially one that must penetrate every living cell of the city, the lines of transportation naturally become the chief organizers of urban integrity. That is why access controls are designed for highway efficiency rather than for the benefit of civic and social behavior.

Historically, access controls applied to land, most notably in the completely enclosed Spanish courtyards. In the heyday of the growth of the American city and the open-ended grid system of rectangular streets and blocks, access was virtually universal for both land and roadways. But when the automobile ascended to dominance in the 1920s and 1930s, the exchange of access between the land and the thoroughfare began to be controlled in favor of the roadway. The result is today's freeways, which are carefully designed to maintain maximum efficiency of movement but are haphazardly organized to integrate or serve units of land development. Very frequently they disrupt and divide what cohesiveness there may have been in land development, often spilling traffic into the midst of adjacent areas to disrupt them.

When highways become the foundations of urban integrity, land planning becomes defensive—if any character or adequacy is sought at all. Of necessity, planning becomes insular and isolated, depending more and more upon the brute asphalt ligaments that bind the urban structure together. Boxed and segregated industrial districts and civic centers are of this order. The clearest element of insular planning is the shopping center, a cluster of shops surrounded by a sea of asphalt and isolated by six-lane thoroughfares. In character with the times, the shopping center draws consumers to their consumptive chores during certain hours, but becomes abandoned and forbidding at night and on weekends, having had all vestiges of civility, urbanity, and spontaneous association wrung out of it.

Of the same character are the controls applied to give a semblance of order to urbanism. Taking its cues from industry and the discrete segregation of each function, zoning segregates urban functions on the premise that one function is noxious to every other. Similarly the laws of subdivision require a separation of parcels of ownership into little kingdoms, each fearsome of every other. As yet city-making has not reached that state of development in which it strives for integration and unity as forcefully as it strives for specialization and segregation of function.

Modern city planning arose in good part as a reaction to the tradition that any function could occupy any parcel of land—to prevent "conflicting land uses." It used zoning to place similar uses together and began to draw the city out of its heterogeneous agglomeration. But zoning was more of a reaction than a conception, for in rescuing the city from its heterogeneous degeneration it has created a homogeneous sterility, a condition that may very well lead to monotonous decay.

A large part of the problem is that the modern tradition of planning was strictly local; there were but minor or abortive efforts to establish national, state, and regional planning. Therefore planning solidified itself locally just at a time when urban expansion began to appear at the regional scale. Planning took hold most firmly in central cities, which governed but half the population and a tenth of the urbanized area of most metropolitan areas. This reinforced the insular nature of planning and denied it the wholeness without which there is no real planning.

Of course, planning cannot become regionally responsible as long as it is a part of a fractured pattern of local government, where many metropolitan areas cross state lines and span numerous counties, dozens of cities, and hundreds of special districts. The geographic pattern of government provides the only normal framework in which problems of physical development can be clarified to elected officials and administrations, as well as to the electorate.

When we look at the modern city and all of the powerful forces playing upon it, we see ample physical and economic reasons for its misfortunes. However, these conditions and problems have not been unmanageable. The problem lies closer to our attitudes about the urban environment and to our lack of a philosophy of urban life—the absence of an urban chapter in the American Dream.

For example, does our system of local government have a purpose as clear as the preamble to the Constitution, a definition of metropolitan roles as clear as that of the three branches of the national government, or an articulation of state and local interests as pointed as the federal principle? Is a tradition such as the town meeting, which once gave us the grass-roots experience to build democracy, now relevant in mass society? Or has any other tradition arisen that can face up to urbanism in giant form?

There is one certainty. The giant forms that collective living takes in this corporate age are imperialistic. What city does not hunch its civic and social back to get a growth industry? Why? They do not use the growth for self-improvement. Growth and giantism are a habit of mind, almost a faith, and deliver a special profit to a very few, rarely to the majority. What is created is a vastness of area, population, mobility, and organization that is put upon the individual whole, not scaled down to him in any meaningful way.

An urban philosophy is needed to bring the city back to man. Then we might begin to design cities life-size for the man afoot; relevant to his eyes, ears, and voice; enhancing his familiarity, association, and excitement. This must be done in the face of unprecedented change. And it must be done in spite of forces that continue to make the city massive, meaningless, and therefore merciless to the heart of a human being.

SPACE: THE URBAN RESOURCE

Human beings remain finite and space-bound in their daily living despite miraculous progress in transportation and communication. So long as men retain their flesh and blood, human action, association, and simple sense of place will be deeply affected by the physical spaces that frame them. The entire social environment is structured by its urban spaces. But the modern metropolis has shown its capacity to destroy the human scale and human form of spaces that characterized nearly all cities of the past. In concert with many other forces in society the structure of the metropolis has been undermining the basis for humanity, civic purpose, interpersonal association, and urbanity itself.

Apparently we lost our appreciation of the *social* importance of urban space in struggling to master the elements and meet the demands of the industrial age. We strive in the name of high standards of development to multiply the land area occupied by the city and then to dissect every part of it with thoroughfares. Thus we strike at the human essence of urban space, and of what a city is: an articulated concentration of development contrasted with selected open spaces within or about it. For villages and small towns the countryside was always sufficient to retain the quality of spaciousness. But with the emergence of the modern metropolis after 1800 it fell upon man to preserve a spaciousness. And with the rise of the railroad and especially the automobile after 1900 a new burden of maintaining both a concentration and a spaciousness—and of articulating their relationship—has fallen to man. But the present forces of urban population growth, wealth, and consumption and of urban development by marketing procedures do not bode well for the social qualities of urban space.

Compact and open spaces afford a contrast and a maximization of two opposable values: intensively used space and casual open space, and even urban and rural space. But what do we actually do? First, we compact urban development indiscriminately. Then to escape suffocation and congestion the well-to-do go outside the city and buy an acre. Business offices frequently go out and build on three acres. This but systematically chops up land, and sites buildings most effectively to destroy openness. The private urge to enjoy a contrast to urban congestion merely speeds up the process of uncontrolled destruction of that value, for all land is divided into acre modules of homogenized monotony, neither compact nor open. Thus we dissipate the quality, quantity, variety, and intensity of activities operating smoothly together in a limited space.

The social essence of a city, found in articulated compactness and openness, also is dissipated by a homogenous use of space. Whatever the scale or diversity of a city as a whole, a human scale of the spaces that frame the activities of the individual (such as interconnected paths, courts, gardens, play areas) in each part of the city contributes a sense of purpose and importance to the person. But this human scaling cannot exist when every unit of urban activity occupies an acre, or even a fraction of an acre, of separately owned land.

Nevertheless, true to its tradition of undermining the foundations of humanity while it creates new humane possibilities, modern society is destroying the value of urban space while it is creating a new and more dynamic definition of space. As one may expect, the source for both lies in new technology and wealth. For example, by the use of air rights and development rights, the space above railroad lines and yards and over freeways is being increasingly occupied by apartments, commercial buildings, schools, and other structures. In New York a bus terminal and three apartment structures have been built over the approaches to the George Washington Bridge and in Philadelphia the Penn Center has been built over the Pennsylvania Railroad. Although the practice is old (the Waldorf Astoria is built over the tracks of Grand Central Station), the importance is new, for only recently has the practice begun to be varied and regular.

Behind these developments is a highly urban definition of *space*. That definition specifically contrasts with the traditional concept of *land*. The concept of land derived from our rural past; it is that of a natural resource. Land was used *as land*. It was valued in two-dimensional form; growing food and fiber required a flat piece of land wholly exposed to the sun. However, when cities today occupy land, what is important is not the land itself but the space it affords. The significance of this definition of space increases as man is able to build higher structures, free himself of the need for direct access to light and air, and transport all necessary people and goods to a given point. It enables the intense use of space that makes a city great. The value of urban areas rests in the third dimension.

Rockefeller Center is still probably the finest example of modern urban design in the United States, and largely because of its judicious use of space. Such a congregation of 48,000 employees might have justified several times its seventeen acres. Yet spaciousness is plainly evident, far more so than in any comparable group of structures in midtown Manhattan. The Center is outstanding precisely because the designers understood the basic variable to be space rather than land.

Clues also come forth from older sources: space became more dynamic with the introduction of the subway. And freeways, while they perpetuate control of cities by the automobile, sometimes utilize the third dimension effectively.

At least three innovations in the use of space have been proposed in recent years. One is the suspension of structures from cables over water bodies, such as those surrounding Manhattan, or over ravines and small valleys. Another, for Panther Hollow in Pittsburgh, proposed to utilize a whole ravine for a building, the structure rising only to the level of the bordering land. The third is a structure resting on and partly conforming to the major proportions of a large and steep slope.

All this amounts to a gradual and far from complete discovery that three-dimensional space is the real resource for cities, not merely level "buildable" land. With a growing concern for urban space, more attention may focus on the external setting of a building in relation to the internal structure, and stress may center upon the relationships of many structures. The function and purpose of the whole urban environment may then be more easily recognized and supported.

The design of urban space has particular relevance for the living qualities of the modern city. Some beginnings are found in the recent evolution of cluster development. The extremely significant principle behind clustering in communities—as in the city as a whole—is that the social and cultural advantages of proximity can be achieved while the quantity and variety of open space is massively enlarged. Clustering of dwellings avoids the wasteful and burdensome division of land into uniform city lots and the barracks-like destruction of large open spaces.

An excellent example of clustering at the level of community is the new town of Reston, near Washington, D.C. There we find an internal scale in which the automobile is not essential, spaces that are relevant to the man afoot, dwellings that are not beyond range of public activities. Yet there is still a spaciousness affording a generous plaza, a lake, a riding stable, and a golf course.

The dynamics of urban space are illustrated in the table by comparing two hypothetical kinds of clustering with a typical land subdivision. All three examples are based on a community of 7700 people, 3.5 persons per household, a dwelling of 2000 square feet, and a land area of 640 acres. The compactness applied to the row-house and tower cluster cases is higher than is now generally used for developing new land, but the advantages of contiguity on the one hand and open space on the other will arise only from a high density. In neither of these two cases of clustering would a family be required to own an automobile, though it is assumed that each family will own one. The table is designed only for comparative purposes, being based on a uniform set of assumptions that should not exist in reality.

A number of striking facts are revealed. In the single-family example some 400 acres are required in lots to house the 7700 people, compared with only 37 acres in the tower cluster, more than a *tenfold* difference.[2] The area devoted to streets and transit line varies from 140 to 36 acres,

DYNAMICS OF SPACE DEVELOPMENT

	Detached Single-Family House [a]	Clustered Two-Story Row House	Clustered Tower [b]
I Individual Cluster Unit			
Number of families per unit	1	20	60
Number of families per acre	5.5	16	60
Area (square feet)			
Building coverage	2,000	20,000	9,000
Driveway and garage	1,200	8,000	10,000 [c]
Landscaping	1,600	6,000	8,000
Private yard	3,200	8,000	
Commons		11,000	16,000
Total	8,000	53,000	43,000
II Community Cluster Unit			
Number of Families	2,200	2,200	2,200
Number of Local Clusters	2,200	110	37
Area (acres)			
Net residential	400	135	37
Streets	140 [d]	24 [e]	6 [f]
Transit line		40	30 [g]
Community center [h]	100	100	100
Open space [i]		100	100
Golf course		140	140
Surplus		101	227
Total	640	640	640

[a] One Story.
[b] Assumes four apartments on each of fifteen floors.
[c] Assumes three-level parking structure.
[d] 25% of net residential area plus portion of public uses.
[e] 15% of net residential area plus portion of public uses.
[f] 10% of net residential area and portion of public uses.
[g] This acreage might be further reduced by placing public, commercial and residential buildings over the transit line.
[h] Including schools, hospital, activity parks, commerce and public buildings.
[i] This space may be used for a passive park, water, forest, farmland.

and with higher densities much of the space above the transit track could be used for development. Note that in addition to 30 or 40 acres of park (incorporated in the community center), 100 acres could be devoted to open space in both the row-house and tower clusters. Yet, in addition, each permits a 140-acre golf course, and 227 acres remain "surplus" in the tower cluster.

In the mind's eye one may perceive a typical contemporary subdivision with lots averaging about 70 by 115 feet, in which houses are the same in height and spacing. Small, hardly usable spaces are isolated by the houses and fences. Streets, driveways, and garages occupy about a third of the land. And in the mind's eye one may perceive thirty-seven towers of fifteen floors grouped relatively closely about a 60 to 70-acre community center, each tower with a half acre of immediate open space. Very nearby would be an additional 30 to 40-acre park and playground (conceptually and perhaps physically part of community center), a golf course, and open spaces of casual parks, farms, forest, or other areas of natural beauty.

One cannot fail to see the real crowdedness of the immense chopped spaces in orthodox subdivisions and the real spaciousness of compact cluster development, even within much smaller total areas. The principle of clustered development means that *achieving spaciousness in urban design is directly related to compactness of development*. This is precisely why the effort of Americans to individually acquire open space in large lots or small acreages is so self-defeating.

Nor can one fail to note the simple convenience derived from clusters, once we have denied the automobile dominance of the plan design. No person in the tower cluster would live more than 1000 feet from the diverse community center, or more than 1500 feet from it in a row-house cluster. Nor would he be any farther from a major park or open space.

Yet there would be no congestion, for compactness is very different from congestion. If distances to transit, commerce, schools, public buildings, and major open spaces are very short, there is no need for an automobile. Only negligible space need be devoted to vehicular access and parking. Every family could own a car, but each *could freely choose not to own one*. Since up to 100 pedestrians can move easily in the space one car requires for motion and parking, even an intensively developed community center would not be congested. What clustering offers, then, is compactness without congestion; a judicious allocation of different kinds of spaces, each serving a maximum number of purposes; and easy access to both the community center and the larger open spaces.

In reality, of course, many variations should exist in any worthy community cluster design. Physical and institutional diversity will add social and cultural value to the advantages of clustering. Some residences might be integrated into the community center, sustaining the high level of interest of the center of traditional towns. Residential towers might vary in height, bulk, and form and be incorporated with row houses and even some single-family houses. However, with single-family houses, great efforts should be made to minimize the space consumed in traditional streets, setbacks, side yards, driveways, and fenced corners. And clustering vastly reduces these costly and wasteful spaces.

ARTICULATION OF CLUSTERS

The design of urban space in living areas should not only maximize the physical qualities of space and create a human scale in the normal human habitat but establish a physical definition for community. This can be done only if the cluster that forms a community is vitally related to the larger metropolitan structure, which nowadays is often regional in scale.

Although the example above assumed new development in open countryside, the same principle may be incorporated in existing communities close to the dense centers of cities. Through urban redevelopment the same clustered form and integrity of community can be attained, though in some cases man-made improvements such as transportation arteries must serve as community boundaries and open spaces.

Hence, whereas the density of buildings of the present city is highest at the center and tapers off in a nondescript fashion as it spreads out into the countryside, we can now imagine a city, each of whose communities develops its own centrality and simultaneously a distinctive form.

Therefore, while clusters involve compactness, they must be distinguished rigorously from the common practice of endlessly and indiscriminately crowding large buildings side by side and back to back, with streets providing the only significant open space. The cluster is yet in its infancy, and its best development will likely occur when it is (1) conceived of and serves as a social unit with a purpose beyond the function of each of its various buildings; (2) designed with as much concern for the external spaces as for the internal spaces of buildings; (3) formed with a distinctive relationship between dense development and open space; (4) developed small enough to dispense with automobiles and major forms of public transportation for internal movement; (5) related effectively to the city and served by efficient public transportation; and (6) aimed toward a final stage of completion (for, although adjustments will necessarily occur, unlimited change would destroy the principles involved).

Transportation between the community clusters and the major activity centers of the metropolis will be particularly important. The dynamic use of space made possible by clustering requires an advanced system of public transportation. A heavy reliance upon street systems and freeways would not be compatible, though some concessions must be made to Detroit. The problem of all transportation in cities is that while its benefits arise from its proximity to the places it serves, so do its disadvantages—noise, nuisance, and danger.

Unquestionably the finest example resolving the dilemma is the new town of Vällingby, a well-clustered suburb of Stockholm, Sweden. Instead of either skirting the town or slicing its way through Vällingby's vital center, the commuter railroad becomes a subway at the more dense central development. Atop the subway and adjacent to the station is the town center. Nearby are the tall apartments. Farther out are the row houses and detached homes, all with ample open space and relaxed interior pathways. The conflict of transportation is eliminated and its benefits are simultaneously maximized. The value of Vällingby, therefore, is its magnificent complimentarity—open space and dense development, spaces designed for walking and freedom to drive, and compatible transportation at the center of town.

The crucial relationship of cluster development and rail transportation is that both happily function best when focused at nodal points on a map. Vällingby has demonstrated how the nodal points of each may be complementary. For community, the concept of compact space at the center and open space at the periphery best provides for convenient services, growth of indigenous institutions, local diversity, and social coherence for the individual. For transportation, nodal points of population are easier to serve than a population that is spread out along a continuum or throughout a wide area.

Numerous implications arise from the integration of public transportation within concepts of clustering and principles of community. They present the urban designer and architect with a new range of objectives, a new breadth of challenge, and a fuller complement of tools for achieving more socially purposeful variety in the environment. The direct relationship of social values and social coherence to the urban physical form may provoke and assist the designer to achieve more than a usable enclosure and a handsome facade at a minimum cost. Utility, facade, and cost now necessarily dominate design and offer little civilized potential, especially when property is chopped to its minimum denominator of usability.

Enlargement of the *social* horizons of physical design is critically needed to counter the gross alienation imposed by the Big Society in its megalopolitan form. A physically coherent form is the first prerequisite for a *meaningful social variety*, locally rooted but with easy access to cosmopolitan diversity. A future good life may well depend on society's achieving many seemingly contradictory purposes: organization and freedom from organization, work and freedom from work, wealth and freedom from wealth, intimacy and anonymity, commitment and freedom. Many of these apposable values may depend on a combination of intense urban development and a cosmopolitan environment with a natural spaciousness, both in community and in the city as a whole.

Very possibly the most important reconciliations between apposable values may be evolved in the community. And the community's limited diversity may be the most significant social diversity, for it will be a local diversity of, by, and for people.

The diversity that might be resolved within the clustered community may be noted in two opposing concepts. First, one may appreciate the metropolitan milieu of the streets revered by Jane Jacobs in her book, *The Death and Life of Great American Cities*.[3] She makes a telling case for a lot of people living in compact areas with intimate spaces (streets) that are lined with numerous retail shops, workplaces, and cultural institutions. One may just as well appreciate with Ebenezer Howard, Clarence Stein, and other urban planners the carefully planned benefits of new towns, neighborhood unit plans, and "greenbelt" planning. These men sought relief from the debilitating chaos of overbuilt cities by assuring an integrity of the home and living areas, ample parks, a serene setting, and other features of orderly development.

The significance of the two positions is that they are not basically contradictory within the concept of cluster development. Clusters resolve in a structural way the two central qualities of urban living that are often considered most inconsistent: urban vitality and urban serenity. In doing so they create a new social rationality in the use of land and the development of space.

In her own way Mrs. Jacobs values community. Certainly also the community-oriented planners never rejected metropolitan diversity. No doubt the planners overreacted against the bewildering blight and the depersonalized diversity of the industrial city. What both Jacobs and the planners have to say is highly important; what is now required is a synthesis.

It is amusing and a bit ironic that possibly the best example of a consciously designed urban synthesis exists at Disneyland in California. Besides keeping the scale small and giving unusual attention to detail, the designers put together a most exciting open diversity of structures, rides, and demonstrations, yet shielded the visitors in some areas from "outside" annoyance, obtaining undivided attention to these particular events. For example, the ride through the "Congo," though but a few yards from other events, is unusually well shielded from the sights and sounds of these events. Some attractions are skillfully protected for particular effect, others remain a part of a broad milieu of sensation and activity. This would seem to be a quality of a good community and a good city.

But in our efforts to resolve the "problems" of our cities, instead of seeking to bring together and harmonize the diverse physical qualities of urban life, we usually strive only to overcome space. Typical is the project to widen the New Jersey Turnpike from six to twelve lanes, which will funnel ever increasing traffic into the overcrowded Hudson River tubes and into Manhattan at a cost of 350 million dollars. The project, based upon projections of traffic, illustrates the self-contradictory nature of auto travel. In judgment, *Fortune* magazine was led to say that "if this madness continues, cities will have to hang out signs similar to those on the parking lots: 'Full Up.' "

And the more we look at the whole city, the less basic and more costly the solutions seem to be. All transportation efforts will remain partly self-contradictory until an urban form is realized that *minimizes the need for transportation*. Inefficiency tends to feed on itself, and the level of efficiency of the American city now reflects a century of free-for-all growth. In a society devoted to increasing efficiency, it is becoming plain that the city itself is a most important productivity unit, and it may now be the greatest drag on the efficiency of the whole economy. Once again we see society's microcosmic efficiency deranged by macrocosmic chaos. And even more important than productive efficiency is the development of a wholesome and invigorating social habitat, for the city also lacks large social purposes.

The scale and dead weight of urbanism are growing in vast proportions. As our cities now disperse and spread upon each other, it is clear that urbanization is a continental matter, beyond what the cities and states can conceivably manage. This makes imperative the creation of a profound and comprehensive national habitation policy. Recent decades have seen the growth of broad economic, scientific, and educational policies. The impact of urban development dictates a rigorous and liberal concern of comparable intent, for cities are falling to their knees from their own dinosauric weight.

CITY FOR MAN

Inevitably the future city will combine masses of men with masses of machines, more even than it does today. But in developing the future city man must become neither so mixed with machines that he loses his dignity nor so mired in his own urban masses that he loses his person.

For the city to achieve greatness it must first attain *a unique social and cultural place for every person*. It may then elevate its inhabitants, the varied richness of whose accomplishments may in turn prosper the city. The essence of a great city lies in this reciprocity with its people.

A number of difficult questions are thus posed for the contemporary city. Can civic excellence arise as a residue of separate private interests working only for their separate purposes? Can we allow our cities and regions to continue to be developed as marketable commodities? Or should we view them as profound trusts? Is something more than prosperity essential to the attainment of urban value—especially when so much wealth is required to socially ameliorate the means to produce wealth? Are cities, in Mumford's words, to be embodiments of immortal technological forces and institutional practices? Is the city the place to stage a struggle for the survival of the fittest between man and metallic beasts?

These are questions touching upon a deep disorder in civic life today. "The current trend," writes Norton Long, "to reduce citizenship, at least at the local level, to a sort of free-floating consumership, attests to the serious decline in the appreciation of political values. . . . There is good reason to believe that the crisis of our cities is a crisis of our civic life." [4] And does not the crisis of our civic life really rest deeply in the way in which we structure human association in cities? Have we not abandoned our faith in the individual person in favor of the institution, making him institutionally functional but personally irrelevant? Even some three decades ago a public report on cities recognized that "the tenuous relations between men, based for the most part upon a pecuniary nexus, make urban existence seem very fragile and capable of being disturbed by a multitude of forces," and this leaves many men "with a paralyzing sense of individual helplessness and despair." [5]

A new civic faith therefore seems to be called for, a faith that will focus its principal attention upon the individual person in vital association— stimulating and challenging while yet comforting, exciting and also rewarding, commonplace and still meaningful, peaceful while enriching. On the other hand, the city where men reside and associate cannot be fraught with safety problems or even safety precautions, burdened with dead spaces, interrupted by fractious noises, isolated by specialized performance, or overwhelmed by immensity. These suggest that future urban development will have to be far more exacting, requiring a socially purposeful direction that is now the prerogative of economics and technology. Resolute attention must be called to the whole range of conditions affecting human sensibilities in their urban environment.

10

Ethics for Institutions

A. N. Whitehead once warned that "no more deadly harm can
be done to young minds than by depreciation of the present." On another occasion he asserted that "the task of a university is the creation of
the future."

Generalizing upon Whitehead's two views, we can infer a basic ethical
relationship between men and their institutions, a relationship based upon
distinguishing between the present and the future, between rights and
responsibilities, and identifying each of these with men or institutions. In
effect, Whitehead proclaims that the "insistent present" is the *right of men*
while the promise of the future is the *responsibility of institutions.*

Our consideration of institutional ethics will follow from this premise.

ETHICAL UNDERPINNINGS

The corporation is one of society's master tools, argues Adolph
Berle. The corporate society is the result, admits William Gossett of the
Ford Motor Company.

It is hardly surprising that the rush to organize and develop powerful
bureaucratic capacities is central to the struggle for economic growth.
However, the rush might well alert us again as to how essentially new and

193

pervasive are these corporate dynamos of world development in the life of every person.

Of course ancient China, Egypt, and Rome each had bureaucracies of a sort, but theirs were limited and rigid. Ours are developing a virtually infinite repertoire of action, being our chief sources of both technical and cultural innovation and at the same time our most reliable instruments to guide and manage the complex currents of change.

The awesome importance of modern bureaucratic organization, whether business, government, or other, is how it transcends the individuals who are a part of it, being a dynastic object in which both sovereign and subject are subordinate contractors to its ongoing purpose. The individual person is a *conditional participant*, not an *inalienable member*. Yet bureaucracy is second to none as an organizing force in social as well as economic life.

The ethical implications are profound, unprecedented, and deeply disturbing, though not without positive possibilities. For if all social action is ultimately reducible to questions of ethics, organized social action is then ultimately reducible to the institutional patterns in which ethical action is shaped.

This proposition, without removing ethics from the realm of individual conscience, clearly places the ethical underpinnings of a corporate society in the realm of achievable social purpose. Furthermore, ethical purpose becomes a concrete aim of conscious design of institutions, comparable to that of building safety into the engineering of automobiles (as in tires, brakes, headlights, windshields) and highways (alignment, visibility, surface, warning signs). Of course, safety engineering does not eliminate accidents, but it does systematically eliminate specific causes of accidents and injuries. The clear implication is that every institutional feature that organizes or affects human behavior be analyzed and adjusted, sometimes quite radically, more often in numerous minor ways, to improve the moral content of institutions and individuals. Like safety engineering, the task is a never-ending one.

Among the anomalies emerging with the age of industry, none seems to have arisen more silently than this question of the ethics of institutions. The silence is deafening, for while the ethical powers of institutions have rapidly increased, their direct responsibility for the ethical environment of the individual has actually diminished. Rather than being concerned with the whole individual, as a person, as were the churches and the early guilds, their *concern* has shifted to an *interest* in the individual and this has narrowed to special aspects of his being, most often as a consumer or employee.

Unified, distinctive, formal, and authoritarian in their own right, modern organizations are able to combine the capabilities of many kinds of human skills and machines to achieve specific results. But as a consequence, they also command well-developed strategies to employ, manage, influence, educate, or outrightly control individuals in most of their waking moments. Although there is still ample room and stimulation for immoral behavior by individuals, much ethical ground has shifted from the individual acting by and for himself to his institutions. Ethical problems for society are now more likely to reside in highly organized, large-scale, and monotonously reliable bureaucracies than in overt acts against life and property by individuals.

Therefore a striking anomaly lies in the efforts of churches and schools to imprint moral precepts into young minds when the important ethical initiative lies more powerfully in corporations, government agencies, professional associations, and sometimes in the schools and churches themselves. Moreover, the relative futility of individual moral action, when measured against organizational practices, tends to promote disenchantment and engender a take-it-or-leave-it cynicism about altruism in general. Indeed, altruism exists more widely among individuals than social opinion overtly warrants, and must be masked to be tolerated at all in many groups.

What popular fad or style is not stimulated by an organization that has an interest to exploit, regardless of the immediate or long-term social consequences? What organization does not teach the lie or use silence and the half-truth to achieve an advantage? What major course of government is taken without the interest or acquiescence of professional societies, farm organizations, unions, or industrial associations? Acts of government have seriously declined as a consensus of persons and are more deeply the politics of organizations.

Capitalist philosophy argues that human benefits arise from competition. However, in human terms, this is merely organized conflict and tension. Its social shortsightedness is that the playfield for competition is people. The competition tends to become an exploitation of people, whatever the material bounty. Using people to achieve particular or special objectives denies the more basic purposes of human organization: establishing a hospitable setting for human personality, meaningful association, social continuity, and broad cultural challenge. Using people for organizational purposes bites at the roots of institutional ethics.

ANATOMY OF ORGANIZED ETHICS

Until society hammers its ethical theses on the door of the corporation and other bureaucratized institutions, men will always be able to rationalize and say, "What is possible legally, politically, and economically is therefore ethical." Such attitudes may not be momentous at any one time, but over a long span they turn ethical initiative into an easy ride downhill. Institutional ethics requires its own independent foundation.

Every group, every organization produces a distinct moral atmosphere, and this always varies somewhat from the norm of the larger society. The extreme possibility is seen in the euphoric suspension of moral restraints as an individual joins a lynch mob or other mass activity. But to a degree, the same situation exists within particular organizations, for institutional behavior tends to attain for the individual an emotional validity and an authoritative ethic, whatever its level of probity.

Examine, for instance, the statement of one executive who was convicted in the billion-dollar electrical conspiracy case in 1960, involving both General Electric and Westinghouse: "It's the only way a business can be run," he said. Another person who had been convicted said it's a "way of life."

The very nature of the commercial corporation, whose parties (owners, managers, and workers) are unified only by their special interest in profits, tends to assure a narrow definition of purpose (and ethic) that prevents any compromise on making a profit. Narrow interests create narrow interpretations of social action, and there is then a tendency to press on the borders of ethically permissible forms of action. Of course, all exploitive actions are easier when anonymous, when a man is not called upon to look into the bloodshot eyes of those his actions have exploited. They are easiest when one is performing simple abstract manipulations of percentage points, or making informal agreements with a competitor, as in the electrical conspiracy.

An ethical role for institutions, however, involves far more than just remaining "morally clean." Modern institutions are too complex and their effects too far-reaching for this naive interpretation. Institutional ethics involves the whole impact of organizations upon the whole society and the whole man. It means a larger purpose than a highway department's building a highway, a company's profit from a new product, a profession's control of standards. There has been a decided improvement since business held that "the public be damned." But now the power is more complex and pervasive.

Institutional ethics hinge, therefore, upon the development of a systematic way of conceiving the form and function of organizations, more than it does upon a simple change of heart within them. In a society chiefly founded upon formal organizations in which the most important are the most bureaucratized, these inner workings are the principal objects of concern.

Of the few persons who have taken a serious look at institutional ethics, Reinhold Niebuhr is deeply pessimistic about their prospects. He argues that "in every human group there is less reason to guide and to check impulse, less capacity for self-transcendence, less ability to comprehend the needs of others, and therefore, more unrestrained egoism than the individuals, who compose the group, reveal in their personal relationships." [1]

"The relations between groups must, therefore," continues Niebuhr, "always be predominantly political rather than ethical. . . . Whatever increase in social intelligence and moral goodwill may be achieved in human history, may serve to mitigate the brutalities of social conflict, but they cannot abolish the conflict itself. That could be accomplished only if human groups, whether racial, national or economic, could achieve a degree of reason and sympathy which would permit them to see and to understand the interests of others as vividly as they understand their own, and a moral goodwill which would prompt them to affirm the rights of others as vigorously as they affirm their own." [2] Moral progress, then, according to Niebuhr, rests almost entirely upon the personal relation between one man and another. Expressed in an era when a large proportion of interpersonal relationships have become impersonal, and when most of our significant social action is highly rationalized, this attitude of a leading Christian theologian is pessimistic indeed.

I rather take the view that society can and must establish a foundation to elevate institutional ethics. Human ingenuity each decade repeatedly succeeds in arriving at solutions previously thought impossible. And have not man's greatest inspirations arisen within and because of institutions? Has not the growth of institutions stabilized and given a measure of security as well as freedom to the individual? The simple beauty of human institutions is that they have proven to be malleable in man's hand—once man has the vision to demand something more of them.

We have not really examined institutions for their expanded and diversified social potential, as we have arduously sought health in the human body, food from the soil, minerals from the earth. We only inspect institutions for functional effectiveness. Unrestrained bureaucracy is the result. Therefore, we still have extremely rudimentary perceptions of their implications for moral behavior, based on all facets of their action: patterns of organization, systems of specialized or generalized work, varieties of ownership and control, contractual methods, buying and selling practices, personnel policies, training techniques, work schedules, technological alternatives, social uses and limits of money, insurance regulations, and tax procedures. We have yet to search systematically for new forms of organization that might broaden ethical purposes and the *socially* beneficial influences of corporations, federations, cooperatives, nonprofit organizations, professional societies, trade and industrial associations, governments, and churches.

The task is extremely complex, of course. Here we shall merely suggest some initial avenues that might be followed beneficially. The diverse possibilities of organization reveal at least four areas in which institutional ethics may be squarely confronted: (1) Institutions may be identified with *moral purposes,* and these may be found in the reasons for establishment or stated in preambles and by-laws. (2) Institutions behave as *moral agents,* acting by and for themselves like individuals. (3) Institutions are comprised of parts and processes that form *moral structures* with a moral import for all persons involved within them. (4) Finally, institutions radiate a *moral tone* derived in part from the purposes, behavior, and structures that influence the moral behavior of individuals and other institutions.

Each of these areas of confrontation requires further examination.

Moral purposes are set forth foremost in what a particular institution is set up to do: produce, regulate, serve, comfort. But, as we have seen, a single good pursued without limit tends to push other goods aside. Single-minded pursuit of single moral purposes tends to cut brutally through the larger range of human moral requirements—especially the many diverse ideals in a democracy. It is not enough, then, that a single moral purpose reside within an institution. One purpose may well be motivating, as dictated by necessary divisions of labor among organizations, but one cannot be dominating. Purpose should also encompass in some positive way the total effects of organized action upon the whole individual and whole society.

As potential *moral agents,* organizations are capable of applying self-restraints upon their own behavior (notwithstanding the dissent of Reinhold Niebuhr) in about the same degree as individuals, first because they are made up of individuals and do reflect individual feelings, and second because they operate in a social context comparable to that of individuals. More than that, organizations, which after all are but massive abstractions of individual behavior, are regularly created and molded to serve men. Even organizations established for the benefit of certain limited aggregations of men should be able to "affirm the rights of others as vigorously as they affirm their own" in about the same proportion as do individuals, because their directors can shape internal charters and constitutions, codes and regulations, training and work practices, operating policies and the selection of managers and other employees to make them ethically responsive.

Undoubtedly organizations that are controlled by a few persons (establishing special interests), serve single purposes (defining an absolute goal), and specialize (promoting limited perspective) are least likely to develop a broad moral philosophy. These characteristics are precisely those most associated with the drive to production and material abundance—and are the most active power in the society today. Yet even these can reflect larger moral purposes—if that becomes an objective generally sought in the social system.

The *moral structures* of organizations are a most potent ethical vehicle for man, since they shape the ongoing daily events of all people associated with them and give authority and substance to individual decisions and actions. Every organization gives rise to characteristic ways of behavior, which have cumulative moral significance. And few are the organizations that by their patterning of events do not present dilemmas for the individual about his own moral conduct concerning truthfulness, maneuvering for advantage, actions to save face or build image. This underpinning of moral behavior lies within the labyrinth of bureaucratic devices: the wording of questionnaires, the prerogatives and prestige of hierarchies and authority, the kinds and character of anonymity, the uses of cooperativeness and competitiveness, the worthiness and *esprit* of group endeavor, the patterns of communication. These and many more aspects of organization expand or set limits on individual moral behavior.

The broad radiation from an organization having moral purposes, acting as a moral agent, and constituting several moral structures may be described as a *moral tone*. In a society in which we expect large formal organizations to take initiative for us, provide for us, protect us, and discipline and train us, we should not underestimate their power to project their character and values upon us. As a simple example, we often see how the reliability and effectiveness of an organization carries over into the individual behavior of its members or employees. We can readily see a difference in moral tone between participation in the American Friends Service Committee and the Teamsters Union. And we know that individuals transferred between them would respond to the new tone of events. One suspects that only when positive ethical examples of the Big Citizens multiply will there be a sufficient reduction in public cynicism ("I've got mine, how are you doing") to create an atmosphere where moral behavior, especially moral ideals, can be openly espoused without triggering cascades of ridicule.

Despite its superficial vitality the bureaucratic glove fits mutely and servilely the hand of him who controls it. Just as bureaucracy may freely transfer its allegiance from democratic to authoritarian masters, or the reverse, as noted by Max Weber, so also it can be made to serve high or low moral purposes.

ORGANIZED ETHICS IN ACTION

If it is possible to analyze the elements of institutional ethics, it is also possible to examine and evaluate the ethical content of particular institutions and their programs. As examples, we shall review in broad terms the Peace Corps and public housing.

Probably the most significant current demonstration of the positive aspects of organized ethics is the Peace Corps. Small private organizations have long sought to demonstrate ethics in an organized way, but the Peace Corps is an example where one would least expect it: in government. Moreover, the Peace Corps is remarkable in that it is an ethical demonstration on an international plane.

Although America has quite consistently demonstrated its military stance since World War II, it has never fully demonstrated its deeper peaceful intent. America has given overseas assistance for many years—indisputably ethical as well as political—but this deals only with money, material, and technical assistance. Internationally it involves only a few thousand advisers and administrators. The Peace Corps, however, is a national commitment of *people* to assist and to share experience with others face-to-face *as persons*. It establishes a most pertinent feature of institutional ethics: a valid and fruitful interpersonal relationship between individuals. It also establishes an organized outlet for individuals desiring an adventurous, constructive, and ethical experience.

Organization of an ethical experience of the sort provided by the Peace Corps appears to have three principal elements: (1) planning, organization, and placement of volunteers to assure a specific work assignment for immediate involvement and usefulness of the volunteer; (2) orienting and training the volunteer to help him adjust rapidly to the novel setting and to particular work conditions; and (3) covering sustenance expenses and external costs that would be prohibitive to all but an extremely few individuals. Moreover, the Peace Corps provides a continuity and a build-up of benefits by successive volunteers.

To see the alchemy operating, as I have, is nothing less than inspiring. In Sierra Leone the Peace Corps volunteers often worked singly and happily with villagers in very isolated places building roads, schools, and small water systems. It was profoundly refreshing to observe a recent psychology graduate completing with great pride a four-room addition to an eight-room school with over six hundred students. It was no less exciting to observe the deep enthusiasm and genuine rapport of a white volunteer from Alabama working with Africans on village water systems.

Despite prolonged frustrations and constant cultural misunderstandings, the lessons of humanity are endless. That a well-educated man should leave his country to serve strange people in a distant land is a completely unimaginable act to most people on earth. That a man demonstrates both education and intelligence, and then works with his hands, is equally novel for most peoples. But the volunteer himself also finds enlightenment in as many ways: learning how people can be happy without material advantages; seeing one's own society in the perspective of another; working in different systems with different materials for different outcomes.

These experiences must become more common. The present seeds are few and require time to mature and multiply. It is encouraging to see other programs similar to the Peace Corps taking hold in other countries so soon. It is encouraging also to see comparable in-country programs as well, such as VISTA in the United states.

The Peace Corps exemplifies institutional ethics as a purpose, an agent, a structure, and a tone. It begins with a clear moral purpose. It is a moral agent in that it has acted to fulfill a broad ethical purpose. It is a moral structure in that it establishes the means for moral incentives of individuals to find root and enlarges the possibility of moral relationships between individuals. Finally, it has inspired a moral tone and prompted a profound response in many countries and among millions of people, despite its being but one half of one percent of the size of the American armed forces. (Incidentally, the Peace Corps is also unique in permitting a staff member tenure of only five years, thereby assuring an individual freshness and enthusiasm that this type of institutional ethics seems to require.)

The next example, public housing, might also be said to have a moral purpose and be a moral agent, but it better illustrates the crucial importance of a moral structure and how a moral structure reflects back upon original motivations and intent.

The words that best depict the purpose of public housing in the United States are "decent, safe, and sanitary," as incorporated into housing laws. These words are direct reactions to the incredibly bad housing conditions that exist in parts of most large American cities. The words reflect acute problems of water and sanitation, heat and light, space and air; and so public housing sought to remove these aberrations of human habitation. But it sought no more, and it ignored the critical importance of a man's habitation for the social and psychic foundations of his existence. Once again we have a demonstration of society's institutional inhumanity concerning psychic and social well-being. Attitudes about poverty underlying the creation of public housing assured that miserly conceptions of man in social need would prevail. Thus the moral assumptions surrounding the development of public housing prompted the creation of a negative instrument, because they were partial and arbitrarily restrictive when in fact they were creating a complete physical environment. There was a failure to be concerned with the moral structure of the environment created by the housing projects.

The "immoral" structure of public housing is seen at many points. When associated with urban renewal's massive indiscriminate relocation, public housing destroys the complex social relationships found in older living areas. Housing only for the needy (as with prisoners and mental patients) segregates families who are the losers in society into a permanent subsociety of losers. Housing only for decent accommodation creates a sterility of the social environment.

Very largely on this foundation, housing assistance was conceived only in massive, homogeneous, isolated, and sterile terms, though recently some promising departures have begun to be proposed and tried: housing subsidies applied in renovated houses; mixed-income housing (including both subsidized and nonsubsidized); incorporation of varied activity areas, schools, community centers, and commercial shops into housing projects; smaller projects better integrated into the surrounding city. But these experiments have been too few and too slow.

The monstrous gap in the conception of public (and also private) housing is the lack of provision for diverse associations and services. When meeting rooms, informal gathering places, halls, small office spaces, and commercial shop spaces are absent, then in effect both formal and informal institutions are banned, because to function or be effective they require a righful place in a physical plan. A social vacuum is produced when housing is conceived only as "decent, safe, and sanitary." The lack of a social conception in housing therefore epitomizes an "immoral" social structure.

Yet the immorality is not limited to an initial physical design. It exists also in the administrative arrangements. Because rental levels are linked to income and because a low income is required even to remain in a project, numerous unusually cruel conditions arise. For vivid illustration we turn to a report by Mrs. Ellen Lurie, completed in 1956 and involving a public housing project in Manhattan. ". . . A large number of families had not reported salary increases" to avoid paying higher rents. "In several cases, tenants had to pay as much as $400 (for retroactive rent increases). Many tenants, especially the husbands who were interviewed, expressed great bitterness at this system. One woman, who wanted to work for a few months to save some money to send her children to summer camp, wouldn't do so because her husband felt the rent would go up much too high and when she stopped, he was afraid they'd forget to lower it. Another man, Mr. Belton, didn't know how he would ever save enough to move to his own house, because every time he took a raise, he paid more rent. More common were the men who told the interviewers of raises they had refused because they didn't want to move, for if they earned much more than they were already getting, they would be above the continued occupancy limits. In several homes with teenage children out of school, the parents weren't anxious for the children to find jobs because the teenagers usually kept the money and the parents would have more rent to pay. . . ." [3]

In another passage, Mrs. Lurie provides a broader perspective of the effects of the administered living that families must submit to in return for public housing and welfare subsidies: One family has "four children, ranging from 8 years to 14, but they are not allowed downstairs alone, because the parents are afraid someone will hurt them. . . . To protect themselves, they make few, if any, friends. Some are afraid that friends will become angry or envious and make up a story to report to management, causing them great trouble. If the husband gets a bonus (which he decides not to report) and the wife buys new curtains, the visiting friends will see and might tell the management, who in turn, investigates and issues a rent increase. Suspicion and fear of trouble often outweigh any need for neighborly advice and help. For these families the sense of privacy has already been extensively violated. The deepest secrets, all of the family skeletons, are well known not only to management, but often to other public agencies, such as the Welfare Department. . . . Perhaps this pattern is nothing more than an elaborate group mechanism to protect and preserve inner dignity in the face of so many outside pressures to conform." [4]

Do not mistake the purpose here. Public housing assistance is necessary *in some form*, probably more in the abundant future than in the less abundant past. But its problems are many. Its purpose was too narrowly conceived. The arrangements are uniform, rigid, and sterile. It was housing only, not a new social setting, not an environment for people to grow in. The people to be helped were begrudged, and the wholeness of their lives was not considered. Little wonder that crime is often higher in projects than in many slum areas. It emanates from the limited purpose of the endeavor.

Both examples—the Peace Corps and public housing—demonstrate that positive growth in ethics in institutions and institutional endeavors requires the same down-to-earth attention as does producing to make a profit, or engineering to improve safety. Higher ethical behavior can be developed if it is worked into the institutional texture of human behavior. But the efforts must be conscious, forthright, and clear-headed. They must begin and end in the highest human ideals, operate with an effective strategy, and yet be pragmatic in practice.

COUNTERPOINT TO SPECIALIZATION

The ethics of institutions are found not only in the nature of particular institutions but implicitly in the larger social structure within which organizations are created. One condition that vastly affects ethical action is specialization.

Jacques Barzun argues that specialization has become ritualized into "specialism," an "etiquette which decrees that no specialist shall bother with the concerns of another, lest he be thought intruding and be shown up as ignorant." [5]

When men are specialists within organization, the coherence of their behavior or completeness of interest lies only within the organization. Specialization means that the behavior of the individual is incomplete, reinforcing Peter Drucker's observation that organizations produce, men don't. Consequently the relationship of the individual to the organization is not that of a *member*, but that of a *part* to a whole.

The importance of this relationship is that the individual is less complete, less useful, less functional than the organization. This is another way of saying that in the new "natural" order of things the individual has become intrinsically less important than the enterprise to which he applies his talents. And the more highly specialized men are, the more critical this *organic subordination* becomes. A modern operative enterprise thus creates a new level of subordinate dependence for the person.

Today's specialization is hardly comparable to that of a traditional craftsman, who was but partly specialized. His specialty included all of the steps and skills required for at least one product—a shoe, a pot, a garment—not one phase of a lockstep process. The craftsman was largely his own entity, able to make his own decisions. And the major determinants of his life remained within the total physical, economic, and cultural interplay of his family and community, not so singularly within his occupation, employer, and economic conditions.

As specialization becomes more pronounced and is reinforced by highly specialized training, another subtle effect occurs. Special purposes, special functions, and special processes in organization—the ideal form of contemporary bureaucracy—focus interest and insight more pointedly on means and special benefits. By contrast, the broader realizations of human life, requiring free interplay of many purposes and ways of doing things, atrophy like unused muscles.

One of the more important effects of specialization, therefore, appears to be a narrowness of purpose, whereas the ethical development of institutions seems to require a broad range of purposes.

John Dewey recognized these implications when he said that "compartmentalization of occupations and interests brings about separation of that mode of activity commonly called 'practice' from insight, of imagination from executive doing, of significant purpose from work, of emotion from thought and doing." In the end, Dewey continued, we "suppose that these divisions inhere in the very constitution of human nature." [6]

And science is hardly helpful. We may observe with the late Kurt Riezler that, although many sciences look through their special lenses at man, there is not a science of man. Equally, there are many professions dealing with man, but none with a concern for man as a whole. If the professions were to be reconstituted anew under the present pressure for specialization, one might ask whether medicine, for example, might not become ten or twenty completely separate vocations. How might this affect our view of health?

Thus, while the sciences place man in a glass house and the professions process him and coddle his ailments, there are no institutions to study and guide the impact upon man of the sciences and professions themselves. Keen on specific measurements of specific effects, both the sciences and professions are unfocused to their own combined effects and long-term implications. The critic Sigfried Giedion plaintively notes that "there is no institution to help us understand the interrelations that exist between the different sciences and the realm of feeling." [7]

If as individuals we have become less whole and less able to see wholes in life, the same disability has descended upon society. Could our society today—fragmented by special interests, skills, and knowledge—produce a politically viable document as broad, complete and simple as the American Constitution? Do we have men in public affairs as diversely capable as Jefferson and Franklin, or as widely penetrating as Madison and Hamilton? And if we should be so fortunate, would our institutions permit these men to make their contributions? And, once made, could those contributions be accepted after the field maneuvers of mammoth interest groups?

One way or another this reflects Western society's many centuries of learning how to divide tasks. In the process some tasks have been misplaced and forgotten. Those forgotten most deeply are the undivided wholes—the whole man, the whole society. It is now imperative that we learn to reunify the dismantled parts of our lives, especially feelings, freely made associations, locality.

Certainly, a simple reversal of the trends of specialization will serve no purpose. But might we not begin to seek a reintegration of our divided heritage? Rather than a counteraction, we may be in want of a counterpoint, like that of community to the cosmopolitan world. But the counterpoint would need two parts—one for the society and one for the individual.

For the individual, a counterpoint to specialization might be incorporated within a redefinition of the human career, which we have previously discussed, to enlarge upon the personal benefits of work. This might coincide with a restructuring of education to stress the inherent human benefits of learning rather than the specialized utilitarian applications. Specifically, we might seek, first, a deeply humane orientation of the specialist to his specialization and, second, his broad understanding of the results of his specialization. This will be considered in the next chapter.

For the society, a first essential step in creating a valid counterpoint to the specialist is a development of the role of the generalist. Like the specialist, the generalist must be prized, trained, given scope, and rewarded before he can begin to bridge the many minute divisions of social interest of the specialist and become a responsible force in society.

Neither specifically academic, scientific, nor professional in outlook, but all three in part, such generalists might become cultural balance-wheels. Instead of seeking complete effectiveness for particular kinds of knowledge, they would seek balance and order in the larger frame of knowledge. Interrelationships, composite results, and lasting influences would be their vital concern.

There might be numerous kinds of generalists. Perhaps each generalist might define his own scope and focus of interest. This does not imply a new array of specialists but rather that the generalism has its degrees. There can be no ultimate generalists, just as there can be no ultimate specialists, however we try. Each generalist might spread his umbrella over a number of specializations. Some generalists might span the physical sciences, some the social professions, some all the sciences and professions.

But a span of concern is meaningless without a focus. One science generalist might attend to the future of science, another to the future effect of science upon man, as do C. P. Snow and the technological prognosticator, Richard Meier, each in his own way. A generalist might begin with a problem, such as the future biological evolution of man, and then select the span of knowledge that bears upon that question. In turn, his work might have influence in other arenas, such as specialized research, public policy, and social attitudes. Another generalist might begin with a span of interest, such as the social sciences, and gradually focus upon a problem.

Evidently generalists must be relatively free of the categories, rankings, registrations, and discipline imposed by the contemporary specialized professions (academic, scientific, and professional). In other words, there might be a lot of the amateur in the generalist, to assure that his interest will guide his own line of investigation and permit him a free range of movements and contacts. As it is, a man's responsibility tends to be rigidly boxed, in both content and character, and to be circumscribed by his profession and employing organization. Whatever his particular orientation, what the generalist requires is a broad, open-ended responsibility ultimately focused on the whole society.

Western society has always had a few generalists by the grace of individual genius. They have been extremely few, however, and have penetrated but a few of the broad problems and possibilities of the present time, though their influence has been disproportionately great.

The contemporary character of education, the pressures toward a specialized career, and the niches in which society organizes its members and compensates and honors individual endeavor have all combined against the generalist. But still the generalists have emerged: Churchill and his breadth in public affairs, Toynbee and his historic scope, and the social criticism of De Voto and Mumford. Other contemporaries come to mind: Peter Drucker, Paul Goodman, Jacques Barzun, Gunnar Myrdal, and Barbara Ward.

That these and other leaders have arisen independently in no way implies that persons should not or cannot be educated for such broad tasks, which every specialized advance in society makes more urgent. Given time, a form of education can be evolved to train generalists and evolve a generalist tradition. Current curricula in the liberal arts, for example, are inadequate because they are essentially specializations and emphasize a professional methodology. Furthermore, there is not presently a positive ethic or methodology appropriate for the generalist. Especially the compartmentalized treatment of subject, theory, and responsibility—whether in physics, psychology, or art—places a steel band about the thinking of a potential generalist. Even the field of philosophy has been narrowed to fit this mold.

Although we may not know how to educate generalists, as we do specialists, we can shape education to the generalist's clear potential. We can aerate the curriculum and recompose it to stimulate thought on the interconnected results of action. We can find ways of stimulating minds toward both the macrocosmic and the microcosmic arena. We can bring many of our most able minds to explore the broadest questions with indifference to the jealous etiquette of specialism.

Of course, any preparation for generalization must lead to involvement and usefulness. Perhaps every corporation, every government agency, every large association, every community, should have its "philosopher." But he must remain without authority, and outside normal hierarchy and responsibility, for the generalist's broader and longer-term contributions may well thrive on a new level of freedom. Such a person might be given a "commission" instead of being a "member of the staff." He must always be free to serve the higher claims of social responsibility, perhaps allowing only his judgment of posterity to impose itself upon his thinking. Probably his sanctity should transcend even that of the scientist, calling for every protection of his breadth, integrity, and ultimate responsibility.

The generalist is also needed in administration to create the kind of order required for personal and social coherence of bureaucratic action. That cannot occur until organization is restructured in a way comparable to its restructuring for functional effectiveness. We shall now consider the ethics of the generalist administrator and the integration of administrative action.

INTEGRATION FOR COMMUNITY DEVELOPMENT

This chapter has dwelt upon institutional ethics. Earlier, in Chapter 7, we discussed three objectives of community development: the use of community for development, the amelioration of development, and the development of community. Now we shall illustrate certain possibilities for achieving all three objectives of community development as well as a more humane structure of organization.

To an important degree, institutional ethics may be equated with order. The order most important to ethics is that which affects the individual. The kind of order most important to the individual is that which is felt personally and emotionally every day, not that which is technically or economically or administratively smooth for the society.

One vital determinant of order for the individual is the governmental framework, especially the branches of government that deal directly with him or his community. If they are many, if they tend only to their special functions, if they have varied jurisdictional boundaries, and if they have uncoordinated programs, they then have a splintering effect on community. To splinter the community is to splinter the environment of the individual. Under the American federal system today this is the effect of federal and state agencies upon local government. In large cities this is the effect of numerous municipal agencies upon local living areas.

When we look at federal programs designed to provide assistance to local areas, we find that in 1963 there were over 70 agencies administering more than 140 types of services or assistance to localities. The varied antipoverty programs have since come into being. (Some years ago it was noted that there were over 140 *sets* of federal field service areas, and now the Bureau of the Budget is unable to say how many there are.) Such programs are born of different legislation, and carry with them separate purposes, qualifications, timing, and administrative requirements. Since grant-in-aid type programs usually are special-purpose, develop under rigid administrative regulations, and yet arise out of complex local political circumstances, the benefits are often questionable: agricultural improvements where agriculture is obsolete and declining; housing in isolation from commercial services, social institutions, welfare services, and urban planning; highways to depressed areas without means to make them useful. And because the channels of assistance and the means of initiative are so complex and cumbersome, devising unified programs to do justice to local circumstances and local institutions approaches the impossible. A planning report termed it an "exponential hardship . . . beyond belief." [8]

The question is one of comprehensive responsibility, requiring reasonably balanced progress and a salutary influence upon local government and other local institutions.

This approach is also highly consequential for the objectives of community development. When varied programs are integrated for comprehensive benefits, they are—at least by their form and structure—a community development program. Community development is not just a program among programs; it is a combined effort for a combined effect. In a large sense community development gives social structure and quality to what is done; it has relatively less to do with the quantitative aspects of what is done.

This means that community development, stripped to essentials, is closely tied in with the structure and practices of public administration. Therefore, a philosophy of public administration oriented to the individual and the individual's context in society, and incorporating this philosophy into a unified framework of action, becomes largely indistinguishable from community development.

In our present structure of public administration the multiplicity, inconsistency, and incompleteness of assistance and service to local development through isolated lines of management frustrate those who struggle for better over-all planning of physical development, public services, and the development of local institutions. The frustration centers upon the allocation of authority to specialized agencies at the expense of coordinated interdisciplinary administration in the field.

Historically, three major principles of structure have come to dominate organization today. *Hierarchy* concentrates authority in one head and maintains control through strict lines of subordination; this serves the integrity of the organization. *Staff and line* separates counsel from command; this serves the integrity of the decision-making process. Functional or specialized *departmentalization* is simply group specialization; this serves the integrity of particular functions. But as yet there is no widespread use of a principle serving the integrity of many activities upon one man or one community.

If we examine the constellation of action in the federal government, we soon observe that the highest level at which the specialist functions is the level to which legislation is most frequently directed, the level at which program policy is most effectively advanced or frustrated, and the level that most effectively controls the organization of program. The level of the highest specialist is also the level from which field administration usually branches out: the Bureau of Land Management rather than the Department of the Interior maintains the significant operative field organization. So do the Social Security Administration; the Office of Manpower, Automation and Training; and the Area Redevelopment Administration in their respective departments. Except for departments that have a degree of functional specialization at the secretarial level, such as Post Office or Justice, departments are hardly more than umbrellas for household administration. The significance of this is indicated by wide use of the term "operating agencies."

Administrative organization by functional departments or bureaus is integrated vertically. That is, the only valid responsibility of the field officer of the Area Redevelopment Administration in Palo Alto, California, is directly to his superior in Washington. Horizontal coordination with other field headquarters in the western part of the country, such as the Office of Economic Opportunity, has no authority behind it and must overcome unrelated and conflicting administrative patterns. Consequently, coordination between agencies in the field is isolated from the normal course of events. This has led the administrative theorist James Fesler to comment that ". . . to a remarkable extent the only line of relationship of a field agent is vertical. With his eyes so strongly developed for looking upward and downward, the muscles that would turn his eyes to the right and to the left tend to atrophy." [9]

Remarkable too is the fact that while vertical coordination is seated in firm authority at every level of administration, the only structural and authoritative means for horizontal coordination of many federal agencies is with the overburdened President. In effect this means that while specialized functions deserve integration, broad programs for whole regions, states, cities, and communities do not. At the end of the administrative line, the citizen is greeted with a plethora of action and motion, but little sense of purpose, certainly no sense that he is worth any unity of federal action. Here is a pointed illustration of Nisbet's observation that the theory of administration has not done justice to the complexities of personality and culture.

When government fails to achieve a comprehensiveness (or unity of effect) and when it fails to plan flexibly for regions and local areas, for local government and local institutions, people are inevitably dealt with in pieces rather than as wholes. Underlying this pattern of organized action is a basic disregard for people, however the "problem-solving" bureaus and compensatory benefits may multiply. It is a disregard for their integrity, their common or unique aspirations, their persons.

Historically the domination of organization by functional departments has made possible the concentration of technology for new achievement in *particular* spheres of endeavor. We can now see that this line of development has left the organization by specialized departments with a reduced *over-all* unity of effect.

Fortunately the history of administration also provides examples of strong horizontal coordination. The best example exists where there is the most pressing need for a unity of effect by many disciplines: in military organization. The military is also where the generalist maintains a clear superiority over the specialist, at least in field command. Nevertheless, specialization is highly advanced and effective.

Although there are numerous variations, the Army is basically composed of three organizational elements. The fighting forces are the means of action; all military organization serves to make them effective. Then, there are the support forces (quartermaster, transportation, signal, medical, engineers, and so on). Except at central terminal and service points service forces are *attached* to combat units. Finally, of course, there is the staff, which *facilitates* decision and control by gathering and managing information and by analyzing and planning the mass of detail required for unified action by a complex organization. Yet, the central and significant line of authority always remains—as if there were no specialists.

Fesler suggests essentially the same features for civil administration: "Perhaps the most promising opportunity . . . lies in the perfecting of machinery for vertical coordination of single functions among several real layers." [10] That is, many functional specialists in a given region or district would be responsible primarily to a *general administrator* in that region or district, rather than directly to numerous specialized supervisors, as is now the case. Fesler also notes the direct human implications of this kind of adjustment. "It would appear," he says, "that functions must draw together and abandon some of the niceties of specialization when brought face to face with the ordinary citizen in his local setting . . ." [11]

The implication of such a change is that the functional role of the specialist would not diminish, but his sweeping authority would. This is realistic and socially just, because the specialist deals with means and has only a distant connection with the broader ends of a government or any large institution. Certain lines of authority would very likely always remain with the specialist to assure continued vertical integration: qualifications of personnel, training, performance standards, and procedures. Variations of this arrangement are in use; for example, some specialized staff divisions were classified in this way in General Motors' reorganization back in 1921.

The generalist described here is an administrator and should be distinguished from the generalist discussed in the previous section (or the generalist we shall discuss in Chapter 12). Although both may seek a wide perspective, the general administrator is of necessity confined by organizational imperatives, and this inevitably limits his interest and outlook, as well as his behavior.

For organization, the crux of the matter again is that a general authority is required at each appropriate level before an administration can even begin to perceive and clarify an entire problem, and before anything like a general combined approach is feasible. Getting a whole view and dealing with the whole question is the first requirement. In human terms, that is what is so central to community development. Unmistakably the critical question lies in organization, especially in achieving a more humane or ethical responsiveness *within organizational structure*.

Undoubtedly, the question of institutional ethics is as diverse as that of institutional effectiveness—a task that has occupied men's attention and inventiveness for centuries. The question of ethics is significant for all subjects we have discussed. In considerable measure it may be equated with planning, especially that part dealing with goal formulation, which will be considered in Chapter 12.

11

Unleashing Liberal Education

One of the current challenges to education is the astonishing hypothesis "that any subject can be taught effectively in some intellectually honest form to any child at any stage of development." In support Harvard Psychologist Jerome Bruner adds that "no evidence exists to contradict it; considerable evidence is being amassed that supports it." [1] And, according to the foundation studies of Jean Piaget, the earlier one's education begins in life, the more of one's intellectual capacity can be developed. Both propositions imply a more advanced education beginning at an earlier age.

James Conant has taken a similar position in *Slums and Suburbs*, stressing that what the schools can do with a child from the slums is limited by the educationally deprived environment of the home and neighborhood. Basically the same assumption lies behind current programs to break into the self-defeating cycle of the "socially disadvantaged." Questions of racial equality also may be reduced to questions of cultural deprivation.

These are challenges of education. What are we to do about them—or, really, what are we to do about the coming generations? If we respond only to the problems or opportunities that force themselves upon us, then the objectives of education have no greater merit than expediency. That is dangerous but not uncommon. For instance, Peter Drucker, who normally maintains a wider vision, has stated what has long been an

213

underlying assumption of educational purpose: "Education has become," he says, "the most advanced form of capital investment today. The more advanced a capital investment, the more productive it is, and the higher rate of return . . ." [2] If this motive is the main response to Bruner's challenge and Conant's plea, then the outlook is bleak indeed.

A century ago, when education for most people consisted largely of the three R's given a few months a year for a few years, the direction and form of instruction were not critical for the main course of society. Now, with over fifty million Americans (over 25 percent of the population) in highly organized school systems, the individual is subjected to between twelve and twenty years of systematic efforts to influence his outlook and shape his thought. The development of education therefore will help determine what the future society will be.

PERSON—A LIBERAL FOCUS

Psychology demonstrates ever more forcefully the plastic potential of human nature, especially the intellectual capacities. Slowly the work of such men as Piaget and Bruner is becoming understood: that intelligence without early stimulation is largely lost intelligence. Now dawning upon us is the realization that the later a person embarks upon education, or the less "intelligent" his formal or informal education is, the more definite is the loss. If intelligence is a highly plastic substance, then what we consider to be innate intelligence is hardly more than a mute power quite incapable of any growth or form until experience triggers and shapes its activity—not a particular value, form, or direction of development, not a particular vessel with a particular fulfillment.

These views emerge from over six decades of intensive studies of intelligence. We do not have a comparable range of study and achievement concerning other human qualities: individual worthiness, strength of character, or well-being. Evidently the overwhelming interest of society exists in the instrumental rather than the purposive values of human development. Consequently we educate almost solely for external effectiveness.

However, we can imagine some dynamic qualitative possibilities of life arising from education. Plasticity of intelligence implies a plasticity of personality as a whole. If the instrumental spirit of education were less dominating, then emphasis might shift to many qualities of being human, such as inner vitality and stability, social good will, cultural depth, independent judgment. Qualities of person arise from qualities of experience. If a person has a value-building experience, he also develops a value-rendering potential. Obviously, education must also be utilitarian. But ultimately the only justification for any social action is the complete worthiness of being human. Education is the principal institution determining the extent to which this objective can most directly be realized.

The stressing of a wider range of purposes and human qualities in education would obviously require profound changes in our approach to learning. Of course, education would be sought more for its own sake—for the experience associated with inner personal growth. The many inspirations arising from personal discovery, always highly varied and unique for every child, might outweigh our present preoccupation with routines of adding utilitarian building blocks of knowledge bit by bit.

Education will become exciting when its immediate and distant possibilities become evident and enticing to the child, when it deeply but freely involves the child and intermingles his creativity and initiative with that of his society. The principle is one of *provoking* and *responding*. First it might provoke the joy of seeing, perceiving, manipulating, relating, enlarging, creating, sharing, questioning, and reconceiving. Society might then respond by creating the conditions for a new and wider circle of discoveries—but always related to the child's own drive for understanding.

At present we constantly emphasize the endings or completedness of knowledge (that is, its fragmentary and isolated elements) by preparing students for tests that measure how completely and uniformly a group has digested each discrete block of knowledge. We ignore the open-endedness and relatedness of knowledge, as well as the more deeply questioning, imaginative, and exciting qualities of moving toward a mature and profound understanding of the world. We seek specific uniform proficiencies while diverting or killing individual thrusts toward deeper, if more unique, understandings.

Whitehead himself fought to eradicate this "fatal disconnection between subjects which kills the vitality of our modern curriculum. There is," he said, "only one subject-matter for our education, and that is Life in all its manifestations." [3]

Instead of presenting materials in minutely graded portions as building blocks for more complex concepts, to be digested in steps by means of drills and tests, we could greatly expand the provocative potential by directly confronting each child with important propositions and questions as quickly as he could even partly understand them. As he is drawn into the vital centers of knowledge—that is, as the horizons of knowledge are revealed to him—he is spurred to fill in, extend, relate. Then the flesh can be added to the bone structure almost as a matter of course.

This appears to be implicit in Bruner's proposition that any subject can be taught to any child at any stage of its development. And it was also anticipated by Whitehead when he said that "it is not true that the easier subjects should precede the harder. On the contrary, some of the hardest must come first because nature so dictates, and because they are essential," such as oral and written language.[4] Cannot serious questions of contemporary society, of science, and of the humanities be introduced in early education just as well? The perspectives thus gained—even though incomplete—then strengthen the child's perceptive grasp of the environment and make each experience more relevant, coherent, and important to him. Certain elements of advanced mathematics have already been taught successfully to young children.

This approach depends on making questions of great importance vitally important *to the student*. Questions provoke a seeking and create the sharp focus for accumulation and interpretation of factual knowledge. Emphasis is placed on the seeking of knowledge rather than on drill-forced consumption of facts, rules, and propositions. The latter is still necessary, of course, but is secondary to the wide expanses of possible knowledge and wisdom (note how in contemporary learning we slight wisdom while propounding the effectiveness of knowledge). The wider awarenesses are far less amenable to tests and drills, and can easily be destroyed by them.

Tests and grading designed for lockstep progression thus appear to defeat a deeper purpose of education, since they emphasize immediate performance, conformity, and knowledgeability over a fuller and deeper maturity. This would seem to occur especially during the earlier years. Of course, for the production-oriented society the tests and grades become the chief measure of the "product" of the school.

But this is illusory. We haven't greatly improved our education in this respect since 1952, when Arthur Bestor made his biting criticism of American schools: "Academic courses which teach men to perform mathematical computations but not to think mathematically, to manipulate laboratory apparatus but not to think scientifically, to remember dates but not to think historically, to summarize philosophical arguments but not to think critically—these advance no man toward liberal education." [5] The educational values men require most are those qualities of thought that can lead them to whatever sources of knowledge they find necessary. In this day of rapidly changing demands upon individuals even the bureaucracies are beginning to call for persons with more basic and flexible abilities.

We have been measuring education by the performance skills it develops; henceforth we might evaluate education by the depth to which it provokes inquiry in a child and by the breadth of enthusiastic challenges that can be provoked within each person. We have measured education by the minimum it should do; now we might also judge it by the maximum it might do. If deep challenges can be conveyed to the person, we need not be seriously concerned about training him for minimum utilitarian proficiencies.

The approach is one in which the frontiers of each person's understanding are stimulated far in advance of (and are generally far more important than) efforts to consolidate and test digested knowledge. There is a parallel here with discovery in science, in that the breakthrough of knowledge is infinitely more important than the filling in and elaborating of knowledge.

Yet we still process children uniformly, giving them minute undifferentiated doses of information. This but convoys the child's mind from infancy to adulthood. What value has this education for its own sake? Or what creativity arises from it? Nevertheless, we somehow expect to have a plural society and a complex social order maintained by persons with an independent judgment and a personal maturity.

We can always be relied upon to correct a child for the meanest trifling errors, but we almost completely fail to encourage broad vision or daring imagination, precisely because it involves errors. We denounce trivial error when we should applaud the quest, the daring, and the imaginative thrust. But quite characteristically, a single scale of grades is all that separates the bright from the dull, the imaginative from the sterile, the involved from the resistant.

How would the proposed provocative approach to learning contribute to the inherent values of education? If "instruction" centers upon provoking each child to seek out through his own process of discovery the heart of important questions, it necessarily responds to his own personality and his own unique development potential. Guidance may influence both the provoking and the responding, but the interest, initiative, and discovery are uniquely the person's. He is stimulated to develop his own understanding to the farthest reaches of his ability. This frontier is strikingly personal and a rewarding achievement in its own right. This magnifying of the mind-stretching qualities of discovery enlarges the inherent values of education, making it simultaneously more enjoyable, challenging, and beneficial.

A unique individual response to each person gives education a means to compensate the culturally disadvantaged child, possibly magnifying his psychic and social development early enough in life to break the cycle of social deprivation that is so easily carried from one generation to another. In the past, society's goals of equality in education have foundered upon unequal social conditioning. When students come to school with unequal backgrounds, equal opportunity in the classroom too often becomes farcical. Positive equality cannot arise until education can adjust for the handicaps many children bring with them. Positive equality will emerge only when every individual is assured an optimum and unique response to his own potential.

Another condemnation of the dull cadence of the monolithic educational procession is the kind of commitment and conformity it promotes. Are schools to turn out graduates capable only of commitments to organization and their special interests, as our corporate society seems inclined to demand? Or can we educate individuals capable of original commitments to independently determined ideas and ideals? To speak of a truly independent commitment is to speak of individuality. And, sooner or later, strong individuality is a matter of defense of the humblest freedoms: to disagree, to speak out, to go one's own way. This is one reason for alarm as many large corporations move forcefully into the subject content of education.

The crucial question becomes ever more insistent: what is the purpose of education? Is it only to concern itself with effective action? Or does it include goals and the consequences of action as well? We must ask first *what* we do, not how much we can do, or even how well we do it. Society is improving its technical competence but floundering in its purposes, precisely when the growth of powerful undirected forces creates an urgent need for clear purposes. If goals remain undefined or uninterpreted or mute, excellence in education, like excellence in technology, is likely to focus more and more on less excellent ends of society.

COMMUNITY—A LIBERAL CONTEXT

One symbolic mark of education in our time is its new massive scale: education parks of ten to fifteen thousand students and university campuses of thirty to fifty thousand. And while schools grow and become more impersonal, their administrative organization increasingly stresses specialized instruction and administrative methods. The cost is inevitably the loss of integrity for the student.

The concept of community—a scale and form of social organization to enhance social coherence and continuity for the individual—has a particular relevance to education. In this light let us consider two radically opposed experiments that have appeared almost concurrently in higher education. The first illustrates the essence of the prevailing trend; the second reveals a new trend, not yet widely accepted, of creating small colleges in clusters, thereby attaining some of the qualities we have attributed to community.

Near downtown Chicago the University of Illinois established in 1965 a major new campus for 20,000 commuting students on 100 acres reclaimed by urban renewal. The initial campus plan of buildings, completely specialized by type of function (rather than by traditional departments), will consist of: (1) twenty-one general-purpose lecture halls and an amphitheater in a Great Court, the central element of the campus; (2) a structure with sixty-five science and engineering laboratories; (3) seven buildings exclusively for general classrooms; (4) a large library and instructional resources building; (5) a twenty-eight story administrative and faculty building; and (6) three structures for student activities.

The concept is plain. Whereas on most campuses each building usually contains several kinds of facilities that serve one or more departments, each building at the Chicago campus, according to a prospectus, "will have a specific function which will enable it to be used interchangeably by all academic disciplines and will be a major factor in keeping construction costs to a minimum."

The University of Illinois thus has moved entirely to the opposite pole from the English residential college, out of which it evolved, and whose buildings, students, books, and laboratories with their varied associations and facilities of scholarship form an intimate *unity for scholars*. The new Chicago campus strikingly expresses the epitome of educational *processing* in a mammoth marketplace of courses. The students (and faculty) must pass from building to building as they progress from function to function: lecture, laboratory, classroom, library, faculty appointment, or recreation. There is no place that a student can call "home," which many students could do in departmental buildings that housed most or all of these functions. Since each student must shift very frequently, the plan (which quite symbolically uses the term "express walkways") is designed for mass movement between buildings.

This campus removes learning as far as possible from the normal behavioral and emotional setting of the person. Learning is conceivable only when the student enters one of his formal educational niches—lectures, laboratory, library, faculty office—at the various corners of the campus. There are negligible chances for casual intellectual association among students or for informal meetings between the students and faculty. Since there are no living quarters, there is little connection possible between the process of learning and one's personal life. Conceived for processing, the campus rationalizes courses, credits, and grades to produce graduates, not mature and well-rounded human beings.

Nevertheless, somehow the president of the university found courage to say that "in its partnership with the community . . . the urban university is more than a teacher of youth and a provider of academic service. It is an instrument for the harmonization of the various elements in the general social structure. Following the scholarly way, accepted by all, it can be a welding force in the inevitable decisions of community life . . ." [6] In reality the planning of the campus would do better justice to the Chicago stockyards (not far away), which have a similar differentiation, as well as express walkways.

The University of California is also establishing new campuses on a very large scale. Like two others planned in the state, the 2000-acre site at Santa Cruz will eventually enroll 27,500 students. But the other two campuses do not reveal the same degree of concern for person as shown at Santa Cruz, where the large enrollment will be *scaled down and organized for the individual student.*

The campus will consist of from fifteen to twenty semi-independent residential colleges and nine or ten professional schools, some of which will have the characteristics of colleges. Each college will have its own small campus, its own library and other essential facilities, as well as faculty and students. Each college campus design will be "inward" looking, expressing its self-containment. Enrollments will vary from 250 to 1000 students.

Each college will develop its own distinctiveness. "A determined effort will be made to reach the whole individual," states the academic plan, and this appears eminently plausible, for the college will be the student's "center of academic life, a place where he lives, dines, leads most of his social life, and centers his athletic and recreational activities." Further, each college will have its own *resident* dean and ten or twelve *resident* fellows and preceptors for informal continuing stimulation of students in an atmosphere of serious interests of the mind. Courses will be small, stressing the seminar and tutorial methods of instruction.

But the advantages of bigness are not lost by scaling the colleges to the individual. "At Santa Cruz the intent is to combine the advantages of a small college with the facilities of a great University." [7] The core of the entire Santa Cruz campus will contain the central library and administration, with a cultural and academic center adjacent to it on one side and a science center on the other. Every student will have access to the central facilities and the courses at other colleges. However, he must take most of his courses at his own college, the home for most of his activities.

Education at Santa Cruz is conceived as a complete *experience,* arising from a whole environment devoted to learning, from a continuing and penetrating dialogue of faculty and students, and from the guidance, frankness, and confidence of those who share an outlook, enthusiasm, or belief. The small scale by itself accomplishes little, but it makes possible many worthy things that can happen between and among individual persons.

Educationally, the college plan epitomizes community: a finite and cohesive environment open to broad aspirations—that is, a partly self-contained society that remains a part of a larger society. It is a scaled setting for the wholeness of the man, but also a doorway into the vast opportunities afforded by the whole civilization.

The University of California faces ominous growth requirements in the decades ahead, measuring not tens but hundreds of thousands of students. Yet even with these masses of students, the University is actually improving its attention to the individual. (We should note that Santa Cruz was planned well ahead of the riots at Berkeley, but reflected a prior and growing concern about the mass dissociation of students.) Whereas "excellence" might have been sought in massive and daring architecture or in a new form of academic or administrative initiative, it was properly focused upon the integrity of the individual and his learning process. As it is, excellent architecture and new academic and administrative forms are in fact arising from the college system.

There are strong reasons for the development of very large university campuses—reasons as varied as the number of specializations, complementarity of fields, and economy of facilities and instruction. The difficulty has been the imperceptible but steady loosening of interpersonal ligaments and the loss of the inner values of education as the scale of numbers multiplies. The plan for Santa Cruz, which owes its American precedent to the far smaller Claremont Colleges system in Southern California, is the first major answer to this kind of giantism in education.

The same powerful arguments for large-scale operation usually do not apply in the primary and secondary schools. Still, as Americans acquiesce toward massiveness, undifferentiated bigness is making headway in the form of education parks—large sites serving a number of schools. Administrators and boards of education are finding many local or temporary justifications for clustering a number of elementary, a number of secondary schools, or both, on one site: the lack of good or inexpensive sites within local service areas, racial integration, and economies of scale.

The meaning of education parks as they have been proposed is: (1) the massing of students in some fashion for administrative (that is, noneducational) reasons and (2) the removal of the students and the institution from the locality where the student lives.

As for massing, the congregation of schools at one site offers a highly tempting opportunity to rationalize facilities, functions, processes—and people. For example, to minimize the necessarily high transportation costs associated with education parks the schools might stagger their schedules to make better use of buses, a simple and unobjectionable change on the surface. But then bus schedules compel a particular kind of coordination for purely administrative reasons. Other facilities are also pressed for joint use: auditoriums, cafeterias, playgrounds. Sooner or later someone will note that one principal and one office are more economical than three or four. More and more decisions will be made for noneducational purposes, and the individual will be more and more lost and imprisoned within larger, more rigid, more demanding bureaucracies.

The second meaning of educational parks is that they rob the already sterile living areas of their last significant institution. They make the overly mobile city more mobile, the overly specialized urban fragmentation more arbitrarily specialized, the overly anonymous life more anonymous, the distant institutions more distant. What deep meaning can a child's neighborhood environment or any environment have when it is socially so barren? A personal value of life is lost when there is no stimulating diversity near the home.

Schools, whether elementary or university, are far more important than merely what they teach. They are important for what they are, where they are, what forms they take, and what larger forms of society they are a part of. The elementary school, the high school, and the university all have an important bearing on the quality of the urban environment. At one level their best place is as a part of community; at another level it is in the formation of student community.

COMMUNITY ACTION—A LIBERAL VALUE

The fragmented fringes of education—the night school, summer school, correspondence school, in-service training, special institutes and workshops—aim primarily at filling gaps left in one's initial training. Despite their evident advantages of open-endedness, opportunity for experiment, potential involvement in local affairs, contemporaneousness, and flexibility, they have not developed more than a patchwork purpose or place in education.

No such confined spirit motivated the lyceums and chautauquas of the nineteenth century. These two movements sought simply and completely both the benefits and the enjoyment of popular enlightenment. From 1826 until the 1860s as many as 3000 local lyceums sponsored lectures and study groups on a wide span of liberal and scientific subjects. Henry Steele Commager says in *The American Mind* that "the catalogue of any lyceum over a period of years suggests not only catholicity of interest but a standard of popular intelligence that could not be matched elsewhere in the world and that was far more rigorous than that imposed by radio in the next century." [8]

Later in the nineteenth century the chautauqua sparked a grass-roots interest and a more definite organization of programs and instruction in languages, speech, music, physical education, science, and theology. Its many lectures, forums, conferences, and cultural programs gained an academic reputation, and its pioneering involved correspondence courses, summer schools, university extension, and book clubs.

Both movements were popularly organized and community based— mostly in small towns, it might be noted, where a social coherence and civic spirit was still capable of mustering enthusiasm and participation. Any subject could be included, and any person might attend the full range of local programs without regard for his background. But the lyceums disappeared for a lack of a properly supported institutional base, and the chautauqua slowly retreated to its birthplace in Chautauqua, New York, as mass urbanization and technical specialization came to dominate the setting of education.

It was also in the large cities with growing industries that the grim night schools of the late 1800s began helping those without a sufficient educational base to become proficient in the technically demanding urban environment. Thus, as the liberal approach of the chautauquas began to recede, the struggles of the urban masses to overcome their technical deficiencies by night study revealed the growing instrumental character of education. It also revealed how the elevating of men's status had come to replace the elevating of man himself.

Such experiences merely suggest the larger role that continuing education might play, especially in countries with a growing wealth and free time: to diversify and deepen human inspiration, stimulate individual and social renewal, bring vitality to local affairs, and give greater enjoyment to learning and doing. The potential might well complement other social possibilities previously discussed: community and community development, redefinitions of careers, the reformation of cities, and the humanity and ethics of institutions.

The great opportunity in defining a fuller purpose for continuing education lies in the possibility of close involvement with the activities and issues of the community, city, and metropolis. On the one hand, continuing education might evolve directly out of the ongoing adult interests, institutions, and traditions of the locality it serves. On the other hand it might tap latent interests and stimulate new institutions and action programs.

In Los Angeles, for example, the University of California Extension Division sponsored the creation of the Theater Group in 1959 with the assistance of many professional actors, playwrights, and directors. In a city previously barren of good amateur theater the Theater Group has not only produced many enthusiastically received plays, but regularly presents symposia on them for their subscription audience.

As yet, however, continuing education has hardly engaged the diverse possibilities of cultural life, especially on a popular basis with a vital role for the amateur. And with civic groups, continuing education can relate understanding to action on issues such as localizing the values of metropolitan government, overcoming the deficit of beauty and creature comforts in downtown areas, or readjusting the role of the automobile in fashioning the form of living areas.

Of paramount importance is the tremendously significant role of highly focused knowledge and a sharp dialogue in any civic action on the more profound problems challenging mass civilization. This is what calls for a contemporary, experimental, and flexible quality in adult "lifelong" learning. This is the open-endedness and involvement most needed in the future of "extension" education. The joining of understanding with action will be necessary for the reestablishment of public or community life in the metropolis—that is, for a level of social intercourse intermediate between family intimacy and metropolitan anonymity.

Very likely the most burdensome task for continuing education will be to help achieve a physical and social unity of the various parts of a city—a civic unity having a common perspective so that dialogues can take place. This foundation underlay the establishment of the lyceums and chautauquas in the setting of independent small towns. And even a degree of physical and social unity in the metropolis will require concerted action among many public agencies and groups.

A step in this direction has been taken in Kansas City, which created a dozen-odd community councils through its municipal Community Services Division. Each council is assisted by a community worker, who acts as executive assistant and as a liaison with the city government. Each council's area is identical with a high-school service area. This common area begins to establish a physical and social unity upon which dialogue can take place in a meaningful context. But it is only a start. Physical planning is required to steadily promote a physical coherence for each of the areas as new highways and other physical developments take place.

Upon these initial foundations for community (that is, the councils, the high schools, and their common boundaries), highly varied and provocative courses, seminars and workshops might also be offered, each focused upon a potential within a particular community. Debates might explore specific topics that attain wide interest. Under the aegis of continuing education, classes might prepare specific prospectuses for consideration by the people. Such activities of education could form the basis for steady long-term community development.

Continuing education, if it is to be responsive to people, their organizations, and their community and metropolis, must achieve a sensitive and full *involvement* with those affairs. Involvement may be the chief distinction between adult education and primary, secondary, or higher education. Involvement may be, therefore, the chief foundation for defining a more independent and purposeful role for continuing education. The definition cannot be satisfied either by vocational advancement or by esoteric doses of cultural knowledge. Involvement seems to be the most vital ingredient for urban educational extension, just as it was with agricultural extension.

Purposeful direction by educators is also required. Education itself needs to take a stand, for example, on what kind of community or metropolis is desirable, before it can be useful in responding to the groping efforts of individuals, civic movements, or organizations. Boards of education and extension supervisors need to learn what is possible before they can help support a social renaissance.

We must breach the isolation and aloofness of the traditional classroom from the affairs of society. The vital interests of adults will be aroused when there can be vital involvement with important affairs. Civic affairs will become more important to more people when there is more coherence in their geographic and administrative form, when there is more knowledge about them, when the issues are highlighted by pertinent dialogue, and when the work of a "class" will have a clear connection with what might be accomplished. Classes must go into the community; the community must get into the classroom. Therefore, teachers in their own way need to be leaders in the community—cultural, civic, social, or economic. Similarly school budgets need to cover more than the cost of instruction.

It is necessary to distinguish between collegiate and continuing education. Collegiate education is directed to the future contributor who has not begun to put his education to use, while continuing education is directed to those who are already in the mainstream of life, already in the position to make immediate contribution, already active or influential. This may seem obvious, but to date the content, method, or tone of learning-related-to-action of adult life has not been affected. Are classroom lectures, recitations, and tests appropriate? Do credits and grades serve reasonable purposes of motivation and evaluation? Are the traditional fifty-minute periods and semester-long courses the right pattern? Are fields of knowledge a more appropriate organization of content than problems, issues, and social possibilities that cut across traditional academic boundaries?

Might not a community's continuing education program be in part an extension of the work of its many civic organizations: community council, city council, arts society, associations, youth groups, and even the board of education? Might not civic matters be taken up in occasional intensive four-to-eight week sessions, completely removed from the distractions of the day, and comparable to programs for middle and senior management in business? If civic life is to gain the importance it once had in Greece, one could well imagine the civic possibilities being explored just as intensively by local groups from sunrise to midnight in special programs at universities, summer camps, and retreats.

Our discussion of adult education, like so much of what is said in these pages, emphasizes civic life, for that seems to be crucial in our time. Civic life is really a funnel wherein institutions and activities can develop a new bearing toward the individual person, whether at the scale of the metropolis or the community. Perhaps this kind of involvement will give virility to continuing education.

DEVELOPMENT—A LIBERAL FORCE

After almost eight centuries of evolution, the university is now moving dramatically from the periphery to the center stage of society toward a time, according to John Gardner, when "society will be organized around the university." Notwithstanding its conservative traditions and inhibitions, higher education has already become society's most seminal and directive institution of development.

The university, more than most institutions, perhaps more than all, reaches farther into the past and farther into the future, deeper into the means and deeper into the ends, more into the relationships and possibilities, more into the character and content, and more into the successes and failures of development. For a world society that is increasingly founded upon explicit and articulate forms of knowledge the university is now becoming something of a microcosm of the future: what it does now, society will do later.

But the university's recent appearance at center stage has been anticipated—in the United States at least—by its association with many development objectives for over a century. This association took definite shape with the creation of the land-grant colleges of "agriculture and mechanic arts" after 1862. The private institutes of technology, beginning with Rensselaer in 1824 but gaining new momentum with the establishment of M.I.T. in 1865, slowly began bridging the gap between the theories and laboratories of science and the practical operations of machine shops and foundries. Finally, the lowly normal schools contributed large numbers of teachers and now are gradually rising to university status.

Other specific changes occurred within both the private and public universities to adapt them as agents of development. Especially evident is their willingness to admit large numbers of students and new fields of study. The rapid growth of schools of business after World War I reflected the growing complexity of commercial organization. More recent research contracting with government indicates a direct and purposeful development role for universities, as do the contracts of many universities to provide overseas assistance. Clark Kerr, former President of the University of California, has affirmed this in his comments about the *federal contract university* and the *multiversity*.

Almost a century ago President Charles Eliot of Harvard emphasized the development uses of universities when he said that "the University must accommodate itself promptly to significant changes in the character of the people for whom it exists." So did President Rainey Harper when he organized an extension division simultaneously with the founding of the University of Chicago. James Perkins, President of Cornell, recently reaffirmed for advanced societies the same development uses of universities. Perkins' remarks, however, did not stress the particular uses and results of knowledge but the "dynamic nature of knowledge." This knowledge, he said, is founded upon an "interplay and tension connected with its acquisition, transmission and application. It is this interaction . . . that shows the world what could be rather than what is." [9]

What now stirs President Perkins is that the university "has transformed our whole society—and the university with it." In effect, Perkins amends the timeless—and static—ideal of university teaching and scholarship to incorporate a dynamic stimulus and response between the university and a whole society, raising the university in the process to a new epochal level of cultural leadership.

Still it cannot be said that the university as it has evolved is ideally suited to fulfill the mandates of its inheritance. It is seminal, indeed radical, in its scientific and technical explorations and yet extremely reticent in philosophical and social innovations. Its work serves society in a thousand particular ways and yet, despite its relative independence in society, presents no consistent direction and perspective to society broader than its particular specializations. And it is specialization "in the name of untrammeled inquiry," writes Jacques Barzun, that plants restrictive "citadels throughout the realm of the mind." [10]

But can we remain so partial and narrowly extravagant? Are not the combinations and patterns of knowledge and the purposeful uses of knowledge becoming more critical than the bare creation and effectiveness of knowledge? The form of a city is more important than any number of brilliant devices designed to overcome its defects. The character and pattern of productivity looms above hosts of new products. The importance of the use of knowledge becomes more critical as the quantity of knowledge grows, as the total social power increases, as aspirations diversify, as interdependence and common perils magnify.

If the university as a whole has played a major, if somewhat unconscious and indirect, role in past development, its position is eminently powerful today, perhaps even paramount. Although the expansion of specialized skills and research remains an important challenge, more pressing for the universities in the decades ahead will be the guidance they can give to the diverse technical and economic capacities already in motion. The universities might well strive to make every technical and economic advance in society richly rewarding in personal and cultural terms—a conspicuous failure of development to date. This massive, complex, and urgent challenge calls for a new purpose and a new foundation for acquiring, transmitting, and applying knowledge.

What universities might now strive to do is effectively unite the old Greek ideal of philosophy (that is, to seek a purposefulness and directiveness in human affairs) with the boundless technical powers being derived from science. This is the imaginative challenge facing the whole university, not merely isolated test-tube research. A. N. Whitehead has said that "a university is imaginative or it is nothing—at least nothing very useful." [11] The central challenge, therefore, is more than technical, scientific, or organizational. At base, it is ethical and cultural. It is no less than giving civilized definition to the immense capacities all parts of world society are setting into motion. "A university's major task," Harvard University President Nathan Pusey once said in an annual report, "is to respond to the deepest needs of the time, and now as in the past a university will be measured by its capacity and willingness to do this." But, as it is, universities may be forfeiting their larger cultural leadership when they allow themselves to be nationalized merely to train manpower and maintain a flow of specialized research.

Even Abraham Flexner, founder of the Institute for Advanced Study at Princeton and no friend of direct public service in higher education, had this to say about the role of the universities: "Societies have to act—intelligently, if possible—if not, then unintelligently, blindly selfishly, impulsively. The weight and prestige of the university must be thrown on the side of intelligence. If the university does not accept this challenge, what other institution can or will?" [12]

The highest potential of the university tradition, that of giving scholarly attention to the compelling intellectual challenges of society, now appears to be the least activated. Universities would seem to have a natural role in fostering the larger human purposes and in creating culturally worthy philosophies and strategies of development. But strict compartmentalization and narrowing of the university intellect has not yet permitted this role to emerge.

One compelling challenge—certainly comparable to the most advanced questions of physics or genetics—is the contemporary city. As yet the benefits of urbanism are specious indeed. It appears that the many new institutes of urban studies at the universities are not going to vitally affect that condition. But the universities do have a magnificent opportunity to experiment in creating a more livable urban habitat. Many universities are nowadays created on large virgin tracts of land, offering them an unprecedented opportunity to experiment with various urban forms, both on their campuses and in the area that will inevitably urbanize about them.

For all its range of possibilities and profound significance, urban habitation has had less systematic concern than the family kitchen. We have yet to imaginatively explore the many possibilities of multifamily structures, semipublic spaces, or family-related institutions and facilities. Nor have we considered the urbanity that might result from such simple measures as conserving urban space (for the same reasons we conserve kitchen space) and minimizing the need for both private and public urban transportation. It is fair, I think, to say that the university will be delinquent if it does not combine its experimental method with the influence it will have over urban growth to enlarge a quality of life.

Western universities have now articulated themselves to press upon far-out scientific frontiers and are but slowly recognizing the disruptive cultural whirlwind generated by growing technological capacities. If development is multiplying man's capacities, it also increases the need for command of those capacities by and for man. This imposes a responsibility, perhaps the most profound in human history, to examine, assess, and set a clear course for man's journey on earth. Yet, in this age of man's greatest surge to develop, the mood of men and the character of organization conspire to dissect and splinter thought and overlook the major questions of the age.

The university might therefore seek to awaken a new outlook and engage it to the epic questions posed by development in all parts of the world. It will not be sufficient to set up special centers and institutes to tackle these questions. The problem is deeper than that, for if the legitimacy of broad and penetrating thought about human development is questionable in the mood of our specialized times, as there is ample reason to suspect, then new institutes would soon find the means to fracture their assignments into the formless bits that give them entree into the contemporary faith. In the end, we may call for changes in the foundations and patterns of thought as great as those appearing in the shift from medieval disputations to empirical investigations.

A new purpose-giving spirit is needed in the university's missions of acquiring, transmitting, and applying knowledge. Fragmentation of issues must be brought under control. The university needs to create operative knowledge with social pertinence and intellectual plurality and to inject this human relevance into the whole generative process.

Henry Steele Commager, speaking of the newly developing countries, says that their "prodigious revolution—the greatest since the Renais-

sance . . . will make ceaseless and importunate demands upon our resources of organized intelligence. . . . That is another way of saying that
the responsibility will fall upon the university." [13] The universities' task is
to give value as well as effectiveness to development, "to make," in
Toynbee's words, "the benefits of civilization available to the whole
human race."

12

Goals and Guides
for Democratic Change

Contemporary science and technology are setting into motion a radical and incomprehensible power in society, a power in some ways as complex and as baffling as the mysteries of nature. A new kind of mystery is being created, and it holds a new magical quality for us. Our resistance to examining it honestly and facing it squarely is not unlike that of the Church four centuries ago when it resisted and condemned the investigations of Galileo.

The magical quality is admirably depicted in the old English parable of *The Monkey's Paw,* as related by the late Norbert Wiener, mathematician and father of cybernetics, in his splendid little book, *God and Golem, Inc.* In this tale a sergeant-major back from the Indian army shows an old English couple a dried monkey's paw, which is a talisman with the virtue of giving its owners three wishes. His own experience with the paw was too terrible to relate and so he casts it into the fire. But his host quickly retrieves it and wishes for £200. Soon a gentleman knocks gently on the door and solemnly tells the couple that their son has been killed at the factory, and leaves them £200 in solatium. The distraught parents quickly make a second wish to have their son back again. Soon there is another knock at the door. The parents know it must be their son, but not in the flesh, so quickly make their third wish for the ghost to go away.

The theme, Wiener warns, is the danger of magic. "This seems to lie in the fact that magic is singularly literal-minded, and that if it grants you anything at all it grants what you ask for, not what you should have asked for or what you intend. If you ask for £200, and do not express the condition that you do not wish it at the cost of the life of your son, £200 you will get, whether your son lives or dies.

"The magic of automation and in particular the magic of an automatization in which the devices learn, may be expected to be similarly literal-minded. If you are playing a game according to certain rules and set the playing-machine to play for victory, you will get victory if you get anything at all, and the machine will not pay the slightest attention to any consideration except victory according to the rules. If you are playing a war game with a certain conventional interpretation of victory, victory will be the goal at any cost, even that of the extermination of your own side, unless this condition of survival is explicitly contained in the definition of victory according to which you program the machine." [1]

Of course literal-mindedness is not only a feature of single machines and computers, but also of most modern technological and bureaucratic establishments: the factory (products), the corporation (profits), and even the economy (growth). And the more we submit them to single-purpose performance tests of output, profit, and linear economic growth, the more literal-minded and narrow become their effects upon the whole society. Thus, the more a society is dominated or deeply influenced by single-purpose institutions, the more it becomes a talisman with its special wishes and undetermined effects.

Our struggle for development in the past was intellectually simple: to achieve the necessities of life in the most direct way. Wiener seems to say that simple goals and unquestioned assumptions are no longer tenable, because the action may achieve not only the goal but also uncontrolled ramifications.

Wiener concludes: "It is relatively easy to promote good and to fight evil when evil and good are arranged against one another in two clear lines, and those on the other side are our unquestioned enemies, those on our side our trusted allies. What, however, if we must ask, each time in every situation, where is the friend and where is the enemy? What moreover, when we have to put the decision in the hands of an inexorable magic or an inexorable machine of which we must ask the right questions in advance, without fully understanding the operations of the process by which they will be answered? Can we then be confident in the action of the Monkey's Paw from which we have requested the grant of £200?

"No, the future offers very little hope for those who expect that our new mechanical slaves will offer us a world in which we may rest from thinking. Help us they may, but at the cost of supreme demands upon our honesty and our intelligence. The world of the future will be an ever more demanding struggle against the limitations of our intelligence, not a comfortable hammock in which we can lie down to be waited upon by our robot slaves." [2]

FOUNDATIONS FOR PLANNING

In this age of kinetic organizations and exotic technologies we must make diverse knowledge more comprehensible and give more penetrating guidance to awesome new powers of society. The essence of what is required—and the essence of Wiener's advice—is planning.

However, because of the peculiar experience of the Western democracies with ideologies since World War I a rather sharp ambivalence about planning has appeared. On the one hand broad planning is eschewed as a tool only for authoritarian power. On the other hand, planning in particular fields is everywhere in the air, popular in almost every organization, promoted for the effectiveness it prompts in hundreds of special areas of life.

Widespread special uses of planning arise from the technological complexities of advanced industrial systems. "Through its application," writes Robert Brady, "processes are being linked to processes, plants to plants, firms to firms, and even industries to industries in such a way, and under such ordering disciplines of integration and synchronization, that the relating plans and management procedures must keep in step on pain of crippling breakdowns, any one of which may threaten to ramify endlessly throughout the system." [3] Other particular forms of planning have arisen. Corporate planning now links research and development with long-range marketing strategies. Economic planning, though hardly formalized in the United States, seeks to stabilize the economic fluctuation and stimulate economic growth. Urban planning strives to put order into cities, increase their efficiency, and improve their amenities. Military planning is undoubtedly the oldest and most thorough, arising with the general-staff concept over a century ago.

The current basis for planning in many areas evidently arises out of the immensity, complexity, and rapid change of the economic and social system.

But special-purpose planning poses a unique problem for men. Planning, like the organizations it serves, seeks only the objectives set for it, and subordinates all others. Specialized or limited-purpose planning serves only specialized or limited purposes. It implies that certain aspects of life—economic growth, corporate wealth, vigorous cities, and military power—are worthy of planning, whereas other areas of life, including diverse social goals, may be left to the random impact of powerful changes in society.

The great significance of the special forms of planning we now undertake is this. What we plan for is a measure of what we consider valid and worthy in society and worthy of men's attention. What we do not plan for we consider unworthy of attention in the centers of decision-making. But *the values we consider unworthy of planning are the very ones we wish to protect from the kind of "planning" associated with autocratic regimes!*

Therefore if planning is to be made worthy of democracy—indeed, if democracy is to last in a society in which planning is required for its functioning—planning must serve not only the powerful special interests but all worthy elements and values of society. Inevitably the rapid currents of change will bring about successive enlargements of planning power in special areas of life. If the central values of democracy are not also supported by planning that can defend and enlarge them, they will become progressively isolated and fall to the mercy of the special-purpose, literal-minded technological systems. Again Wiener gives us a view of the possibilities, particularly those involving automation:

"A goal-seeking mechanism will not necessarily seek *our* goals unless we design it for that purpose, and in that designing we must foresee all steps of the process for which it is designed, instead of exercising a tentative foresight which goes up to a certain point, and can be continued from that point on as new difficulties arise. The penalties for errors of foresight, great as they are now, will be enormously increased as automation comes into its full use. . . .

"As engineering technique becomes more and more able to *achieve* human purposes, it must become more and more accustomed to *formulate* human purposes. In the past, a partial and inadequate view of human purpose has been relatively innocuous only because it has been accompanied by technical limitations that made it difficult for us to perform operations involving a careful evaluation of human purpose. This is only one of the many places where human impotence has hitherto shielded us from the full destructive impact of human folly." [4]

When Wiener says that "we must foresee all steps of the process," he inevitably implies the necessity for the most comprehensive planning possible (under whatever name it might be given). Unintended results in any economic, social, or cultural sphere of life will likely be too destructive to be tolerated. When Wiener stresses that we "must become more and more accustomed to *formulate* human purposes," he stresses the terribly vital role that goals must play in planning. We cannot avoid unintended results in society unless we know exactly and completely what we want from the machines and organizations we set into motion.

These two imperatives—to give comprehensive guidance and to fully comprehend and carefully set our goals—are the essence of the planning that is necessary for our time.

Planning, however, is primarily a methodology, not an idealogy, as many people mistakenly believe. It is, as the remarks above indicate, a goal-related or goal-seeking methodology. Being highly variable, it is therefore comparable to other major social tools, such as bureaucracy. Bureaucracy is not an idealogy, but it can support almost any ideology. Planning is a similar tool, now ripe for evolution—as were exact systems of administration in times past.

The connection with bureaucracy is not incidental, for planning may well represent a wide new corollary development of bureaucracy. Bureaucracy is essentially a social instrument to *control the normal process* in government, industry, and so on. Planning, however, seeks to *control the changes in the normal processes* of large organizations. Planning has always been implicit in bureaucracy, but it was nonsystematic, just as administration was nonsystematic until the rise of modern bureaucracy.

Seen in perspective, administration is a method for mobilizing and organizing social and technological power. Planning, however, is a method for giving purpose and direction to social and technical power. Planning is concerned with proposals for action, whereas administration is concerned with the management of action. A primary difference is between the *instrumental* and *purposeful* aspects of action.

Planning, as an entity linked with but going far beyond present bureaucracy, may be associated with the steady development of a number of specific tools, including: (1) the precise and comprehensive information control and multifaceted analysis made possible by the computer; (2) large-scale and systematic application of research to whole areas of theory and knowledge; (3) precise projection and simulation (pretesting through hypothetical or real models); (4) complete evaluation or diagnostic investigation of the results of action (as in the detailed search for the causes of aircraft accidents); and finally (5) the formulation of plans of action that define objectives and coordinate sectors, stages, processes, and the like.

As an instrument, planning seeks a smooth bridge between theory and practice, and it appears to be a social tool comparable in significance to technology and bureaucracy. Whereas technology organizes materials and machines and bureaucracy organizes people and institutions, planning organizes objectives and information (or ideas and facts).

Systematic planning is a modern development. It appears to be as inevitable for the twentieth century as systematic bureaucracy was for the nineteenth. Planning is therefore fundamental to the kind of society we are developing. Actually, "only the completely static and traditional society can escape the need for planning," writes Luther Gulick. It constitutes a new power—for organizations and for the whole of mankind. That power may be directed solely to serve the purposes of organizations, or, if carried out on a socially comprehensive and liberal basis, it may serve the individual and his extremely broad requirements of democracy and development, opportunity and community. At present the momentum vastly favors organization.

Planning as a methodology is, like any tool, valid only to the extent it serves human purposes. Evidently human purposes require highly sophisticated definitions and astute interpretations. Democratic planning will begin with these purposes and manifest them at every stage, enhancing the accepted way of life and enlarging the human horizons. In short, planning will serve a democratic purpose to the extent it serves a worthy democratic ideology.

There are, to be sure, dangers associated with planning, just as there are in bureaucracy. The most imminent and real menace to democracy lies in the exclusive application of planning to certain highly organized sectors of life, while larger human purposes remain vague and inactive. What the planning we want presupposes, then, is a broader social foundation for planning than is presently in prospect.

The awesome powers this century has set into motion must be made fully manageable and benign. To act without the guidance of broad social planning—honest, purposeful, and effective—is to wish upon the Monkey's Paw while the awesome powers move undaunted among us. "The possibility poised by history is not that of denying the advent of planning," stresses Robert Heilbroner, "but of seizing control of it." [5] The crucial question of planning is not its application in society (for that is inevitable) but the philosophy we apply to it and the inner structure we give it to serve human dignity, justice, and freedom.

In a world made powerful by human organization, planning can not only increase the effectiveness of action but also clarify human purposes and incorporate them into the machinery of organization. Specifically, planning can be a way of sustaining diversity in a world tending toward corporate and technical homogeneity.

PLANNING FOR PLURALITY

Almost every major worthwhile social tool—science, technology, bureaucracy—develops the specific potential dictated by the broader trends and intent of society. If the tendency is simply to augment national power, these tools can be organized to multiply power. If they are intended to contribute to the worth of men's life in democracy, they will be fashioned, adjusted, and channeled to amplify a quality of life.

Planning is one such tool—age-old in its informal development, new in its formal methodologies, and as inevitable as the laboratory, the production line, or the productive enterprise. What is not so certain is that planning will serve a democratic purpose.

Therefore our aim must be the development of the specific democratic potential of planning, to determine both how it can be effective in a plural society and, more important, how it can help sustain and perhaps amplify democratic values.

Put most simply, planning will serve a plural society to the extent it is developed as a plural instrument, serving many purposes, applying to many organizations and special fields, using many methods, relevant to various spans of time and geography, and (still a part of its diversity) developing a guiding consensus.

The plurality of planning is evident in the three major features that always accompany its application: (1) the clarification and interpretation of *goals;* (2) *analyses* of the human condition and of social capabilities; and (3) *plan formulations* that convert the goals and analyses into guides for institutional action. These three characteristics suggest a tentative definition for planning: *a method of clarifying human individual and social goals, of understanding human conditions and possibilities, and of formulating these criteria and findings into various guidelines for social change and development over a period of time.* This definition applies to all kinds of planning but especially to what is called comprehensive planning. As the term is used here, comprehensive planning pertains to a diversity of content and applications, a diversity of method, and particularly a diversity of purposes.

For democracy, the most vital feature of the plural nature of planning—and, so far, the least developed—is that it is a goal-seeking mechanism. Now very nearly dormant, this feature will be democracy's best assurance that planning will serve a broader purpose than bare instrumental effectiveness. When full attention is given to the goal-making and goal-seeking qualities of planning, we may then predict that the democratic potential of planning will be appreciated and emphasized.

Since our concern here is with the plural nature of planning as a whole, we shall defer briefly a fuller discussion of planning goals.

Considering the entire range of planning in society, we may envisage a diversity based first on all institutions that are at the grass roots, second on the major national operative organizations (the large corporations, agencies of government, unions, professional societies), and third on the highest or societal level of social determination. A certain tension may be assumed between the various kinds, levels, and sources of planning. And yet, since planning naturally seeks a reliable and predictable environment for organized action, we may also assume a reciprocity, cooperation, and mutual interdependence among the various centers of planning. Such a decentralization may encourage a flexibility of institutional behavior beneficial to the individual, stimulating an expansion of human freedom.

But this diversity also has a central focal point. Of course, the essential and terribly complex economic and technical integration of modern society must stem from a central source. Furthermore, the flexibility of social action and the many concrete qualities of human freedom can be advanced from a central position, sometimes more effectively than from local bastions, because some social ideals require a universal concern before they can be realized at all. Both the ideal and the practical purposes require their own form of central planning.

Some important variations of planning are illustrated by the varied objectives assumed for it. Robert Brady observes that the necessity for planning arose as if it were by "some grand historical conspiracy to force the human hand—not in a few isolated spots, but everywhere. It is now a problem of plan or cumulative breakdown." [6] The economic planner Jan Tinbergen claims that the greatest need for planning arises during emergencies, such as war, or when the new countries struggle to initiate development—that is, when there must be a maximum utilization of resources.[7] Peter Drucker associates the need for planning with society's massive drive for innovation. Innovation is, he says, "not only opportunity. It is not only risk. It is first and foremost responsibility. . . . The risks and responsibilities of innovation require themselves major innovation." To Drucker, the best hope for responsible innovation lies in decentralized planning.[8]

In 1946 the sociologist Karl Mannheim proposed that planning should strive to reduce social maladjustment and to enlarge freedom and social justice.[9] It was implied by Norbert Wiener that our technology, especially the more sophisticated variety, plays grand games with human beings unless comprehensively controlled.

Here we have five significantly different views of planning: Brady emphasizes integration and maintenance of the industrial system; Tinbergen points to economic effectiveness; Drucker seeks innovation; Mannheim stresses social values; and Wiener is concerned about social control of advanced technology. Evidently, there is no inherent and precise application for planning.

The variable possibilities of planning are seen again in the many relationships it may take into account: between ends and means, present and future, theory and action, general and special (or comprehensive and precise), local and regional (or national), technical and administrative, public and private, pragmatic and ideal. Diversity may also be found in the sectors of interest (economic, physical, social, cultural) and among various kinds of institutions that sponsor planning. By its nature planning tends to be predictive, integrative, comprehensive, practical, and purposeful, of which any combination may be emphasized. Plans may be acted upon legislatively, administratively, morally.

Plans may also be of diverse kinds. Some may emphasize goals, others analysis and prediction, and others policy and integration. They may be broad, long-term guides or precise, short-term implementation programs.

Of course, there is an equally wide diversity in the use of plans. Some may guide the making of other plans. Some may be implemented only by major reorganizations, while others may be adopted for ongoing administration. Each type requires its own theories and expertise. But all establish a cohesive guide for some form of effective action for defined purposes over a definite length of time. And all require some formal consensus, approval, or adoption before they can be acted upon.

The diversities of planning—objectives, types, uses—promise a diversity of results, especially since plans will be formed by a variety of organizations. Each plan, however, should be framed with reference to the larger purposes of society as a whole.

How can the larger purposes penetrate independent organizations? If strict legal restrictions and other means of compulsion are to be ruled out, there remains only moral persuasion. However, if the moral is focused upon an organization's publishing certain features of its planning—its institutional and social goals, its performance record on certain public matters, and its proposals that will affect the public—the persuasion is immeasurably strengthened. In effect, organizations are asked to explain themselves, to enter into a public dialogue on their role in society, to justify themselves *as institutions*—as all organizations should—beyond their particular commodities or services.

Dissemination of succinct plans of large and small corporations, agencies, and other organizations in effect puts a big neon sign at the front door telling what they are, what they do, and how they operate. Stated goals and proposals may be contrasted with actual performance. Institutions thereby become more highly visible and socially accountable.

SOPHISTICATION OF GOALS

Planning began in a very primitive way when one act was undertaken as a prelude to another. Since that time in man's dim past civilization has grown by means of increasingly involved preliminary actions to achieve more distant desired ends.

As a hunter and scavenger, man could hardly forget his goals in making bows and arrows: he was taking a necessary and obvious step toward obtaining food and clothing. Lacking the confidence to consciously devise new tools and products (a process now formalized in research and development), he concentrated on his own prowess and on understanding the behavior of his prey. Basic innovations usually awaited clumsy accidents. Only in the refinement of accidental discoveries were modifications consciously evolved. Gradually the more basic process of innovation was internalized (as revealed by the Latin source word, *inventus:* to come upon, find) and made more thoroughly experimental.

Today the rush into research, ranging from outer space to the deep sea and from the cellular foundations of life to the nuclear basis of matter, symbolizes how much of our daily behavior is removed from such fundamental goals as procuring food and shelter. Merely by forming vast organizations we remove the action of individuals from the goals they seek, even if organizations in the long run are usually a more effective means of fulfillment.

The more we are able to shift our attention from the necessities supporting life, trusting our organizations to provide both necessities and amenities, the more we risk a drift of gross effect and influence away from the more humanely beneficial possibilities. We have extremely little experience in the higher uses of wealth, and so we tend to reduce it to bare consumption. And the organizations that have created our wealth are pleased to support this simple consumption; they also promote an incestuous redundancy in the economy by systematic advertising, research, financing, and corporate organization. Hence, as our wealth increases, we acquire a new burden: we must see to it that organized action serves human interest. We need to make our goals explicit (and perhaps to create entirely new, more worthy goals) and to direct our organizations to open the way toward them for us, without diverting or reshaping our intent.

As Wiener implies, modern society has created in its industries and institutions a gigantic mechanism that is "more and more able to *achieve* human purposes." Therefore, as human goals become more fully realizable, society must "become more and more accustomed to formulate human purposes" of the highest human potential. Moreover, since thousands of powerful organizations are intermediary between the individual and his goals of life, these goals must be sensitively and continuously interpreted to assure that all organizations can and do respond to human intent.

Modern complexities require that goals be formed into a highly sophisticated system. The more powerful and complex the means of achievement, the more astute and articulate must be the guiding goals. As commercial aircraft become supersonic and multiply their passenger capacities, for example, they require ever more sophisticated flight controls, navigation equipment, and landing systems to assure safe arrival.

Certainly, broad social goals are not so simple that they can be drawn up in a list and then readily approved and acted upon. Rather, an important public dialogue taking place over time makes possible a broad consensus of many particular goals. Such goals then require careful interpretation to make them realistic for each location, time, and circumstance.

Thus, two major hurdles must be overcome to give goals a measure of sophistication. First, the definition of goals, seemingly simple, is really an awesome task. Not only must they be comprehensive to match the range of possibilities of social action (not leaving room for the talisman to choose), but they must be realistically adapted to human motivations, social imperatives, and social conventions. Arrival at both theoretically and practically viable goal definitions entails the formidable task of understanding man's nature, of perceiving the fulfillment of that nature, and of comprehending society's minimum necessities of cultural discipline, personal freedom, and technical and organizational framework. Any valid social goal must satisfy these requirements.

Second, goals require interpretation in various and precise ways to assure that social power actually responds to the defined goals. Of course a given goal may have one possible interpretation when it pertains to the creation of new knowledge and another when it pertains to the production of houses. It would also have one meaning in a world strained by possible atomic annihilation and another in a world where basic order was guaranteed. Each goal needs to be acted upon in the light of both the special and general circumstances in which it is employed.

Goals are formative and primary for democratic planning, for they set forth the aspirations and expectations of a society in individual and cultural terms. Through a process of goal definition or formulation, vague but important motives or values may be shaped into clear purposes and "constituted" through various forms of planning to take hold of organizational behavior. What we would seek through goal formulation is a closer fidelity to all worthy social values by all organizations in all of the ways in which they affect society.

Unquestionably, defective goals are the soft spot in contemporary planning. Our planning to date remains socially derelict, reflecting the instrumental character of contemporary action, the sterile "objectivity" imposed on imaginative thought, and the specialization of our behavior. It is hardly surprising that many people believe planning only serves to augment authoritarian power. Yet such attitudes only help make it so.

But how can social goals be given valid definition and effective interpretation to make them articulate for modern society? We might differentiate goals into several levels according to their precise functions, so that broad definitions, concrete organizational purposes, and particular performance standards can be spotlighted during decision-making.

For example, the most fundamental or primordial social goals might first consist of a number of *ends*. Each end might be derived from the observation, evaluation, and generalization of a number of values—for example, the values that might constitute such ends as opportunity and community, as they were discussed earlier. Ends would be basic premises for all forms and steps of planning.

But ends would not usually be directly usable for planning until they were redefined into *objectives* at a subordinate level. Whereas ends might be formative and basic, objectives would be operative or programmatic. That is, objectives might convert certain ends or combinations of ends into specific purposes for particular organizations. Thus the preamble to the Constitution briefly and pointedly states the objectives of government: "to form a more perfect Union, establish Justice, insure domestic Tranquility, provide for the common defense, promote the general Welfare, and secure the Blessings of Liberty."

A third level of goals might consist of *principles* that interpret objectives in terms of every kind of organized action. Planning principles might be comparable to the articles of the Constitution.

Since many apparently contradictory motives and behavior dwell within people, indeed within the same person, goals might be expected to encompass certain contrasting or seemingly contradictory avenues of behavior, and even to encourage them. The contrasts are seen in such "values" as seeking after security, association, and strong personal identification on the one hand and pursuing opportunity, action, variety, and even a certain turmoil in human affairs on the other. Goals must represent both sides—in a kind of planning equation—as well as many values not identifiable with either.

These human purposes expressed through group life surely deserve the same intense investigation and constructive effort that mankind has given to his material growth. Lacking this intensity of concern, much of our most worthy heritage has fallen into decay. Does our society express the goals that challenge and comfort the urbanite, give faith to youth, engage a renewed spirit among the aged? Have the goals we always thought abounding within the self-reliant individual silently passed on to organizations? What goals are expressed in the anonymity of cities, the mechanistic directiveness of technology, and the blind momentum of change? Quite appropriately, E. H. Carr argues that "we should be nearer the mark . . . if we spoke of the need, not to defend democracy, but to create it." [10]

These attributes of life are the proper subject for goals. Evidently goals need to be comprehensive in spanning all human values, for whatever human purpose we fail to consider will assuredly slip from the sight of society. Already we have lost many features of life attributable to community—a small society aimed at understanding and sharing, an association based on the simple importance of being human, a local plurality of life. The comprehensive planning necessary to balance out the powerful and constricted focus of present planning may therefore depend upon a comprehensiveness of goals.

Furthermore, a comprehensiveness of goals may be the best means to unify society sufficiently to assure a satisfactory environment for the individual. A comprehensive philosophy might unite what we do with cities with what we do in education, science, and conservation and with what we do with technology, the economy, and corporate forms of organization. In a complex world comprehensiveness is vital—perhaps essential —in keeping the individual in view. Comprehensive goals clarify the human values.

The American Constitution illustrates the necessity to succinctly spell out what a society deems of value. The Founding Fathers first thought that specific rights could be inferred by the kinds of constitutional machinery they set up, but then decided it was best to incorporate a specific Bill of Rights. We now know that inferences of social purpose are weak guides for the strong masters of history, and perhaps they restrain the pervasive technological and bureaucratic power of large institutions least of all.

Like the Constitution, planning presents a method of squarely recognizing the kinds of powers we must contend with and of devising means to organize these powers according to our purposes. Professor Charles Haar has described the urban master plan as an "impermanent constitution." [11] This is very apt; it would seem to be an appropriate metaphor for all uses of planning (though perhaps this carries it beyond the original meaning intended by Haar). I suspect that the validity of planning as an impermanent constitution rests primarily upon the definitions and uses of goals.

Goal-making is the application of method to human value. It is the necessary equivalent of the application of method to the organizations that now simultaneously endanger human value and raise its potential.

It is difficult to overstate the extraordinary possibilities that the conscious evolution of goals may have for society. Very many of the discussions in these chapters have concluded that there is a need to shift the magnetic poles that organize society. In the end, as we have noted, changes in the foundations of thought may be as great as those appearing in the shift from medieval disputations to empirical investigations. Vital action in future society may turn on the formulation of goals as it now turns merely on pragmatic research and development.

SOCIAL SELF-CONSCIOUSNESS

Broad and sophisticated goals do not in themselves support the preparation of plans. All relevant conditions of society must also be analyzed and evaluated. Analyses in turn require accurate and complete information, a conclusion hardly surprising to the modern pragmatist.

Yet despite the mountainous volumes of information produced and consumed by corporate society and despite computers and information-retrieval systems, the methods we apply to information remain about where manufacturing was before Henry Ford began to mass-assemble his automobiles. Consequently the service we get for our gigantic investment in information is primitive and of extremely limited use.

That is our backwardness as the pragmatist might state it. But what about the idealist's broad goals of humanism for society? Might they not also benefit from better information about the condition of men? In an early chapter we noted how society maintains quite complete information about what are considered the positive values of economic growth while maintaining incomplete information concernng social values—that limited information being focused primarily upon the festering social disorders that mar the complexion of our institutions.

The advent of planning—both the practical and the ideal—will make unprecedented new demands upon the range, completeness, and flexibility of virtually every source of data in society. New concepts and procedures will be required to bring the management of information to a par with automated production.

It is especially in the formulation and interpretation of goals that great new pressure for data and analyses will arise, for social goals are directed to human aspirations, and aspirations arise from the society's self-consciousness of its own being and potential. As it is, our social self-consciousness and *esprit* today center upon what are ultimately *psychic* and *social* irrelevancies: exotic technological performance, bureaucratic health and power, economic growth.

If a society, like an individual, is to develop and mature upon its *humane* potential—upon the excitements of life in society—through a social self-consciousness, how is it served by the present narrowly pragmatic uses and propagandistic influences of data and lines of communication? How will modern society create its cultural and democratic *élan*—an infectious inner vitality of group life affecting every individual—if it does not develop the many subtle variations of social understanding, collectively seeking after the Socratic dictum to "know thyself" ?

The purpose of planning analyses is to clarify human conditions, problems, motivations, and potential. Information for such analyses should be continuous, systematic, and comprehensive. Of course, the *frontiers of knowledge* expanded by scientific research are an important source, but more useful normally are the *completeness of information* and the *combinations of information* that permit maximum use of the theoretical knowledge that already exists. It is of little use to know the theoretical chemical qualities of soil until complete and regular sampling of specific farmlands gives us an understanding of the precise qualities of every field for every possible use; and of course both the uses and the soil might change and influence each other over time.

What, then, is meant by continuous, systematic, and comprehensive information?

Statistical information about society is important according to the number of ways every statistic may be compared to all others. Any single statistic is meaningless until it is compared with another statistic (perhaps only implied) or a norm that establishes a standard of evaluation. Particular statistical facts usually bear meaningfully upon each other in one of three definite ways: (1) the fact of one time with the fact of another time, as the population of a central city in 1900 and in 1950; (2) the fact of one place with that of another, as the population densities of two cities; and (3) the fact of one subject with that of another, as population density and property valuation.

These three relationships are very simple, but they are basic to a system of standardized, versatile, quantified, and comparative control of information. More important than the fact itself is the number of its useful comparisons with other facts.

The obvious prototype is the census of population. In the United States this information has been standardized for the most part since 1790 and is now essential for innumerable historic and other perspectives. Today the census also covers such fields as agriculture, manufacturing, and housing. But the fact that each field in itself is relatively complete, continuous, reliable, and comparable does not also make each type of census comparable to the others.

Suppose, for example, there is a city in which information about people's income and expenditures, health and education, housing and property values, vital statistics and other conditions of life is regularly tabulated by enumeration districts and "census" tracts. Suppose, too, that these district and tract boundaries coincide with those of public administrative jurisdictions, public utility service areas, and commercial service zones and that all appropriate data are serviced in a common bank. All data for all fields may then be compiled and made available for an infinite variety of computer analyses. Computers are now being adapted to plot information on maps, and this greatly expands their analytic potential in a graphic direction. It then becomes possible to achieve all three basic elements of comparability. All field data can theoretically be compared, not only by gross summaries, but in detail by area, time, and subject.

These qualities are particularly significant for planning. Unlike science, which seeks deep penetrations into the unknown and uses unique combinations of methods and information to make this possible, planning seeks combinations of data and knowledge bearing upon the selection of alternatives, the integration of programs, and other aspects of proposal formulation. Planning must bring wide ranges of information together to achieve numerous objectives. It requires a grasp of, or at least a concern for, the whole social fabric: its balance, order, purposefulness. A broad grasp of understanding is fundamental.

By contrast, a given research project might compare the economic performance of different urban transportation systems or might analyze the variables of a potential new urban renewal program. But as useful as these and hundreds of other research projects may be, they do not compose the broad and balanced foundation of information required for the comprehensive concern of planning—in this case for cities. What is needed is comprehensive, continuous, and standardized information to give valid and balanced illumination to the whole range of planning responsibility.

This is not to say that planning has only a passing interest in academic research or its technological applications. Its interest, however, is chiefly to evaluate specific untried plan possibilities and the results and implications of scientific and technological innovation itself. The latter might involve the following: First, research could evaluate the specific *capabilities* and uses of each new body of scientific knowledge, such as that concerning new structural materials. Second, it might consider the general long-term *implications* of these materials when applied to various kinds of construction. Third, it might note possible *qualifications* or *reservations* about their use as may be pertinent to planning goals. Fourth, evaluation might seek an understanding of how a new concept, device, technique, system, or movement might be *integrated* into the existing social milieu.

Still, the primary need is for broad comprehensive information, far more than it is for research knowledge. The possibility is that, with computer capacities, comprehensive information about society may become useful for an infinite variety of purposes. Perhaps we may achieve a clarity of knowledge about society comparable to the granular fidelity of a photograph, whereas our present statistical basis hardly gives us a rough pictograph of social reality.

At present, in gathering and making use of statistics by a multitude of discrete and isolated methods, we are being archaic and wasteful in the extreme. As a rule only gross statistics are comparable. Different sets of facts cover different areas or time spans, define their terms incompatibly, or have varying reliability and validity. If a laborious search in libraries and offices should bring together widely different but relevant information (such as divorces by neighborhood, income level, and education, compared with the same factors for delinquency), then only total figures for whole cities or counties are likely to be comparable. Such statistics are of limited use. The sensitive variations and connections between events in social life are simply not revealed. At present, only statistics of the national economy form anything like a complete barometer of a group of conditions in society.

That is why our handling of data—uniquely and incompatibly—is so much like manufacturing before production was rationalized. With computers, we have established the technical means for automated processing of comprehensive data of society before we have rationalized the larger system of conceiving and managing data. In industry the rationalization occurred before the cybernetic revolution and laid the foundation for automation when those capacities arose.

Presumably the initiative in establishing a time, area, and subject "grid" for the development of a highly articulate system of information lies with the Federal Government, probably growing out of the Bureau of the Census. A grid rationalization allows us to multiply the quantity of useful information, make it more readily accessible, and, most of all, make it highly comparable for infinite varieties of analysis and research.

(Certain similarities exist between this grid information proposal and the various proposals for a national data center or bank, about which a sharp debate has arisen concerning the threats to privacy and the danger of undermining civil rights. This debate is valid and critical. I shall not enter into it here except to emphasize that it would be dangerous indeed to seriously consider any proposal until *all* aspects of protecting the complete personal and social integrity as well as civil rights of the individual have been thoroughly investigated, and until *all* necessary and contingent protective measures are firmly established.)

Of course, even when such a system matures, it still cannot provide the special and unique kinds of information required to advance the frontiers of social knowledge. What it does do is establish for the investigator a very broad base of data as an advanced point of departure for his studies. In many cases, moreover, the time, area, and subject grid provides him with a sound frame of reference for the collection of his own data, and in turn for the contribution of his findings to the central system of compatible data.

Yet, however complete and versatile a central and standardized system becomes, it must always be viewed as an aid to analysis, not its substance. Nor can we slight the qualitative observations and insights of the individual observer. Statistics of income or health or housing cannot convey the meaning of being poor. Only the most superficial aspects of disenchantement and meaninglessness—or of challenge, *esprit,* and security—can be made statistically measurable. It will always be the person himself, partly involved and partly observer, partly objective and partly subjective, who will ultimately give us the clues as to what statistics to collect, how to interpret them, when to ignore them—and how to go beyond them.

But an articulate informational base for analysis should broaden the scope of social insight in society as well as being directly applicable to planning and many practical uses. If the information is thorough, succinct, and comprehensive, and if both the information and the resulting analyses are fully disseminated—especially if they stimulate a well-focused public dialogue—they can enlarge the collective intelligence about public affairs and contribute to a new dimension of social self-consciousness.

Coming to grips more firmly with knowledge as a process and as a whole, as well as with the particular elements of knowledge, we build upon the foundations that have made us civilized. Civilization not only requires an accumulation of knowledge; it also requires a control over knowledge. Control of knowledge is new knowledge itself—and of the highest order. We need to become as scientific about our knowledge as we are now about the subjects to which scientific knowledge applies.

The highest service of knowledge is to give pointedness to human questions. The highest service of planning is to bring questions of the future into focus and into a clear continuity with the past. If planning can bring human goals, conditions, and possible plans into sharp focus for human dialogue, it will then certainly serve a mighty human purpose.

The *Federalist Papers,* about which debate on the ratification of the United States Constitution revolved, were a landmark of public dialogue about the future course of a society. They were important not only because they helped assure ratification, but because they contributed to a social self-consciousness of what the country aimed to be. They were also based on a society far more comprehensible than is ours today.

As our society is vastly complex, it also changes rapidly. Yet we have not set out with determination to learn what we are or to determine what we aim to be. Both the understanding and the dialogue drift in a social eddy.

ARTICULATING PURPOSE AND PERFORMANCE

The chief human value of planning lies in assuring that *human purposes* are paramount in guiding *organized action.* To this end we have examined the need for sophisticated goals and goal-oriented analyses of man's condition. Now we shall consider a few aspects of plan-making that seek to convert these goals and analyses into definite guides for organized action.

Plans, whether governmental or corporate, are weighted with the necessities of functional performance. Human purposes can be made paramount in such plans to the extent that goals penetrate every plan's operative elements. Whereas *goal clarity* is crucial in earlier stages of planning, *goal penetration* is crucial in the plan product. The effective inclusion of human purposes in planning depends partly on how plans are prepared and related to one another by *time, space,* and *subject.*

To maintain continuity from one era to the next, planning must be a continuous process rather than a series of discrete actions laid end to end. Today many countries have embarked upon a series of five- to seven-year plans, each plan guiding a new step of development. The process is made smoother when, as in Pakistan, a twenty-year "perspective" plan frames the long-term questions posed by the five-year plans, and also when annual budgetary programs interpret the five-year plan's short-range objectives for fiscal and administrative purposes.

However, most five-year economic plans are tied to each other end to end, just as one calendar year ties into the next. This makes integration between plans brittle. Arbitrary breaks of policy may be expected. However, continuity and smoothness can be served by formulating a new ten-year plan each five years, revising each time the final five years of an old ten-year plan, and extending it another five years into the future. Only the first half of the plan would actually be carried out. The second half of the plan would always serve as a means of comparing earlier plan choices against the realities of changing times, and would offer five years of living with and revising the recommendations of the plan before they were put into effect. In other words, the best planning might result from a process of revision and extension. This principle is sometimes called a "rolling plan."

Similarly, continuity would be advanced if "perspective" plans extended, say, forty years into the future, with extension and modification each decade. And budgetary plans might be projected two years, with annual revisions and extensions.

These three varying terms of planning—one to two years, five to ten years, and thirty to forty years—offer two benefits besides continuity. First, they allow each subject to be taken up with an appropriate lead time, so that action in the present will be fully effective for an appropriate future date. Each term plan allows each subject an appropriate time for the future to be "brought into the manageable present." [12] Planning for education might thereby extend to the length of time required to take a child from elementary school through university, especially since certain advanced subjects are beginning to be introduced at very early ages.

Second, goals and targets are important in long-range plans, while integration and staging are generally more crucial in shorter-term plans. In other words, a division of labor is worked out among the parts of planning while an integration from long-term to short-term objectives is maintained.

When we consider space and subject, the two remaining variables, plans that span a continent, region, and locality conceptually follow approaches like those of time-span plans. For example, a scheme has been put forward for the integrated *water* development of the western parts of Canada, the United States, and the northern part of Mexico. A fully developed plan of this nature would necessarily be long-term and comprehensive (in the sense that all uses of water would be taken into account). The continental plan, requiring three or four decades and many billions of dollars, would also require complementary plans for each region and locality.

But such a plan for western North America would, when founded solely for water development, once again pose the problem of single-purpose planning and its customary biases. What would the effects of the plan be upon the continental population pattern, the continued dispersion of cities, the character of recreation, and the conservation of open spaces, wildlife, and wilderness areas? The plan could be a constructive instrument in these matters, if its founding purposes were enlarged, or it could be a source for severe problems, calling into question the billions of dollars spent on it. Despite its publicity, this is a lesson only partly learned in the "multipurpose" TVA.

The point is that the coordination of plans must not only reach into the future for the length of time required to finance and construct the water plan, or across the continental space required for its integration, but must also focus all development more fully and equally upon the numerous subjects and goals for human betterment—human betterment as a whole, not only in acre-feet of water or in dollars.

The concern here parallels the three elements in a system of comprehensive information: coordination from time to time, area to area, and subject to subject. The merits of comparability in information also apply to a comprehensiveness in planning. Planning is now beginning to approach a broad span in time and space, but *comprehensiveness of purpose* remains largely undeveloped. While time and space are fundamental to practical achievements, comprehensiveness of purposes is essential to serve the diversity of goals for men in an advanced and liberal civilization.

When the objectives of planning are divided—particularly when the objectives of immense plans with a wide impact upon men are reduced to certain utilitarian benefits—those objectives and working methods tend to advance only special purposes, such as water development or the organizations that manage water development. These objectives then tend to override and disrupt other social benefits. And new, powerful interest groups are formed that seek their own welfare more heartily than that of the people as a whole.

Organizational self-welfare becomes virtually inevitable when a public body must be financially self-sufficient. This figures in TVA's increasing interest in power development, and in the Port of New York Authority's refusal to develop and manage an integrated transportation system—since some elements would not be self-sustaining. The balance sheet effectively reduces their operations and philosophy to those of a profit-making corporation. A larger view of human purposes then becomes unrealistic because of the narrowly practical terms of necessity.

However, the "hard facts" of financial self-sufficiency for such bodies become increasingly fictitious in a society that spends many billions of dollars to promote consumption through advertising and wastes many more billions on other make-work economic redundancies. The more important question is how our institutions are conceived, how their goals are defined, and how comprehensive goals are fitted into their plans.

Organizations can be better turned from self-welfare motives when their planning can be founded upon a broad span of human goals. The organization is made more clearly subordinate to the individual via those goals. This is in keeping with the idea that the present is the *right* of the individual and the future is the *responsibility* of organizations.

However, the subordination of institutions to the freedom and vitality of the individual should be as much as possible a matter of self-control concerning institutional ethics. This will emphasize diversity and decentralized planning. Yet a broad, commonly accepted social ethic should always exhort organizations to consider deeply their wider social purposes.

The diversity of planning may seem to work against the integrative purposes of planning, but it need not. Planning and uniformity are not the same thing. Planning, like all elements of life and society, derives interest and vigor from diversity. Although not all institutions may define their own goals in exactly the same fashion or even interpret national planning goals in exactly the same way, planning can help each of them appreciate more keenly its own effect upon the human equation.

Planning is as much as anything a magnification of social purposes through more pointed dialogues and more systematic procedures about means and ends, immediate decisions, and long-term direction—and about institutions and individuals—in a world in which the foundations of human value often shift swiftly and ominously. Although planning must concentrate the bulk of its energies upon technology and bureaucracy, it should first of all maintain their focus on human purposes—thoroughly and constantly.

INDEPENDENT FRAMEWORK

Having considered the major elements of planning—goals, analyses, plan-making—we now briefly consider how planning might be incorporated into the processes determining the course of social change. In keeping with our focus upon comprehensive, goal-formulating planning at the highest level in society, the discussion here will center upon instituting planning at that level. The major consideration is the independence and integrity of that planning function.

Plans are the focal points at which society comes to select its basic course and devise the appropriate coordinative means to carry out its aims. The term "society comes to select" is used advisedly, because the plans (that is, the planners) do not select; they only recommend. It is only for duly constituted legislatures and administrators to make selections according to their authority. Adoption is and should be distinct from the plan-making process. Plans are not final determinations, that is, they are not decisions. This is a very important distinction, and is comparable to the separation of powers basic to the American tradition of democracy.

The separation of powers is particularly relevant to planning. At high political levels it may well hedge the authority of an unscrupulous leader who would seize and distort the processes of a free society. The position of a potential autocrat is further weakened if there is wide public consensus on planning goals, for if he cannot easily take command of goal-making and broad social planning functions, his departures from established practice quickly and sharply isolate him from the conscious expectations of men.

Here, then, is an important principle: *the more general and more central planning is in a society, the more its goal-making and broad social plan-making functions should be separated from the normal channels of authority.* That is, the more central and general planning is, the greater is the ethical potential. If ethical potential is protected from the grasp of misdirected ambitions, one basis for usurping power is considerably inhibited.

On the other hand, where planning is more localized and specialized, whether in corporations, associations, or local governments, and where the broad social goal-making tends to be derived from other sources, there is less necessity for a formal separation of planning from the ongoing behavior of these organizations. Nevertheless, every organization still has its impact upon human values and social goals. It is therefore the first task of every organization in instituting planning to determine the position and role of planning vis-à-vis the protection and enhancement of these values.

Further, the separation of planning from administration can be important for the long-term stability and effectiveness of organizations themselves. A formal separation assures that there will be an independent voice on all critical matters. For example, James Mooney and Alan Reiley in *The Principles of Organization* note the significance of the Jesuit Council,[13] an advisory body to the Roman Catholic order. Although direct authority lies with the Jesuit General, the Council always has the *right* to be heard by the General. Independent staff advice is guaranteed by the appointment and dismissal of the Council by the Jesuit congregation as a whole, not by the General. The General may disregard the Council's advice, *but he cannot rid himself of the advice.* He does not have arbitrary power over the Council to persuade them against their independent judgment. Hence, there is at least moderate protection against the compelling misjudgments of a person who might permanently damage the work of the order.

Planning is therefore essentially an extension of the staff concept. Its independence is a form of staff independence. A large degree of independence for staff planning (staff advice relating to change) therefore has merit for institutional as well as democratic purposes.

At the national level, where staff independence is the most essential, where the ranges of planning purposes and functions are bewilderingly complex, two major forms of planning appear to be appropriate. (1) The first will have an unlimited concern for the whole society, its cultural *esprit,* its ethical content, its freedom and opportunity, its community and security. This planning will emphasize the formulation of goals, the framework for analyses, and criteria to assist plan-making throughout the society. (2) The second form of central planning will provide guidance and coordination directly to the operative branches of government via the legislative process and, where appropriate, directly by the administrative authorities. Responsibility will be highly defined and fixed. Our interest dictates a focus upon the first, more independent form of central planning.

The breadth of scope, the concern for the basic direction of change, the intent upon achieving the most profound human values attainable in society call for a planning institution akin to a "Constitutional Convention" sitting in permanent session.

This institution—perhaps a Commission of the Society—would strive to amplify the honor, inspiration, and excitement of every person living in the society. Yet, its "constituency" would also reach into the future generations. Its "advisors" would include all teachers throughout history. Its function would be a continuing search for consensus through a continuing dialogue about the role of society and all institutions. It would have no power save its moral authority.

The Commission would be free to carry on planning (and initiate the dialogues underlying planning) for any level or part of society, to cover any area, length of time, or subject, and to direct the results of its planning to any level of government, any other institution, any or all persons. It might stress any arrangement of goals, analyses, or plan proposals.

The Commission's obligations would be to every individual in society, and this would be defined by the Commission itself. Its obligations to government would be none. Government would have three obligations to the Commission: to guarantee (1) the right of access to information, (2) the right to be heard, and (3) the right to minimum financial support (comparable to that of the judges of the Supreme Court).

The Commission might consist of a moderate number (ten to twenty) of full-time members: persons whose breadth and human purposes are beyond question and whose outside interests are minimal. Nonrenewable long-term appointments (eight to sixteen years) might be made from federal, state, and private candidates, though none should be ex officio, even implicitly. A staff of advisors on nonrenewable shorter-term appointments might augment the work of the Commission members.

In recent years the need for broad social direction has become increasingly recognized. Following World War II the two Hoover Commissions on governmental reorganization showed some of this character of planning. Then, about 1960, national goals rose to a temporary prominence with the President's Commission on National Goals; the series of articles on national purpose sponsored by the *New York Times* and *Life;* and the Rockefeller Panel Report, *Prospect for America.*

Probably the closest approximation to a Commission of the Society was proposed by James Conant in his book, *Shaping Educational Policy.* His plea for an "Interstate Commission for Planning a Nationwide Educational Policy" was realized with the establishment of the Educational Commission of the States by interstate compact in 1966. The Commission will "facilitate the improvement of State and local [educational] systems to meet adequate and desirable goals. . . ." Each state entering the compact names seven members to the Commission (the governor, two legislators, and four educators). A staff will undertake numerous studies pertaining to policy questions at all levels of education.

The long-overdue creation of a national educational policy body at the highest level simply emphasizes the urgency of similar action in other spheres of public life: urban development, environmental conservation, a wide range of social development, and commercial and industrial evolution (especially considering the impact of automation, and corporate evolution)—to name only a few. However, the Educational Commission also underscores the necessity to examine the wider question of the joint impact of all institutional activities upon the life of the individual.

In this age of development, it is ironic, as we have noted, that the mood of men and the character of organization conspire to dissect and splinter thought and disregard the major questions of the age. Wherever groups of men or new organizations are asked to take a fresh look at a broad institutional or social question and to consider the most profound social interest, they almost inevitably divert themselves from a concern for broad purpose to one of method, from general to special matters. Judging from the ex officio composition of the Educational Commission and its initial list of studies, there will be no exception in this interstate compact. There is little possibility, then, that the Commission will energetically seek to relate education to larger social purposes; rather, it will work almost solely on the "pressing" policy questions facing educational administrators.

All such bodies, which deal with special fields such as education and bear upon the individual only in a partial or indirect way, almost inevitably carry a professional bias or special interest. Conant himself has argued for the participation of many disciplines in education to overcome its closed and sterile nature. Something wider, something not tied so directly to politics or any particular field, something with only an allegiance to the good life is evidently required to bring broader purpose to the unnumerable special endeavors, and most of all to the good works of bodies like the Educational Commission of the States.

Another interesting—and wide-ranging—proposal for national planning was recently put forward by Harvey Wheeler,[14] a staff member of the Center for the Study of Democratic Institutions, itself an institution having importance for the broadest span of planning in society. Wheeler proposes a completely new "political" branch of government, equal to the present "governmental" branch (the legislative, executive and judicial functions), which "would deal with the infrastructure of society, the sources out of which responsible citizenship, consensus, long-range goals and candidates arise." Paralleling the new branch would be a new division of the Constitution incorporating "constitutional statutes for exercising the office of citizenship."

The political branch would consist of three parts: education, planning, and political. Education is considered responsible for the cultural and educational welfare of the people, possibly carried out by such means as a "TVA for the mass media." Planning would be "more detailed than idealogy but short of a legislative program." The political division would formally institute the political parties, subsidize their structure and campaigns, and strengthen their ability to coalesce public opinion and transfrom plans into platforms and legislative programs.

Wheeler's planning is of the scope of the fathers of broad planning, Plato and Bacon. His object is a far broader dimension for democratic society. Thus, says Wheeler, "When goalsetting and planning are submitted to the popular processes, social and economic democracy will join political democracy and give an expanded and more positive meaning to both democracy and constitutionalism."

Planning holds whatever virtues we give to it. If its development is directed to enlarging the democratic potential, our society may find that the results of planning will be exactly contrary to the constrictive regimentation once expected of it. Considering the self-will, powerful authority, and unchecked momentum of corporate institutions—supported by the weight of technology and the pervasive and penetrating bribery of economics (the bribery that becomes possible when independent subsistence is no longer tenable)—our social system may find that only through articulate planning can freedom, opportunity, and community, for example, be assured *for the individual.* Only through some form of conscious planning can apposable and plural values be guaranteed, such as industrial affluence *and* environmental serenity. Only through some form of conscious planning will the citizenship of institutions give way to a renewed sovereignty of the individual person.

13

Destiny of Change

Sometimes a personal experience has a way of enlarging itself far beyond the apparent significance of its occasion.

Not long ago I went to observe a Boys' Club program in Paterson, New Jersey. The club was new, housed in a very old, unattractive, abandoned fire station provided by the City of Paterson in a run-down neighborhood. The two-story brick structure badly needed repairs. Floors were unevenly worn, walls were dingy, and peeling paint hung from the ceilings. The equipment consisted mostly of three old billiard tables, a gymnastic mat, and hand bars. Yet the club signed up more than 700 boys in its first year. About thirty-five boys of various ages were busily occupied while I was there. The director was encouraged by a budget—largely contributed—of a little more than $20,000 that first year.

Talking with him, I discovered that the City of Paterson had long had a serious deficit of agencies to serve youth, particularly for lower-income children. There was a vital need to serve between 5000 and 7000 lower-income boys alone. Yet the Boys' Club program was extremely meager even for its present 700 members. Expansion would inevitably be slow and painful, since the club depended almost completely upon contributions. The onerous burden and probable frustrations of establishing an adequate program were dismaying at best.

Leaving Paterson for New York City, I drove on a very new portion of

257

the twelve-lane Interstate Highway. Just having left the dingy Boys' Club, I was impressed to see how many costly specimens of molded glass, steel, and chrome were traveling upon a highway costing $11,000,000 for each of its thirteen miles—$145 million, all told.

The costly highway and the high-powered cars suddenly seemed cheap and absurd. Slowly the social meaning of a Boys' Club struggling on a budget of $20,000 and a highway for which even a single overhead directional sign may cost that much became starkly evident.

Normally, the precision and thoroughness of engineering on highways, automobiles, refrigerators, and television sets gives us the impression that our society has a confident grip on itself. But that is not only a facade; it is a complete social fraud, and not the least for those who are caught up in the rat race for its inane results.

The contrast of what we do for mobility and what we do for youth carries throughout modern man's range of accomplishment. It is simultaneously success and failure, vision and blindness, intelligence and stupidity. It is simultaneously society's inspiring ideal for democracy and its willingness to forget that ideal in deeper cultural terms. It is our willingness to be simultaneously aggressive in business, subservient to organization, passive to political leadership, pragmatic in science, and utilitarian in education.

It is the social tragedy of our promising times: it marks the decline of what Walter Lippmann calls the "public philosophy." It is the transfer of personal commitment from precepts and ideals to the interests of specialized institutions. It is the rise of administration as the inheritor of rights and privileges in public affairs. It is the rise of science and technology as the new natural environment to which man must adjust.

TOTALITY OF CONQUEST

Accompanying the technological debasing of social values through the new "natural" environment of science and technology are many deep-rooted reinforcing attitudes. We tend to view the social incoherency of change as if it were the weather, to be accepted as it is found. Individually we buy automobiles and then collectively treat their vast numbers as it they were as essential as food and shelter. We accept the random forces fracturing the urban environment, such as the automobile, as if they shaped the ideal city.

We expect a man to commit his whole mature life—his whole pattern of living—to an organization whose sole obligation to him is pecuniary compensation. We expect him as well to develop a personality resembling his occupation, believing it remarkable when a minister, soldier, scientist, businessman, miner, machinist, engineer, or doctor does not reflect the conformities of his occupation.

The reinforcing attitudes follow closely from the growing impact of modern denominators of social opinion—the newspaper, television, utilitarian knowledge, money, functional organization, advertising. All of these tend to flatten individual values. Newspapers treat all subjects with the same seriousness or, rather, emphasize the sensational and momentary more than the significant. College courses on retail marketing carry the same credits and increasingly achieve the same status as courses in international relations or social philosophy. All companies on the stock exchange are equal in the price mechanism, regardless of whether they publish college textbooks or sell cosmetics. Money, now that independent subsistence has vanished, is the most universal denominator of society, grading all goods from slum properties to "priceless" art on the same hierarchy, and frequently at similar prices.

Permeating us deeply and underpinning so much of our behavior is modern man's pervasive drive to conquer. Western countries sought to conquer the sea and distant continents in the same spirit in which they sought to conquer each other. Today it is still our tradition to push back the frontier, clear the forest, dam the water, and mine the ore in a single-minded conquest of the elements. We are a society whose ethic of competition begins with sports and carries on into struggle within organizational hierarchies and between businesses. Conquest is the motive of corporate strategy. We are now conquering the north and south poles, the depths of the sea, and outer space.

Not by coincidence, then, we describe science as a conquest. It is a conquest by knowledge; in the end it enlarges our capacities but ignores the worthiness of our performance. Modern conquest at once displays meticulous order and purpose set beside disorder and lack of purpose—contrast the freeway and the social services for youth in Paterson. Nor are the old conquests any longer satisfying. Each new cycle is more powerful, penetrating, dominating, overlapping. Each new round becomes more massive in relation to man, makes him in some respect less significant and less worthy, and leaves him less important than the machines and organizations required for the conquest. The struggle for conquest tends to be monolithic in purpose and to press individual behavior to the bounds of human tolerance.

Man does not conquer so broadly without the conquest's becoming part of him; and if he sees his ambition only in terms of external conquest rather than inner achievement, the conquest inevitably centers upon himself most of all.

There is a fearsome oneness about conquest, no matter how materially bountiful its results may seem. Our modern powers are becoming too great, our world too small, for such unqualified conquest. Competition, whatever its output, has become exploitive, now mainly of the individual as worker and consumer, in the personally schismatic grappling between corporate Big Citizens.

We are a society aimed at capacities—the last margin of efficiency, the all-out war, the costliest highway system, the largest cities. We see world development almost wholly as a matter of increasing the capacities of organizations. The training and skills of individuals are but the atomic additions to that capacity.

The modern society accomplishes approximately what it sets its mind to do. It has sought abundance and power, and those are evidently approaching a world-wide realization within the next generation. Science has sought the power of knowledge. It now works toward synthesis of life. That prospect opens an incredible portent—and speaks not a little of scientific shamanism, all the more because it may be realized. For what purpose do we seek to uncover the natural basis of our own existence when we haven't decided what ends such a discovery should serve, and when we haven't even considered the means to protect human biological integrity?

The threat to biological integrity only highlights the actual loss of human integrity that has taken place piecemeal in the course of contemporary technical and economic development. We are seriously confronted by the attitude of conquest associated with our institutions and the attitude supporting submission by individuals. It seems to be a part of our tradition that the *powerful uses* of knowledge should overwhelm the *reasoned uses* of knowledge. The present assault on the biological basis of life (and its integrity) is but a hulking specter in the long shadow of past events.

Can we permit our attention to be monopolized, as it so often is, by the dramatic problems of nuclear or population explosions? Much of our best attention is required there, of course. Yet even these problems are unlikely to be resolved as long as man denies himself a valid social and psychic franchise in society.

We must therefore seek new ways of perceiving what social development can do for men. We must seek the avenues that enlarge human purposes and more completely accommodate human pursuits. Then we may find that the attention we give to immediate and urgent world questions may become more real and the results more manageable.

IMBALANCE OF SOCIAL PROGRESS

The common terms that most fully describe the Western social system—political democracy and economic capitalism—also parallel the two main thrusts of historic effort in recent centuries. It is in the political and economic areas that the greatest triumphs have been recorded for large numbers of men.

Political democracy, though under strain, now rests upon a broad base of theory and a history of growing maturity. Human political rights are a truly revolutionary attainment in any country at any time, though they are always an unfinished business. The other generalization we can safely make is that the economies of the West, based upon technological exploitation of scientific discovery, are expanding beyond all previous imagination. Although many persons do not yet share its largess, there is little question that a few decades will see poverty virtually disappear in most Western countries.

Contrasted against these advances is an increasing *social* subordination of the individual to the prerogatives of the very organizations that made it all possible. Historically, men have often been cruelly treated within organizations, but it has remained for modern institutions to systematically disenfranchise the social foundations of behavior. Consequently the individual has become a psychically isolated and socially undifferentiated particle of society.

Then, too, the professional specialized performance of organizations has left us—as persons—culturally shallow. The attainments called excellent are really the attainments of corporately organized universities, museums, theaters—and of high finance, specialized skill, and professional exclusiveness. Little of this involves the layman except as spectator. The socially divisive pattern of urban organization prevents him from becoming vitally and meaningfully engaged. Excellence rarely appears outside a full-time occupation and a bureaucratic organization. The individual is not even trusted outside the medium of a specialization and an institution; all other interests are subordinated in the mind as well as in social organization. Herein lies the basis of our shallowness.

These generalizations but emphasize that society in general accomplishes what it sets out to do. It is plain that the material basis of life has been remade and that political liberty has evolved at the cost of long and inspired struggles. It is equally plain that society has *not* sought to accomplish goals of comparable social and cultural importance. There has not been the equivalent of a "political struggle" or "economic drive" for diverse *social* opportunity, for a "social grace," for a rich cultural challenge, or for the rights of personality. We have not sought the intimate psychological integrity of the person (or the corollary structural context of personal integrity). We have not sought a personal richness in education. We have not sought to make civic life a source for or a memorial to the good life. Indeed, there have been serious recessions in the face of the resounding economic and technical forces of our times.

These questions naturally reflect upon our way of acquiring and using knowledge. Today we create a flow of innovation. The flow, especially that of the physical sciences, may be likened to a flow of water spreading out into a parched plain. The land desperately needs the new water, just as man requires new knowledge. But what is becoming more critically important is that the knowledge flowing from the mountains of science is year by year breaking out of its channels in ever larger quantities, causing deep erosion and spreading debris and damage along with its life-giving fluids. One may be sure that a water development scheme that enlarged the sources but failed to control the uses of water would be an inconceivable lapse of human thought. But that is precisely what is beginning to occur today in the flow of innovation and knowledge.

The absence of clear channels for human purposes to give direction and meaning to the flow of innovation has left us with an uncontrollable intellectual flood. We suffer, even as the ancient Greeks, from what they called *polygnosia,* or too much knowledge, and from *minisavvy,*[1] or too little understanding. We have come a long way since Alexander Pope wrote the famous line, "A little knowledge is a dangerous thing." Now, ironically, we might be in greater danger from the converse: "A lot of knowledge may be a more dangerous thing."

Taken together, our flow of innovation, our technical and bureaucratic aggressiveness, our willingness to acquiesce to the "necessities" of change, and the absence of a rich variety of inspiring social goals have left us with progress but without renaissance. We seek excellence but are not sure what purpose excellence should serve. We believe implicitly in advanced research but hold a naive faith that the knowledge from research will, on its own, find its highest and best use. We have a passion for creating new capacities and improving efficiency, but capacity and efficiency are increasingly irrelevant to the most serious problems and greatest possibilities in the industrialized countries.

ENLARGING SOCIAL PURPOSE

It would indeed be a tragedy if man allowed his purposes to be governed by the direction of his movement. But that is the ponderous weight upon society at the present time. Economic analysts too easily convert their predictions into recommendations; one reads, for example, that "man must learn to adjust to the requirements of the computer." A growing number of writers exalt the rationalism that computers will bring to society—and they mean a binding of a society of men to the peculiar characteristics of the computer, rather than a harnessing of rational computers to the service of men.

Persons who argue this way are not new among us. This is the direction we have been setting for society for several centuries. This is the common attitude among us that accepts in hundreds of little ways that organizations have a life above men—that men are the "human resources" for organizations to control or exploit. Put in terms of economic and social necessity, this belief in a superior welfare for institutions is a spiritual descendant of the "divine right" of kings and the "will of the state" of earlier times. And any organization that rises above the individual becomes to some degree totalitarian.

Part of the explanation, one suspects, is that social capacities have seriously outrun social goals. Human goals have often been perverted, but has a society ever changed so radically that it made its traditional goals irrelevant or impotent? For instance, in Western history we see the slow evolution of the importance of individualism; but now the meaning of being an individual has turned upon us, converting our individualism into individuated bits of behavior. Ethically, what has happened to man dominates what man seeks in himself.

The task ahead is the magnification of the individual, the establishment of a new honor that sanctifies him, a new belief that enlarges him, a new role that invigorates his whole existence.

New human goals will, however, necessarily focus great attention on institutions, just as the growth of industrialization and bureaucracy focused much attention on individualism. Primary attention will be given to the social and interpersonal context of the person, as the emergence of industrial organizations gave primary attention to the functional structuring of many individuals. The questions of both times are similar, but the purposes are reversed. Heretofore the abilities of the individual were harnessed to build powerful organizations. In the future we may hope that the capacities of organizations will be harnessed to support a psychosocial coherence in society that will in turn promote inner growth of the individual person.

This is one dimension of—or one requirement for—a new shift in the magnetic field of social organization, reversing the drift of the past century of change, in which very many prerogatives of men have shifted away to become the imperatives of corporate institutions. All of the discussions in this book but suggest the range and depth of the past magnetic shift and the future possibilities. Yet possibilities are such only insofar as they are recognized and demanded by men.

This optimistic view can well be challenged. For instance, the French writer, Jacques Ellul, argues that the imperious force of "technique . . . cannot be escaped or mastered," that "it is vanity to pretend it can be checked or guided." [2] But the trend that Ellul sees bringing about a society completely subordinated to "technique" reflects his preoccupation with the technological extrapolation. He does not take into account the turns and reversals in history, because he restricts himself to but one relatively recent trend in history.

Specifically, Ellul does not consider the changing will of people. If we observe only the various protest movements in the United States at one point in time, it appears evident that powerful counterforces can and do emerge, and they may well have a lasting and telling effect on deep-rooted social assumptions and human organization. Given four or six decades of such historic events and a growing awareness and determination, a new *social* renaissance could get underway.

Of course, the crucial contemporary questions are not changed: Is social endowment the property of the individual or of his organizations? Is freedom to be the possession of society's Big Citizens? Is world development to be a development of social virtue, or will it become solely the development of institutional power?

Put most simply, recent centuries have occupied men in making machines and organizations effective. But man has yet to learn to fully control the larger purposes to which these developments are directed. This may become the preoccupation of men in the coming decades.

The ultimate question rests not so much upon what is happening or what the trend is but upon what man determines is within his reach. This question underscores again what was stated at the outset: *the enormity of our task in world development is inspiration and conception, not achievement.*

DEFINING A HIGHER HUMANITY

Man has always thought best of himself for his aspirations. In recent centuries his aspirations have become increasingly externalized as the possibilities of exploiting the natural inheritance of the earth have become ever more evident. The result is a wondrous system of technology and bureaucracy. But at the same time these master tools have taken command over many of the externalized aspirations of men. The consequence is a progressive removal of social action from human sensibility.

And in recent decades, as institutions have acquired aspirations, initiative, privilege, and naked power, a plateau in the distinctly human spirit seems to have appeared. The hippie and the protestor engaged in their demonstrative struggle reveal one feature of the plateau. The social isolation of the suburbanite, the social numbness of the commuter, the inanity of the redundant economy reveal another. Jacques Barzun is so very right when he says, "Man is *not* flourishing."

Perhaps the successes of our externalized aspirations have been too much for us, too dazzling and too powerful, too beautiful and enchanting.

Those successes distract us from some basic facts of life: the spacebound and timebound organism of the individual person, the emotional and interpersonal underpinnings of happiness, the inner beginnings and endings of aspirations themselves.

Perhaps, one day, man will learn that his highest aspirations are those that are closest to himself, and that all external aspirations must serve an inner growth, or they are nothing.

The question urgently facing us is to find a definition for a higher humanity—a higher development within and among men, a closer subservience of institutions to human sensibilities: psychic, social, cultural.

If we were to view society with the broadest possible lens of history, it might become evident that society has for the first time—in this, the latter half of the twentieth century—begun to realize the material foundations of a completely liberal society for *all* men. This is a truly astounding accomplishment. And all men are beginning to know this, or feel it.

However, the same wide lens might also reveal that in creating the technical base for the humanely liberal society we have also been creating an institutional antibody to liberal human action, except in the narrowest sense that we call institutional humanity. This is equally portentous. And it is not recognized, except by a very few.

Why have we been so gullible about the things we have created? Are we afraid of the renaissance that should be bursting about us? Are we afraid of the good will that can result from wealth, or the excitement and grandeur of existence that can be underwritten by powerful institutions, or the freedom that can result from advanced technology?

Somehow our success has gotten the better of us. So much success derives from our response to problems, so little from our vision of the good life. This is the failure of pragmatism (as a purpose, not as a method). As our cities so dearly reveal, solutions to immediate problems seem only to expand the scope of our problems. Witness the totally self-defeating solutions that shape cities to the automobile.

And somehow success has come to serve institutions more than men. What men need is a healthy invigorating environment, and this requires astonishingly little success in material or technical terms. But instead of creating a congenial society, we face ever larger problems with ever larger institutions that report ever greater successes.

Old shibboleths must go. The social spirit we need must be simultaneously more liberal and more conservative: more liberal in seeking new human values, more conservative in preserving established human values. For fulfillment we need to become more radical about our institutions, to assure that they become more provident, even if less profitable or less successful.

Pope Paul was indeed inspired when he said that "the new word for peace is development." The danger remains, however, that development will but magnify the prevalence of narrowly focused institutions with exploitive interests and schismatic influences. This kind of development is not a foundation for the peace the individual needs. Nor is it likely to inspire the "social grace" for which Reinhold Niebuhr pleads. A definition for a higher development, a higher humanity, a more personally spirited civilization, is the inspiration we await.

Footnotes

CHAPTER 1

1   LEWIS MUMFORD, *The City in History* (New York: Harcourt, Brace & World, Inc., 1961), pp. 42–43.
2   H. H. GERTH and C. WRIGHT MILLS (eds.), *From Max Weber* (New York: Oxford University Press, 1946), pp. 196–244.
3   Mumford, p. 103.
4   BARBARA WARD, *Five Ideas that Change the World* (New York: W. W. Norton & Company, Inc., 1959), p. 54.
5   ROBERT NISBET, *Quest for Community* (New York: Oxford University Press, 1953), p. 22.

CHAPTER 2

1   ROBERT BRADY, *Organization, Automation and Society* (Berkeley, Calif.: University of California Press, 1961), pp. 6–10.
2   PALMER C. PUTNAM, *Energy in the Future* (Princeton, N.J.: D. Van Nostrand Company, Inc., 1953), pp. 214–215.
3   BRADY, p. 3.
4   BERNARD F. TOBIN and HENRY B. ARTHUR, *Dynamics of Adjustment in the Broiler Industry* (Boston: Graduate School of Business Administration, Harvard University, 1964).
5   TOBIN and ARTHUR, p. v.
6   EDWARD HIGBEE, *Farms and Farmers in the Urban Age* (New York: The Twentieth Century Fund, Inc., 1963), p. 3.
7   *United States Census of Agriculture*, 1959, vol. II, chap. 4, p. 1206.
8   ROBERT S. MCGLOTHLIN, "Trends Within the Agricultural Industry," *Journal of the Stanford Research Institute*, Third Quarter, 1960.

9 *Forbes,* March 1, 1966, p. 20.

10 HIGBEE, p. 82.

11 *Fortune,* July 15, 1966.

12 WILLIAM T. GOSSETT, "Corporate Citizenship," address delivered at Washington and Lee University, 1957.

13 DANIEL BELL, "The Subversion of Collective Bargaining," *Commentary,* March 1960.

14 ADOLF BERLE, "On Living in Freedom with Bigness," address delivered at the Tenth Anniversary Convocation, Fund for the Republic, New York, January 22, 1963.

15 ADOLF BERLE, *The 20th Century Capitalist Revolution* (New York: Harcourt, Brace & World, Inc., 1954), pp. 180–181.

16 EDWARD S. MASON (ed.), "Introduction," *The Corporation in Modern Society* (Cambridge, Mass.: Harvard University Press, 1960), p. 4.

CHAPTER 3

1 ALEXIS DE TOCQUEVILLE, *Democracy in America,* Reeve translation, ed. Phillips Bradley (New York: Albert A. Knopf, 1945), vol. 2, pp. 318–319.

2 PETER DRUCKER, *The New Society* (New York: Harper & Row, Publishers, 1949), p. 11.

3 JAMES G. MARCH and HERBERT A. SIMON, *Organizations* (New York: John Wiley & Sons, Inc., 1958), pp. 13 and 14.

4 MARCH and SIMON, p. 210.

5 MARCH and SIMON, p. 212.

6 HAROLD J. LEAVITT and THOMAS L. WHISLER, "Management in the 1980's," *Harvard Business Review,* November-December 1958, pp. 41–48.

7 A. N. WHITEHEAD, *Whitehead's American Essays in Social Philosophy,* A. H. JOHNSON, ed. (New York: Harper & Row, Publishers, 1959), p. 70.

8 ROSSER REEVES, *Reality in Advertising* (New York: Alfred A. Knopf, 1961), p. 76.

9 PIERRE MARTINEAU, *Motivation in Advertising* (New York: McGraw-Hill, Inc., 1957), p. 15.

10 MARTINEAU, p. 32.

11 MARTINEAU, p. 33.

12 MARTINEAU, p. 101.

13 MARTINEAU, pp. 101–102.

14 MARTINEAU, p. 105.

15 MARTINEAU, pp. 111–112.

16 MARTINEAU, p. 188.

17 VANCE PACKARD, *The Hidden Persuaders* (New York: David McKay Company, Inc., 1957), p. 9.

18 PACKARD, p. 266.

19 DRUCKER, p. 8.

20 DRUCKER, p. 8.

21 *Life,* November 14, 1949.

22 ROBERT NISBET, *The Quest for Community* (New York: Oxford University Press, 1953), chap. 1.

CHAPTER 4

1 ROBERT NIBSET, *The Quest for Community* (New York: Oxford University Press, 1953), pp. 195–197.

2 SIGMUND FREUD, *Civilization and Its Discontents* (New York: Jonathan Cape & Harrison Smith, 1930), p. 92.

3 A. N. WHITEHEAD, *The Function of Reason* (Princeton, N.J.: Princeton University Press, 1929), p. 2.

4 ALLEN WHEELIS, *The Quest for Identity* (New York: W. W. Norton & Company, Inc., 1958), pp. 87–88.

5 FREUD, p. 63.

6 FREUD, p. 139.

7 FREUD, p. 105.

8 KENNETH E. BOULDING, *The Organizational Revolution* (New York: Harper & Row, Publishers, 1953), p. 213.

9 DON K. PRICE, *The Scientific Estate* (Cambridge: The Belknap Press of Harvard University Press, 1965), p. 101.

10 LLOYD WARNER, *The Corporation in the Emergent American Society* (New York: Harper & Row, Publishers, 1963), pp. 4–5.

11 WARNER, pp. 62–63.

12 WARNER, p. 23.

13 WARNER, p. 60.

14 BOULDING, p. xv.

15 ROBERT L. HEILBRONER, *The Future as History* (New York: Harper & Row, Publishers, 1959), p. 158.

16 LEWIS MUMFORD, *The City in History* (New York: Harcourt, Brace & World, Inc., 1961), p. 106.

17 MUMFORD, pp. 167 and 169.

CHAPTER 5

1 BRUNO BETTELHEIM, "The Ignored Lesson of Anne Frank," *Harpers,* November 1960, p. 49.

2 GEORGE MEAD, *Mind, Self and Society,* ed. Charles Morris (Chicago: University of Chicago Press, 1934), p. 255.

3 PAUL GOODMAN, *Growing Up Absurd* (New York: Vintage Books, 1960), p. 238.

4 HERBERT BLOCK and FRANK T. FLYNN, *Delinquency: The Juvenile Offender in America* (New York: Random House, Inc., 1956), pp. 57 and 79.

5 ROBERT K. MERTON, "Social Structure and Anomie," *American Sociological Review,* vol. 3, no. 5 (October 1938), p. 673.

6 MERTON, p. 681.

7 GOODMAN, p. 160.

8 ROBERT NISBET, *The Quest for Community* (New York: Oxford University Press, 1953), p. 199.

9 NISBET, pp. 198–199.

10 NISBET, pp. 200–201.
11 NISBET, p. 201.
12 NISBET, p. 193.
13 W. W. ROSTOW, *The Stages of Economic Growth* (Cambridge: Cambridge University Press, 1960), pp. 166–167.
14 ROBERT BRADY, *Organization, Automation and Society* (Berkeley: University of California Press, 1961), p. 19.
15 ADAM SMITH, *Wealth of Nations,* various editions, chap. VIII.
16 PIERO SRAFFA (ed.), *The Works and Correspondence of David Ricardo* (Cambridge: Cambridge University Press, 1952), vol. VIII.
17 PAUL GOODMAN, *Community of Scholars* (New York: Random House, Inc., 1962), p. 139.
18 JOHN W. GARDNER, *Excellence* (New York: Harper & Row, Publishers, 1961), p. 151.
19 OLIVER C. CARMICHAEL, *Graduate Education* (New York: Harper & Row, Publishers, 1961), p. 68.

CHAPTER 6

1 WILLIAM E. MAYER, *Communist Indoctrination—Its Significance for Americans* (Searcy, Ark.: National Education Program, April 1957). Pamphlet.
2 GEORGE MEAD, *Mind, Self and Society,* ed. Charles W. Morris (Chicago: University of Chicago Press, 1934), pp. 254–255.
3 MEAD, p. 270.
4 ROBERT NISBET, *The Quest for Community* (New York: Oxford University Press, 1953), p. 52.
5 NISBET, p. 70.
6 ALEXIS DE TOCQUEVILLE, *Democracy in America,* ed. H. S. Commager (New York: Oxford University Press, 1946), p. 46.
7 LEWIS MUMFORD, *The Transformation of Man* (New York: Harper & Row, Publishers, 1956), p. 196.
8 MUMFORD, p. 196.
9 ROBERT PARK, *Human Communities: The City and Human Ecology* (New York: The Free Press, a division of The Macmillan Company, 1952), p. 26.
10 NISBET, p. 49.
11 MUMFORD, p. 196.
12 LAWRENCE HAWORTH, *The Good City* (Bloomington, Ind., Indiana University Press, 1963), p. 24.
13 ROBERT REDFIELD, *The Little Community* (Chicago: University of Chicago Press, 1955), p. 4.
14 LEWIS MUMFORD, *The City in History* (New York: Harcourt, Brace & World, Inc., 1961), p. 85.
15 NISBET, p. 53.
16 MEAD, p. 206.
17 GRANVILLE HICKS, *Small Town* (New York: The Macmillan Company, 1946), p. 163.
18 HICKS, p. 110.
19 HICKS, p. 107.
20 HICKS, pp. 85–86.

21 LEWIS MUMFORD, *The Social Foundations of Post-War Building* (London: Faber and Faber, 1943). Pamphlet.

CHAPTER 7

1 S. R. VERMA, "The Gurgaon Scheme," *Evolution of Community Development Programme in India*, Ministry of Community Development (Panchayat: Raj & Cooperation, Government of India, 1963). Pamphlet.

2 ALBERT MAYER and ASSOCIATES, *Pilot Project, India* (Berkeley, Calif.: University of California, 1958), p. 17.

3 MAYER, p. 132.

4 CHARLES FRANKEL, "Obstacles to Action for Human Welfare," *The Social Welfare Forum*, 1961.

5 *American Community Development* (New York: Ford Foundation, 1964). Pamphlet.

6 RICHARD LICHTMAN, *Toward Community, A Criticism of Contemporary Capitalism* (Santa Barbara, Calif.: Center for the Study of Democratic Institutions, 1966), p. 45. Pamphlet.

7 LEWIS MUMFORD, *The City in History* (New York: Harcourt, Brace & World, Inc., 1961), p. 501.

CHAPTER 8

1 GILBERT BURCK, "The Magnificent Decline of U. S. Farming," *Fortune*, vol. 51, no. 6 (June 1955).

2 A. N. WHITEHEAD, *Whitehead's American Essays in Social Philosophy*, A. H. Johnson, ed. (New York: Harper & Row, Publishers, 1959), p. 64.

3 ARTHUR C. CLARKE, address delivered at the National Conference on Air Pollution, Washington, D.C., December 10, 1962.

4 HANS H. LANDSBERG, *et al.*, "Resources in America's Future," *Resources for the Future, Inc.* (Baltimore: The Johns Hopkins Press, 1963).

5 GERARD PIEL, "Consumers of Abundance," *Center for Study of Democratic Institutions*, 1961. Pamphlet.

6 JOHN KENNETH GALBRAITH, *The Affluent Society* (New York: New American Library of World Literature, Inc., 1958), p. 225.

7 GALBRAITH, p. 240.

8 CHARLES FRANKEL, "Obstacles to Action for Human Welfare," *The Social Welfare Forum*, 1961.

9 PIEL, "Consumers of Abundance."

10 DAVID T. BAZELON, *The Paper Economy* (New York: Random House, Inc., 1959), p. 19.

11 W. H. FERRY, "Transforming Economic Institutions," *Cambridge 38* (February 1963), (publication).

12 HERBERT J. GANS, "Some Proposals for Government Policy in an Automating Society," *The Correspondent*, January–February, 1964.

13 GANS, "Some Proposals."

14 GANS, "Some Proposals."

15 Statement, Ad Hoc Committee on the Triple Revolution.

CHAPTER 9

1 KINGSLEY DAVIS, "Urbanization in India: Past and Future," *India's Urban Future*, ed. Roy Turner (Berkeley, Calif.: University of California Press, 1962), pp. 22–26.

2 For an excellent visual illustration of varied densities see: Christopher Tunnard and Boris Pushkarev, *Man-Made America* (New Haven, Conn.: Yale University Press, 1963), pp. 68–71.

3 JANE JACOBS, *The Death and Life of Great American Cities* (New York: Random House, Inc., 1961).

4 NORTON LONG, "Citizenship or Consumership in Metropolitan Areas," *Journal of the American Institute of Planners*, vol. 31, no. 1 (February 1965), pp. 2–3.

5 National Resources Committee, *Our Cities* (Washington, D.C.: Government Printing Office, 1937), p. 43.

CHAPTER 10

1 REINHOLD NIEBUHR, *Moral Man and Immoral Society* (New York: Charles Scribner's Sons, 1932), pp. 11–13.

2 NIEBUHR, pp. 11–13.

3 ELLEN LURIE, Community Worker, New York, "A Study of George Washington Houses: The Effect of the Project on its Tenants and the Surrounding Community" (New York: Union Settlement Association, 1955–1956), p. 31. Mimeo.

4 LURIE, p. 16.

5 JACQUES BARZUN, *Science, The Glorious Entertainment* (New York: Harper & Row, Publishers, 1964), pp. 26–27.

6 JOHN DEWEY, *Art as Experience* (New York: Minton, Balch & Co., 1934), p. 21.

7 SIGFRIED GIEDION, *Space, Time and Architecture* (London: Oxford University Press, 1949), p. 16.

8 MALCOLM and GOLDIE RIVKIN, "Area Redevelopment, Comprehensive Planning, and Regional Development," *Proceedings*, 1965 Governmental Relations and Planning-Policy Conference, American Institute of Planners, Washington, D.C., January 1965, pp. 98–99.

9 JAMES FESLER, *Area and Administration* (University, Ala.: University of Alabama Press, 1965), pp. 98–99.

10 FESLER, pp. 127–128.

11 FESLER, pp. 124–125.

CHAPTER 11

1 JEROME BRUNER, *The Process of Education* (Cambridge, Mass.: Harvard University Press, 1960), p. 33.

2 PETER DRUCKER, *Landmarks of Tomorrow* (New York: Harper & Row, Publishers, 1959), p. 127.

3 A. N. WHITEHEAD, *The Aims of Education* (New York: The New American Library of World Literature, Inc., 1929), p. 18.

4 WHITEHEAD, p. 27.

5 ARTHUR BESTOR, *Educational Wastelands* (Urbana, Ill.: University of Illinois Press, 1953), p. 20.

6 "The University of Illinois at Congress Circle," n.d. Mimeographed.

7 "Long Range Development Plan, University of California, Santa Cruz" (Santa Cruz, 1963).

8 HENRY STEELE COMMAGER, *The American Mind* (New Haven, Conn.: Yale University Press, 1950), p. 38.

9 JAMES PERKINS, "The Three Missions of a University," *University*, Spring 1966, p. 3. Also in James Perkins, *The University in Transition* (Princeton, N.J.: Princeton University Press, 1966).

10 JACQUES BARZUN, *House of Intellect* (New York: Harper & Row, Publishers, 1959), p. 19.

11 WHITEHEAD, p. 97.

12 ABRAHAM FLEXNER, *Universities: American, English, German* (New York: Oxford University Press, 1930), p. 13.

13 HENRY STEELE COMMAGER, "The University and the Community of Learning," *The University in the American Future*, ed., Thomas B. Stroup (Lexington, Ky.: University of Kentucky Press, 1966), p. 83.

CHAPTER 12

1 Reprinted from *God and Golem, Inc.*, by Norbert Wiener by permission of the MIT Press, Cambridge, Mass. Copyright 1964 by the Massachusetts Institute of Technology. Pp. 58–60.

2 WIENER, p. 69.

3 ROBERT BRADY, *Organization, Automation and Society* (Berkeley, Calif.: University of California Press, 1961), p. 4.

4 WIENER, pp. 63–64.

5 ROBERT L. HEILBRONER, *The Future as History* (New York: Harper & Row, Publishers, 1959), pp. 188–189.

6 BRADY, p. 424.

7 JAN TINBERGEN, *Central Planning* (New Haven, Conn.: Yale University Press, 1964), p. 68.

8 PETER DRUCKER, *Landmarks of Tomorrow* (New York: Harper & Row, Publishers, 1959), pp. 49–51.

9 KARL MANNHEIM, *Freedom, Power and Democratic Planning* (New York: Oxford University Press, 1950), p. 29.

10 E. H. CARR, *The New Society* (London: Macmillan & Co., Ltd., 1951), p. 76.

11 CHARLES HAAR, "The Master Plan: An Impermanent Constitution," *Law and Contemporary Problems*, vol. 20, no. 3 (Summer 1955).

12 Quoted from Norman Martin in connection with decision-making by Lloyd Warner, *The Corporation in the Emergent American Society* (New York: Harper & Row, Publishers, 1962), p. 56.

13 JAMES D. MOONEY and ALAN C. REILEY, *The Principles of Organization* (New York: Harper & Row, Publishers, 1939), p. 121.

14 HARVEY WHEELER, *The Restoration of Politics,* (Santa Barbara, Calif.: The Center for the Study of Democratic Institutions, 1965). Pamphlet.

CHAPTER 13

1 These terms were brought to public attention in an editorial by Sidney Hertzberg in the September 1960 issue of *Current* magazine.

2 JACQUES ELLUL, *The Technological Society* (New York: Alfred A. Knopf, 1964), pp. 146 and 428.

Index

275